O CANADA CROSSWORDS

BOOK 18

MORE
O Canada Crosswords!

O Canada Crosswords, Book 1 • *115 Great Canadian Crosswords*
8½ x 11, 136 pp, pb • 978-1-894404-02-0 • $14.95

O Canada Crosswords, Book 2 • *50 Giant Weekend-size Crosswords*
8½ x 11, 120 pp, pb • 978-1-894404-04-4 • $14.95

O Canada Crosswords, Book 3 • *50 More Giant Weekend Crosswords*
8½ x 11, 120 pp, pb • 978-1-894404-11-2 • $14.95

O Canada Crosswords, Book 4 • *50 Incredible Giant Weekend Crosswords*
8½ x 11, 120 pp, pb • 978-1-894404-18-1 • $14.95

O Canada Crosswords, Book 5 • *50 Fantastic Giant Weekend Crosswords*
8½ x 11, 120 pp, pb • 978-1-894404-20-4 • $14.95

O Canada Crosswords, Book 6 • *50 Great Weekend-size Crosswords*
8½ x 11, 120 pp, pb • 978-0-88971-206-5 • $14.95

O Canada Crosswords, Book 7 • *50 Wonderful Weekend-size Crosswords*
8½ x 11, 120 pp, pb • 978-0-88971-218-8 • $14.95

O Canada Crosswords, Book 8 • *75 Themed Daily-sized Crosswords*
8½ x 11, 176 pp, pb • 978-1-88971-217-1 • $12.95

O Canada Crosswords, Book 9 • *75 Themed Daily-sized Crosswords*
8½ x 11, 115 pp, pb • 978-1-88971-225-6 • $9.95

O Canada Crosswords, Book 10 • *50 Themed Daily-sized Crosswords*
8½ x 11, 120 pp, pb • 978-1-88971-236-2 • $9.95

O Canada Crosswords, Book 11 • *75 All New Crosswords*
8½ x 11, 175 pp, pb • 978-1-88971-253-0 • $9.95

O Canada Crosswords, Book 12 • *100 All New Crosswords*
8½ x 11, 232 pp, pb • 978-1-88971-257-7 • $11.95

O Canada Crosswords, Book 13 • *100 All New Crosswords*
8½ x 11, 232 pp, pb • 978-1-88971-272-0 • $12.95

O Canada Crosswords, Book 14 • *100 All New Crosswords*
8½ x 11, 232 pp, pb • 978-1-88971-291-1 • $12.95

O Canada Crosswords, Book 15 • *85 All New Crosswords*
8½ x 11, 232 pp, pb • 978-1-88971-304-8 • $12.95

O Canada Crosswords, Book 16 • *100 All New Crosswords*
8½ x 11, 232 pp, pb • 978-1-88971-312-3 • $13.95

O Canada Crosswords, Book 17 • *100 All New Crosswords*
8½ x 11, 232 pp, pb • 978-1-88971-322-2 • $14.95

O CANADA CROSSWORDS

BOOK 18

100 ALL NEW Crosswords

GWEN SJOGREN

NIGHTWOOD EDITIONS

Nightwood Editions
P.O. Box 1779
Gibsons, BC
V0N 1V0
www.nightwoodeditions.com

Edited by Margaret Tessman
Proofread by Patricia Wolfe
Printed in Canada
ISBN 978-0-88971-334-5

Contents

Au Naturel

The beauty of Canada

ACROSS

1. Sounds of thunder
6. Dandy dude?
9. US hip hop trio: Salt-N-_____
13. Fabrics for jeans
19. Pelvis-related
20. Sundial marking
21. Pearson airport postings (abbr.)
22. Guided missile type
23. **Territorial aurora**
26. Retinal depressions
27. And so on
28. Like move-in ready homes
30. Alchemist's concoction
33. Homeopathic medicine term
35. Neighbour of Niger
36. Sixth sense
37. Canadian polling pro Nanos
38. 3-D shape
40. Stop smoking
42. Happen again
44. T-shirt type
46. Que. neighbour
48. Czech or Croat
50. Kitchen appliances
53. A calendar covers it?
54. Legendary tales?
56. Patella places
58. Hyperbolic function, in trigonometry
59. Alphabet gamut?
61. Dampen flax
63. Axl Rose fronts this band (abbr.)
64. CB user's phrase: Roger _____
65. Tarmac building
68. Calgary Stampede event
70. Rule out
72. Anne Hébert novel: _____ *Disturbing You?*
73. **Tidal phenomenon place in New Brunswick**
76. Before, in an old poem
77. Used logic
79. Monarch's measuring device?
80. Not coloured
82. Pond growth
83. Toronto's 64th mayor Ford
85. Egg yolk holder
86. Burst _____ the scene
87. Continental crust layer
88. Flank or sirloin serving
90. Unadorned
92. Bluffers or High, in Toronto
96. Shawl for a señor (var.)
98. Cut a bit short?
100. In vitro fertilization clinic supplies
101. High nest for hawks
102. Love to bits
104. Paste together
106. Classes
108. Aussie sport-utility vehicle, for short
109. Battle of Britain air squad (abbr.)
111. Shut (up)
113. Last Greek letter
115. Astuteness
117. Brazilian boas
120. Makes beautiful
122. Anne Murray #1 country hit: "I Just Fall _____ Again"
123. **Chain in Western Canada**
128. Us and them?
129. Spelling who starred in *Beverly Hills 90210*
130. Title for Mila and Aline
131. Domed abode
132. Thrust out
133. Baseball great Musial
134. Make a query
135. Early Europeans

DOWN

1. RBC ATM no.
2. "Evil Woman" music grp.
3. It's based in Whitehorse: _____ North
4. Paint type
5. Comedian's "bit" (var.)
6. Juno- and Grammy-winning band: Arcade _____
7. Balm
8. Mushroom tops
9. Immortal winged horse
10. Letter in Old English
11. Stanley Park walkway
12. Black tea type
13. Manicurists who corrupt?
14. 1994 film that won eight Genie Awards
15. _____ Scotia
16. **Coastal Newfoundland tourist attraction**
17. You can buy these at Swiss Chalet
18. Brew oolong
24. Hosiery hue
25. Middle Eastern country
29. Gold standard?
30. Jealousy
31. Mason-Dixon _____
32. Swedish retailer with 12 Canadian locations
34. Skim or 2%
39. American R&B group: _____ II Men
41. Space-age drink?
43. Innocent _____ proven guilty
45. Rugged rock
47. Toss, like a pitcher
49. Goods purveyor
51. "More!" says the audience
52. Demonstrated
54. Knucklehead
55. Passover dinner

57. Canada's Lamaze who won Olympic show-jumping gold
60. SUV to drive to a Nevada lake?
62. Canadian cellphone service provider
64. 1980 Canadian radio hit: "_____ That a Party"
65. Hound
66. Earhart who flew to fame
67. **Cascade in Ontario**
68. Freshens decor
69. Pots for paella
71. Malodorous mammal
74. Peppy
75. Right-hand page
78. Side for Caesar?
81. Dumdum's drug?

84. *The Big _____ Theory*
86. Uttered out loud
88. Most placid
89. Metric weight, for short
91. 66-D, et al.
93. Calla lily
94. Christening or confirmation
95. Sharp
97. Yorkshire pudding, say
99. Popular Thanksgiving dinner pie
101. Severely self-disciplined
103. Finale of an affair?
105. Very creepy (var.)
107. Hamilton-born ballerina Karen
109. Employee's increase

110. Forcibly take territory
112. Petite pastries
114. Jones who played Madam Pomfrey in Harry Potter films
116. Common practice
118. Picturesque place: Peggys _____ NS
119. Flue grime
121. Elephant tooth
124. Canada's "taxman," for short
125. Suffering from a sickness
126. Nimoy biography: *I Am _____ Spock*
127. *Titanic* wireless message

ACROSS

1. Old *Hockey Night in Canada* character: Peter _____
5. New Zealand parrot
9. Amino or boric
13. Invites
17. *Maclean's* columnist Solomon
18. Public crier's command
19. Animal's neck hair
20. Toronto-born *Top Chef* judge Simmons
21. Able to bounce back
23. Hebrew month
24. Preminger's palindromic name
25. Ploy
26. Enclosures for pet reptiles (var.)
29. Slippery substance
30. Analyze, at a mine
32. Doorbell sound
33. Window netting
35. Bruce Cockburn classic: "If I _____ a Rocket Launcher"
37. Get ready, for short
39. Edible root
40. Contribute to hearing loss
42. Sponsorship (var.)
44. And
46. Buenos Aires country
48. Excellent employee's annual perk
50. Weddings can require a lot of this
52. Oracle
53. Christmas season beverage
55. Like molasses?
56. AGO collection
58. "There wasn't a _____ eye in the house"
59. World travellers from Harlem?
63. Patsy
66. Dublin nation (abbr.)
67. Armoury stock
68. One or the other of two
72. Sound of thunderous applause?
74. Contradicts
77. Ottawa landmark: _____ Tower
78. Adjective that applies to a decathlete
80. Negative votes
82. Purplish brown shade
83. Long-time sitcom star Ozzie
84. You might do this with your little eye . . .
86. "We _____ to talk"
88. Styling substance
89. Traveller's document
90. Pointed weapon
92. Jewish dumpling
94. Christmas carol contraction
95. Crack a code, say
98. Rockies' ridges
101. Shoe giant formerly based in Canada
103. Plastic cover
104. Stop bleeding by burning
106. Brunswick or bourguignon
107. Algonquian language
108. _____ Domini
109. Colour of grass, in Gatineau
110. Mate of mère
111. Equivalent of *Monsieur*, in Munich
112. Wharf
113. Pitchers' stats

DOWN

1. Shampoo brand
2. Eye membrane
3. Falling, à la Niagara?
4. Makes a scarf, say
5. Native Japanese fish
6. "Yes," on ship
7. Superman's professional name: Clark _____
8. Montezuma or Itzcoatl
9. 1970 Guess Who hit
10. Seafood serving
11. Condition to
12. Grocery store section
13. Once upon a time?
14. Quenched a thirst
15. Ontario city
16. Sour fruit
22. Speech impediment
27. Greek letter
28. Preacher's "Praise the Lord!"
31. High-pitched cry
34. Chows down
35. Daughter of Zeus and Hera
36. Amazed
38. Your doctor might take this
40. Third Ph.D., say?
41. Hardly any
43. Canadian fashion designer Alfred
45. Table condiments combo
47. Midge
49. Singular songs?
51. The usuals
54. Medusa, for one
57. Vacation, say
60. Honey, in Huberdeau?
61. Evergreen shrub
62. Dance move component
63. Photocopy kin
64. Provide pain relief, say
65. Manitoba's 22nd premier Brian
69. More snooty
70. _____ Homo
71. Dance for Virginia?
73. Kicking Horse or Rogers, in the Rockies
75. Songwriter's muse, for example
76. Look for
79. Former CBC series: _____ *to Avonlea*
81. Parliament Hill player?
85. Slangy affirmative
87. Awful

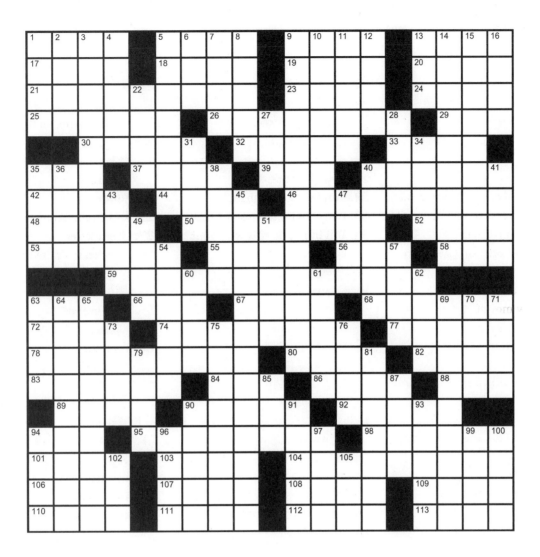

90. Alarm

91. Quick summary

93. Canada's Milos Raonic has a fast one

94. Recipe measurement (abbr.)

96. Carve

97. She's royalty, in India

99. Canadian media personality Levant

100. Eugenie Bouchard's cliques?

102. It can accompany shock?

105. Article, in Abitibi

3 For the Man of the Family

All about Dad

ACROSS

1. BNA, et al.
5. Eject like a volcano
9. They're in business to pamper you
13. _____ code
18. Circle of rope
19. Northern Brazil state
20. The written word?
21. Part of the eyeball
22. Mollusc fossils
24. De-icer ingredient
25. Air Canada Centre and Centre Bell
26. Come due, like Canada Savings Bonds
27. **His mental health treatment?**
30. Met, like a committee
31. Session
33. Network Education Exchange (abbr.)
34. Wild West bars
35. Hit from Alanis Morissette: "You Oughta _____"
37. Some number crunchers
40. Tenant's monthly expense
41. Brainstorms
43. Margaret Atwood offering: _____ and Crake
44. American Paul immortalized in a Longfellow poem
46. Sib of a sis
49. ASAP
51. Goes out with
52. Hair grooming appliance
54. British Columbia island
55. Swear (to)
57. Ocean mammal
58. Virus source
61. Fans' favourites
62. Alter Home Hardware merchandise?
64. Battle recreation participant
65. Catch in a trap
66. Ship's back end
67. Replace one actor with another
68. 1970 Canadian Top 40 hit: "The First _____ the Deepest"
69. With religious reverence
70. Irritates
71. Puts on a production at Toronto's Royal Alexandra Theatre?
73. It might fall from the sky
74. Lascivious looker
76. Divest of weaponry
77. Greek goddess of love
81. Hair colouring
82. Father-and-son Canadian broadcasting magnates Izzy and Leonard
84. Satisfy an appetite
85. Lag behind
86. Bitty bug
87. Speaks like Porky Pig
90. Petulant look
91. Instrument that plays itself
94. I, to Octavius
95. Fork point
97. Canadian rowing icon Hanlan
98. **Cause of his arachnophobia?**
101. Diner's cloth
103. Take off freight
104. Grain storage locale
105. International agreements
108. Some swellings
109. Like speed skaters' tracks
110. Gulf of St. Lawrence animal: Harp _____
111. Number from The Wiz: "_____ on Down the Road"
112. Smart-mouthed
113. Overly studious student, say
114. Chops
115. English actress Lanchester

DOWN

1. Chicken _____ king
2. Military raid team member
3. Spaghetti sauce ingredients
4. Canadian restaurant chain: White _____
5. Ornamental shrub
6. **His prayer?**
7. Earlier, in the Elizabethan era
8. Mud dauber, for example
9. Dummies
10. Criminals, say
11. Fires a logger?
12. Courtroom postponements
13. Exiled
14. Wildcat species
15. Talk for too long
16. Criticizes, in Britspeak
17. Peter Fonda film: _____ Rider
21. Composer Gustav
23. Obsessive person, colloquially
28. Black stone
29. Comforting touch
30. Jennifer Jones, on Canada's golden Sochi curling team
32. Species native to The Rock: Newfoundland _____
36. Timepiece enclosure
38. Strong soaps
39. Bench with a back
42. Makes a movie, say
45. Signs of victory?
46. Little lane
47. Draw back in disgust
48. How most prescription drugs are taken
50. Slangy speeches?
51. **His preferred painting style?**
53. Netherlands city
56. Stencil user, say
58. House of Commons tradition: Question _____
59. Lapse in immunity

60. CFL player's takedown
61. Between Ursa Major and Minor, for example
63. Deeply implant
65. Glucose and fructose
66. His legal advisor?
68. Crutch kin
69. Group of seven
72. Elvis Presley's birthplace
73. Palindrome for a lady
75. You might save for this

78. Sarcastic, say
79. Authenticity
80. Green-_____ monster
83. Mink furs
84. Urban miasma
86. Titles for chairwomen
88. Antediluvian
89. Escargots
91. You can see one at the Toronto Zoo until 2018
92. Doesn't do anything

93. *Happy Days* star Williams
96. US gov. air quality org.
98. Annual club fees
99. Donate
100. Beauty queen's ribbon
102. Mid-leg joint
106. Canadian "Alligator Pie" poet Dennis
107. BC Strait of Georgia locale: Salish _____

ACROSS

1. Impale
5. Poet Ogden
9. Meal where matzos are served
14. British time std.
17. Carson's late night successor
18. Duelling weapon
19. Still in play, colloquially
20. Colin James hit: "Why'd You _____"
21. Little bitty bugs
22. Extremely petite
23. Montréal NHLers
25. Rogers Centre city
27. Jackson 5 brother
29. Former reality show: *Canada's _____ Top Model*
30. Coating for a canine
31. Tortoise's race competitor
32. Put into the post
34. Giving the appearance of
36. Prehistoric tusked beast
40. Height (abbr.)
43. Canadian pharmacy chain: London _____
44. Long-running Canadian kids' show: *The Big Comfy _____*
45. Notable historic period
46. Joseph had one of many colours
48. Type of tree
49. Military services chaplain
50. Not in favour, in dialect
51. They say "Aloha State" in Hawaii
54. 2013 Avril Lavigne single: "_____ to Never Growing Up"
55. Pentateuch
56. Edmonton NHLer
57. Fashion designer Donna
58. Canadian Music Hall of Fame 1997 inductee Breau
59. They're just gems to work with?
62. Eye component
63. Political policy pros
64. Twinings product
65. Grandchild of Abraham and Sarah
66. Came into contact with
67. Immunization injections
68. Paddock newborns
70. See 48-A
71. Unauthorized entries
73. Luftwaffe attack
75. Pads for gymnasts
76. Foundation garments for 4-D
77. Pie-eyed
81. Petro-Canada competitor
84. Societal standards
86. Hotel employee
87. City on Canada's prairies
89. Coke or Pepsi
91. Dryer detritus
92. Famed Cambridge MA uni
93. Draw back in discomfort
94. Aroma, in Arlington
95. Québec diver Montminy who won two Olympic medals
96. Windy City trains
97. Vichyssoise veggies
98. Makes clothes
99. Marsh perennial

DOWN

1. Grey shade
2. Carpentry dovetail
3. Bone cavities
4. Busts and chests
5. Hives outbreak, say
6. Celery, in Seville
7. Hillary Clinton used to be one (abbr.)
8. Canadian Olympic diving medallist Émilie
9. Hôpital du _____-Cœur de Montréal
10. Israeli air carrier
11. Skeletons displayed at Alberta's Royal Tyrrell Museum
12. Fade away
13. Canadian comedy: *The _____ Green Show*
14. Delight
15. Coquette
16. Put to the _____
24. Céline Dion Grammy-winning album: *Falling _____ You*
26. Essential requirement
28. 2014 World Cup finalist (abbr.)
31. Acmes
33. Utmost degree
35. Urania or Erato
36. They keep debaters in line
37. Canadian sprinting star Andre
38. Monopoly game property
39. Grandmothers, for short
40. Ligament in the leg (abbr.)
41. He's just hanging around?
42. Sedimentary rock type
44. Pander to a foodie's whims?
47. Small gulls
49. Turns white with fear
50. Mountaintop nest
52. Opposite of aye
53. Oakville's Glen Abbey, for one
54. Sorceress
57. Australian marsupials
58. Arm or leg
59. Gem for Neil Armstrong?
60. Shakespearean protagonist
61. The end of addition?
63. Formal event sartorial specification
67. Kin of calypso
68. Debacles
69. Casement window feature
72. One way things might run?
73. Pendulum's path
74. Loonie, for example
76. Climbing plant stems

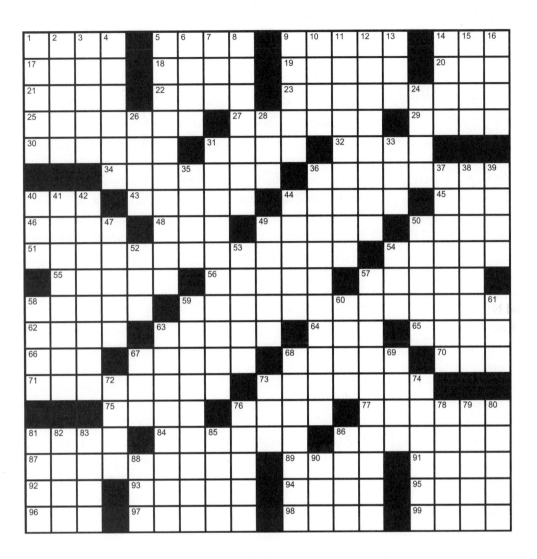

78. Biblical possessive pronoun
79. Metric weight
80. Chose

81. Terry Pratchett series witch Weatherwax
82. Set out on a yacht
83. Concordes, et al.

85. A debtor is in this
86. Snuff out birthday cake candles
88. Pointed punching tool
90. Poem form

Quotable Notables

Which Canadian politician said it?

ACROSS

1. Vacationers' guide
4. Unruly crowds
8. Tremble
13. Calvin's comics compatriot
19. Structural addition
20. It comes before formaldehyde
21. He led before Stalin
22. Not inclined to
23. Like past bills?
24. Ex-premier of New Brunswick Bernard
25. Not with anybody
26. Move a business, say
27. Western Canada province
29. Waspish pop singer?
30. Magnetic field strength unit
31. Final World Series moment
32. Ship-to-ship greeting
33. Ballet costume fabric
34. Discomfit
36. Karate or kendo
41. Evaded
44. Cause damage
46. Sudsy
47. Figure skater's jump type
48. Pop star Mariah
49. Social group for brainy Canadians
50. Compact canine
51. Skedaddle
53. Sought shelter, in a children's game
54. Gripe
55. Ice sculptor's tool
58. Talk like Daffy Duck
59. **"Just watch me."**
62. Provide evidence
64. Torpedo launchers
66. Where to find 64-A
68. Sty swine
69. Get more *Maclean's*
71. Prison in New York state
74. Venus or Jupiter
77. **"Billion dollar boondoggle!"**
81. Marks of Zorro
82. Antelope native to 98-D
84. Head locks?
86. *Lost* actor: Daniel _____ Kim
87. Servers' platters
89. "_____ the ramparts we watched . . ."
90. Minimum quantity
92. Commandeer
94. Have a mental lapse
95. Chinese divination text: *I _____*
97. Place to purchase pastramis
98. Italian city
99. Cause an attorney to be callous?
102. Pose a question another way
104. Big books
105. Arabic leader
107. Hotel that faces Victoria harbour
111. Church bigwigs
114. Levels the score
115. Backyard brazier
116. Not widely understood
117. Shaped like an egg
118. Prickly remark
119. Tolkien creature
120. Body shop's temporary provision
121. Yields control
122. Enclosure for a seed
123. Local Ecological Knowledge (abbr.)
124. Goes through the door
125. Former rulers of Russia
126. Supper or dinner
127. Guitar manufacturer in Italy

DOWN

1. Canadian honour: _____ of Military Valour
2. Gene Vincent classic: "Be-Bop-_____"
3. Common folks
4. **"You had an option, sir."**
5. Pretentious, in literature
6. Criticize
7. Unhappy
8. Spreads shaving cream
9. Multi-Indy 500 winner Castroneves
10. Fictitious name
11. 1926 Parliament Hill brouhaha: _____-Byng Affair
12. Opposite of WSW
13. Disfiguring mouth cleft, old style
14. Superimposes
15. German astronomer Friedrich
16. Kate or Will, by birth
17. Compass point in Cancún
18. It ultimately becomes a flower
28. Chopin's workout?
29. Plain plain?
30. Power supply problem
33. Two-piece outfit: _____ suit
35. Ted Danson's sitcom co-star Perlman
37. Jellied garnish
38. Heart chambers (var.)
39. _____ beef
40. Non-permanent workers
41. Genuine, to Germans
42. Burrow
43. Karachi language
45. **"Let us be English or let us be French . . . And above all let us be Canadians."**
49. Pout
52. Bozo or Krusty
54. Kenyan tribe member
56. Vast
57. _____ eclipse
60. *The Great Gatsby* heroine

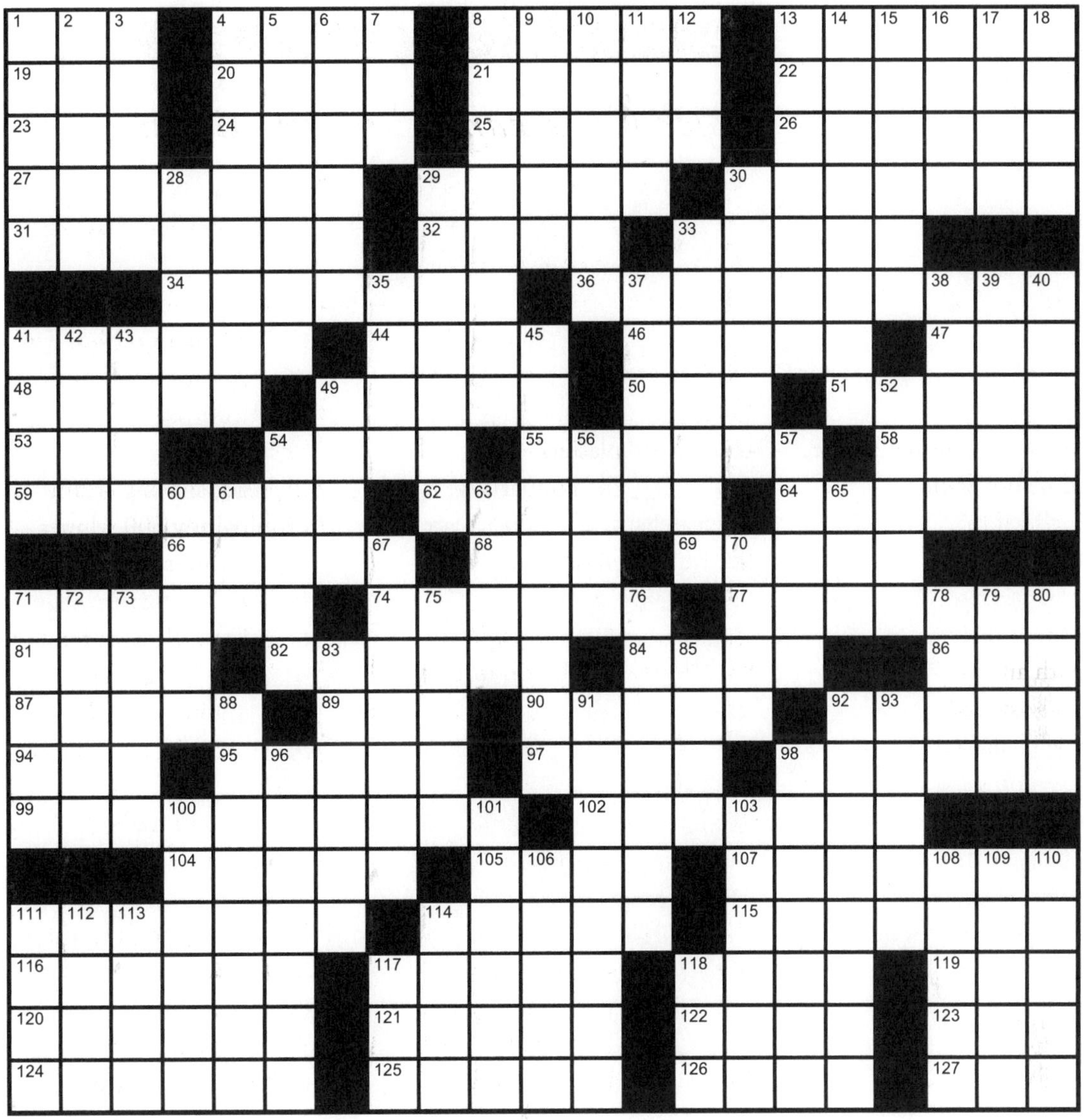

(Crossword grid, numbered 1–127)

Across / Down clues:

61. Additionally (abbr.)
63. Spicy lentil-based dish (var.)
65. k.d. lang collaborator Mink
67. Tacks onto
70. Item anagram
71. Early Mexican empire
72. Southern Ontario conservation area: _____ Cotta
73. Rips apart
75. See 56-D
76. Old European coins
78. False god
79. A scarf covers this
80. Comes down with the flu, say

83. Silks with patterns
85. "_____ I care!"
88. *Bluenose*, for example
91. Creep factor
92. **"Charisma without substance can be a dangerous thing."**
93. *The Magic Flute*, for one
96. Delays a picnic lunch?
98. Botswana's western neighbour
100. Odourless gas
101. There are 12 of these in Canada: _____ Bob's Golf
103. Bring back to the workforce
106. Cabbie's "clock"

108. School, in Chicoutimi
109. Eponymous film franchise about an ogre
110. 2007 Michael Moore health care documentary
111. *The Dark Knight Rises* star Christian
112. Laundry room appliance
113. See 51-A
114. Former Ontario premier Ernie
117. Mo. of fall federal elections, often
118. Product made by Ontario's E.D. Smith

Canada Cornucopia 3

ACROSS

1. Bachelor's buck?
5. Rounded windows
10. Canadian government investment instrument (abbr.)
13. Big bodies of water
17. 30-D, for example
18. Nine-musician musical ensemble
19. Vintage car
20. Acronym for a military deserter
21. They're exhibited at the Toronto Zoo
22. Infield covers
23. Put a monarch in place
25. Gather, at harvest time
26. Dismounted
27. Filled empty shelves
28. Integrate, ethnically
31. Charles Lamb's pseudonym
32. Installed floor tile, say
33. Bone-chilling
35. Give the cold shoulder
39. Casual eatery
42. Canadian comic strip: *For Better or For _____*
44. Muscat citizen
45. Foyer
46. Last wife of Henry VIII
47. Pace for a pony
50. Capture the Stanley Cup, say
51. Seer or sage
52. Pirate's chum
53. Toronto might have one in the summer
55. Atmospheric gas
57. Her statue graces Parliament Hill
58. Canada's 20th Governor General Roland
59. Passerine bird
60. Too smooth, like a salesman?

62. Eurythmics hit: "Don't _____ Me Why"
63. Flit
64. Nettilling or Nipigon
65. Slick
66. Seasonal songs
68. Librans' birthstones
70. Fridge front photo holder
71. She lived at Green Gables
72. Blahs or boredom
74. Have a bite
75. Feather component
77. Reed instrument musician
83. Canvas carryall
87. Choir member's attire
88. Monty Python's Eric
89. Opera opener
90. Hockey great Orr
91. Gordon Lightfoot song: "Early Morning _____"
92. 1960s singer Lesley
93. Unit in the gym
94. Agave, for example
95. Resistance units, in physics
96. Elite police unit (abbr.)
97. EMS vehicles' destinations
98. Went out with
99. Facial feature

DOWN

1. Piece of broken glass
2. Reservation dwelling (var.)
3. Bailiwicks
4. Chaplain's certainty?
5. Smallest Great Lake, by surface area
6. Filled a furnace, old style
7. Dismantle a circus tent
8. Old Athens currency
9. Hit from 92-A: "_____ My Party"
10. Indigenous Canadian
11. Dojo instructor

12. Vino vessel
13. Scornful language
14. Furry *Star Wars* critter
15. Top-notch
16. Toboggan
24. _____ polloi
27. *Cheers* actor Roger
29. Former Manitoba premier Doer
30. Canadian icon Fox
34. Addresses again
36. Like Obama, by birth
37. Old-style gastropod
38. You'll find this many Blue Jays on the diamond
39. Implore
40. All together now
41. Laid low, say
42. Alberta destination: _____ Lakes National Park
43. *Working Girl* character Trask
44. Holy Roman emperor name
46. Wireless communications device
48. A little look around?
49. _____ of office
52. _____ *Lisa*
54. Fancy fence material
56. Merlot and Malbec
57. Medicine container
58. "Give that _____ cigar!"
59. Thrash about
61. Until now
65. Postpaid encl.
67. Hare young 'un
69. Shakespearean troublemaker
70. Rolling in dough
72. Guarantee
73. Closer
74. See 74-A
76. Moose Jaw native Linkletter
78. Odour
79. Man-made "man"
80. Gem State

81. Loses
82. Edgy
83. Some swine

84. Swear
85. Aloe _____
86. Porcinis

90. Like rotten apples

7 Dancing with the Wordplay

Step it up with these puns

ACROSS

1. Source of hemp
6. *Quatorze*, divided by *deux*
10. Old Irish tongue
14. Liver health mo. in Canada
17. Hecuba's spouse
18. Like some chatter
19. Graduate's garb
20. Japanese sash
21. **Jogger's dance floor display?**
23. Crosby hits this occasionally
25. Grand Canyon State city
26. Upper-class Englishman
28. Workplace neophyte
29. Volcanoes spew it
30. Belief
32. Sketched
33. Length in time
36. Across the pond?
39. Itty-bitty insects
41. Crone
42. Canadian aircraft: _____ Otter
43. Kidney bean, in Québec
45. Ready to face the day
47. Canadian entertainers Tyson and Thomas
50. Aroma, in Alabama
51. C sharp or D minor
52. Eye membrane
54. Feeling no pain?
56. "Quiet," sweet Charlotte?
58. Caesar's day of demise
59. **Swing style for an entomologist?**
62. Mozart masterpiece, for example
66. Incite
68. Source of gin
69. Sign up at Seneca College (var.)
71. Goo for a do
74. They can bruise easily
76. Twerp
78. Annual figure skating tour: Stars _____
79. Expatriates
82. Colour of our men's Olympic curling medal in 2010
84. Montréal-born Hollywood star Ruta
85. Prepares the orchestra for a performance
86. California city
89. Offended, emotionally
90. Parkinson's treatment medication
92. Comes down in buckets
93. Computer's innards (abbr.)
95. Groundskeeper's reward?
97. Former premier of Yukon Duncan
98. Pops a balloon
101. Insubstantial
103. **Engineer's dance floor action?**
106. Cancer–_____–Virgo
107. Small sewing case
108. Army group
109. Runner's significant event: _____-marathon
110. Baking powder spoonful (abbr.)
111. Badgers' lair
112. Cribbage sticks
113. God or goddess

DOWN

1. Mo. to submit to the CRA
2. Dry, like bubbly
3. Japanese ethnic group
4. **Gyrations for garbage collectors?**
5. Cockeyed
6. Harbinger
7. Oilers NHL abbr.
8. Woodworker's surface smoother
9. They join with mortises
10. It might be over easy
11. _____ canal
12. Patch of grass
13. They make images bigger
14. **Astronaut's backwards moves?**
15. Roll call no-show
16. Bar mitzvah, for example
22. "When pigs fly," in dialect
24. Instrument for Canada's Marc-André Hamelin
27. Provincial product: Alberta _____
30. Townhouse renter
31. Basque bread
33. Juno-winning vocalist Ulrich
34. Mauled a Manx?
35. Quartz kin
37. Victoria's successor: Edward _____
38. Mystical Hindu figure
40. Home for hogs
42. Jack's inferior, in a deck
44. _____-and-Screw Tax
46. Mouthy greeting?
48. Squirrel's stash
49. Got a whiff of small fish?
53. Mint family plant
55. Hamilton landmark: Mountain _____
57. Rhino's instrument?
60. Clubs for Saskatchewan's Graham DeLaet
61. Subtle shades
63. Verdun soldier
64. Worrier's malady
65. Icy precipitation
67. Sweats
70. Non-verbal "okay"
71. 2014 Nickelback single: "_____ 'Em Up"
72. Imitates
73. **Bunny breeder's boogie?**

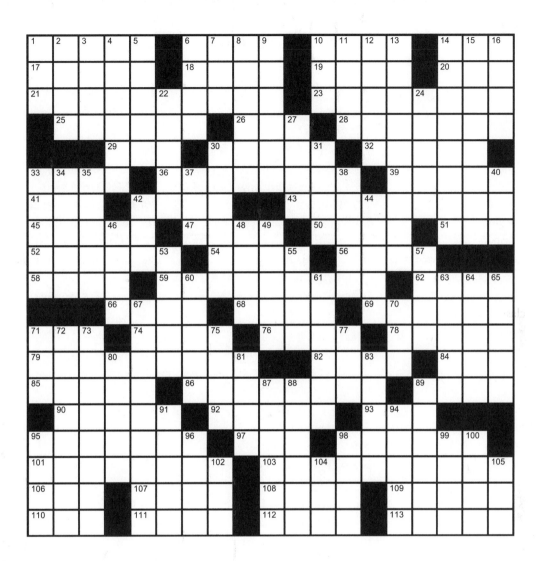

75. Nighttime sky sight
77. Provide duds for
80. Glittering rock
81. It's easy-peasy?
83. Physician's fill-in
87. Give a ring, old style

88. Utter a mantra
89. **Con artist's disco dance?**
91. Ridge in the mountains
94. Quite satisfied with oneself
95. Animal's hide
96. Drawn tight

98. Automatons, for short
99. Ta ta _____ ta
100. Arrange by category
102. Set ablaze
104. Short smoke?
105. Negative vote

ACROSS

1. Dexterous
7. Some mos.
12. Portuguese city
18. Matt Damon film: *The _____ Identity*
19. Use resources wisely
20. Not factual
21. How some cars operate
23. Lubricate
24. Tarts and tortes
25. Pub brews
27. Picked
28. You might have this with ginger?
29. Jump
31. Tree type
35. Guess Who song: "Bus _____"
37. Like a photographic memory
41. *While You _____ Sleeping*
42. Enjoy edibles (var.)
43. Not his
44. Adelaide music performance grp.
45. Some gardeners collect this
47. Diamond ring setting style
48. Rancher's ideal market?
49. Decade components (abbr.)
50. Hadrian's "hello"
51. Noted French wine valley
53. Moderated
54. Beast
56. Drouin who won high jump gold for Canada in Rio
57. Canadian *Company's Coming* cookbooks author Jean
58. Treat from Tim Hortons
60. Trig term
61. Ship's call for aid
62. Siesta
65. "Ditto," in a footnote
66. Throw a salad together?
67. Canadian singer Keith
70. USSR space station
71. She may be sainted?
72. Wizards
73. Group of troops
74. They flap in the wind on sterns
76. Canadian Christmas classic: "Huron _____"
77. Mathematician's bent?
78. Northern Canada borders this sea
80. Cover with asphalt
82. Prize won by Canadians Munro and Mundell
85. Escapes by 33-D
86. Dramatis _____
91. *A Midsummer Night's Dream* king
93. Behind the times navy personnel?
95. United States _____ Corps
96. Punctuation mark
97. Draw into a sting
98. Jean-Luc Picard bridge command
99. Bring into law
100. Behold

DOWN

1. Still under the covers
2. 1996 US presidential candidate
3. Roads, in Rouyn-Noranda
4. *Lord of the Rings* creatures
5. Doctor in training
6. Canada's "Seasons in the Sun" singer Jacks
7. Bursae
8. Oscar-winning actress: _____ Marie Saint
9. Drivel
10. Rudder adjunct
11. More deceptive
12. Oaf
13. Avenues of influence?
14. Siberian tract
15. Badly behaved child
16. Yorkshire river
17. INXS hit: "What You _____"
22. Go over info again
26. Raglan, for one
29. Unscented, in Utah
30. Gaelic name for the Emerald Isle
31. Amiss
32. Use a brand
33. Millhaven Institution inmates
34. Dusk, in old poetry
36. "_____ Got a Crush on You"
38. Becoming more rigid
39. _____ of Capri
40. Chilly
42. Word processing command
43. "_____! The Herald Angels Sing"
46. Plantar problem
47. Pastry chef's graph?
48. Canadian _____ Association
52. Refinable rock
53. Northern Ontario lakes catch
55. Chiclets, for example
56. Juliet's query: "_____ thou love me?"
57. Boston dads' drinks?
58. Canada's features the *Bluenose*
59. Norse god
60. Embassy employee
61. Refined metals
63. Lair anagram
64. 1970s NHL star Mahovlich
66. Feline's food flavour
68. Back then
69. Attila's endearment?
71. Almost everlasting
72. Sweet Italian wine
75. Southwestern Europe locale
76. Shania Twain Grammy winner: "_____ Over"

77. Chemical weapon gas
79. Comedic genre
81. Ready with rifles?
82. Alaska city
83. Western Scotland seaport

84. NL coastline spring site
86. Gasp
87. Food morsels
88. Drug dealer's pursuer
89. Banned agricultural spray

90. Notice James Bond?
92. Maiden name indicator
94. Rest Of Canada (abbr.)

Making It Right

Canadian home reno shows

ACROSS

1. Keep for the sheep?
5. Italian entree: _____ bucco
9. Curse
13. *Caveat* _____
19. Kitchen cooker
20. Social equal
21. *Black Beauty* scribe Sewell
22. High seas criminal
23. **Baeumler show**
26. Pigs' probosces
27. Military camp pests?
28. Elicit a reaction
29. They keep Canadians moving: _____-Richardson
30. Opportunist looking for enlightenment?
32. Some Arabic dignitaries (var.)
33. Should (with "to")
37. Long time
38. Iteration in the gym
39. Fib teller
40. Chamber group, sometimes
41. He meets the bride at the altar
43. Ensconce, like a gardener?
45. Diplomacy skill
49. RBC employee
51. "_____ the night before Christmas . . ."
53. Additionally
54. Too keyed up
55. Morning serving
57. Egyptian boy king, for short
59. Very obvious
61. Group of nine
64. Pan-fry a steak, say
66. Suzanne Somers sitcom: _____ *Company*
67. MLB players' headgear
70. **See 23-A**
73. Elizabethan's eyes?
74. You might stay for this long
76. Creative suggestion
77. Wine type
79. Most inclement, in April?
81. Nada, in a Nottingham match
83. Ditzy pilot?
87. Remove any traces
88. That fellow
90. Front end of a jet
93. Suitable
94. Canine's cry
95. Fabled writer?
97. Appliance distributor in Canada since 1954
99. _____ of passage
100. Recedes
102. Morse code E
104. Group for school fundraising (abbr.)
105. *Titanic* titan John Jacob
106. Oscar-winning actor Kevin
109. You might play tag on these?
112. Tithers give these percentages
113. Rogers Place, in Edmonton
114. Utopian place
119. Loosens laces
120. **Scott McGillivray program**
122. Release an inmate
123. Equipment
124. Cincinnati baseball team
125. Grimace
126. African herd antelopes
127. Ottawa landmark: National _____ Centre
128. Something different
129. British barristers' groups: _____ of Court

DOWN

1. Soft drink
2. Finished
3. Stamps or Flames
4. Green-eyed sin
5. Express a thought
6. United Empire Loyalist, for example
7. Crosses over a threshold?
8. Conquistador's gold
9. Governor General's performing arts award recipient Brent
10. Let loose the oxen
11. Dangerous place for Indiana Jones
12. Less loco
13. _____-Barr virus
14. Smallest possible amounts (var.)
15. **Jonathan and Drew Scott's show**
16. Pantyhose colour
17. Riverbank mammal
18. Has a snooze
24. Where to look for a sunrise
25. Drone
31. Canadian country music legend Hank
33. Palindromic pooch in *Beetle Bailey*
34. _____ formaldehyde
35. Golden coating
36. **One of Mike's series**
39. Predator of 126-A
41. Spanish nobleman
42. Front porch rug
44. Haiti currency
46. More suitable
47. Paparazzi target, for short
48. Long lock
50. Dusky period, to a poet
52. Nourish
54. "What?"
56. Maui visitor's garland
58. Golf peg
60. Fashionable
62. Broad _____ long
63. Canadian actor Ted, to Megan Follows
65. Upper body limb

67. Montréal Canadiens netminder Price

68. Fully cognizant

69. Pharmacy bottle (var.)

71. Dion Phaneuf became one on 2/9/16

72. Irish grp.

75. Fabrication on the fairway?

78. Pacific coast state (abbr.)

80. "_____ Always a Woman"

82. Hit the ball high, in tennis

84. Let off light

85. Saxophone size

86. Canadian international affairs columnist Gwynne

89. More like Millie?

91. Second-year student, for short

92. Preclusion, in a courtroom

95. Chasms

96. Skunk

98. Rumours about Québécois duck hunters?

101. Observed, old style

103. Canadian operatic pop group: The _____

105. "Immediately!" acronym

106. Bonehead, in slang

107. Old-style colony type

108. Sinuses

109. Biome adjacent to tundra

110. Cooking spray brand

111. Jagged, like a leaf edge

115. Moore who starred in *Striptease*

116. Remove wrinkles

117. Wow

118. *Top Gun* hit from Canada's Loverboy: "Heaven in Your _____"

121. Old poet's preposition

Canada Cornucopia 5

ACROSS

1. 1985 Bryan Adams hit: "One Night _____ Affair"
5. All the rage, on the runway
9. Greek letter
14. Everyone
17. Colourful eye part
18. Activity on HGTV Canada shows
19. Brock's Monument at Queenston ON is named for him
20. Canada won 22 medals here in 2016
21. Sty swill
22. Lahore language
23. "Water" pills
25. Decorative metalware
26. Rotate
27. Some salad greens
28. Room warming device
31. Airlines' home bases
32. *Goya's Ghosts* female character
33. Departed
35. "Beat it!"
39. Cathedral keyboards
42. Chatter at length
43. Pro swimmer's suit
45. Seasonal lyric: "Christmas _____ are ringing"
46. Gently boils
48. Made a mistake
49. Pastoral scene (var.)
50. Some vegetable pods
51. Latvian capital
53. Antiquity, in olden days
54. Early Eurasian nomad
56. Churchill's province
58. Middling grade
59. Congregation's interjection
60. Herbivorous South American rodents
61. Arrogant person

63. Straight shooter?
65. Wrinkly-skinned dog breed
67. Suit for designer Kate?
68. "It's all about me" attitude
70. Ondaatje's Giller Prize winner: _____ *Ghost*
71. Knight in training
72. Girl in a Dickens tale
73. _____-Lorraine
75. Unreal?
76. "The _____ the merrier"
78. Gloomily negative
83. Part of speech
87. Open a present, say
88. Order to a broker
89. Middays, old style
90. Energetic '60s dance style?
91. 1970 Crosby, Stills, Nash & Young protest song
92. Young goat
93. 1987 Canadian film: _____ *of Singing Birds*
94. Bellicose Greek god
95. Enjoy an Alice Munro?
96. Some
97. Blows, old style
98. Nerve network
99. Tiny bits of time

DOWN

1. Santa checks these twice
2. Liner's lowest deck
3. String section instrument
4. In particular
5. Adolescent adulations
6. Contagious viral infection
7. It borders Bangladesh
8. Diner employee
9. Iron ore carbonate
10. Egyptian fertility goddess
11. Unmannerly
12. Plunders and pillages
13. Harsh, for short

14. Seed enclosure
15. Scalp invaders
16. Defeat
24. Insomniac, for example
29. Austrian river
30. Physicians' tests?
34. Outdoor entertainment areas
36. Like crossword solvers?
37. Financial district street in Toronto
38. 1980s Canadian slopes star Brooker
39. Samurai's belt
40. RCMP formal wear
41. Moisturizer ingredient
42. Predatory fish
44. Organic source of fuel
46. Heavens above?
47. Peninsula between Asia and Africa
50. Georg's physics unit
52. US Army soldiers, for short
55. Marbles
56. Ingredient in some Canadian candies
57. Despotic rulers
58. Northern France city
60. *The _____ Is Right*
62. Don Adams sitcom: _____ *Smart*
64. Some Western Canada tycoons
66. Poetical cadences
67. Japanese quaff (var.)
69. Cocktail with an olive
71. See 35-A
74. Netherlands city
75. Make restless motions
77. Square dance group, for example
79. Nighttime noise
80. Little guffaw (var.)
81. _____ artery
82. Oafs

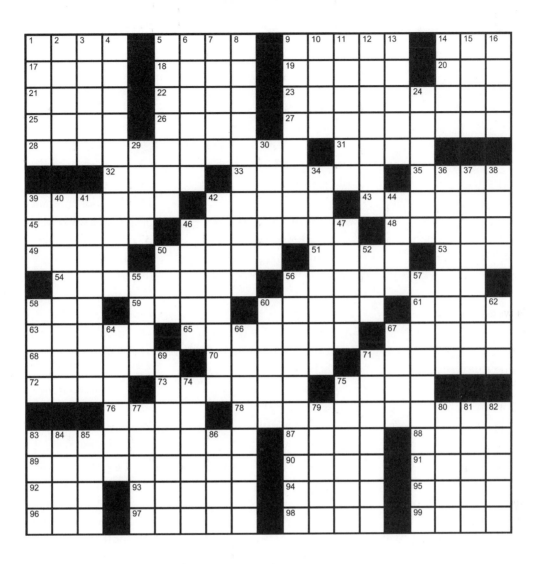

83. Ottawa-born singer Paul

84. Cause the ruin of

85. Ontario-born former NHLer Hull

86. Sleeveless garment

11 Old Occupations

Jobs in bygone years

ACROSS

1. High-fives
6. _____-ran
10. African language
15. Tools for cobblers
19. Black bird (var.)
20. Greek alphabet letter
21. Attempts
22. Swag
23. **Special delivery person?**
25. 1960s painting style
26. Sea mammal
27. Western Canada ruminants
28. Wine aperitif
29. Cape Breton musical group: The _____ Family
31. "Are we there _____?"
32. Initial occurrence, say
33. Giving a new title
35. They're sold at Sleep Country Canada
36. Lawyers' watering hole?
37. Official Languages _____
38. Married lady's letters?
41. Down, in mood
44. *Bluenose II*, for example
46. **Test tube technician?**
49. Special concert?
50. Celebrity chef Bobby
51. Jollity
52. On edge
53. Famed loch
54. Dress flounce
55. Some cookware
56. Appetizer type
57. More insecure
59. "Sure," in slang
60. Preschool tyke
61. **Telephone tag player?**
67. Fled or bled
68. Lumberjacks' tools
69. Collapses inwardly
71. Argentinian grassland
75. Surname seen in elevators
76. Halifax Regional Police personnel
77. Make a new acquaintance
78. Heart hit: "What _____ Love"
79. Rams' partners
80. Unbending
81. Wood-burning appliance
82. **Back alley employee?**
84. Gullible maple syrup producers?
85. Petite keyboard instrument
86. AB educators' grp.
87. NHL stat
88. Old perfect score, in gymnastics
89. Apartment, in Britspeak
90. Pertaining to living things
93. Chip off the old block?
95. Chess pieces, en masse
98. Italian noblewoman Catherine de'_____
101. MacLean who returned to *Hockey Night in Canada* in 2016
102. Female relative
104. Elderly
105. Dodge duties
107. **Modern medicines man?**
108. *Street Legal* actress Cynthia
109. Trace
110. Tease singer Groban?
111. Tailless nocturnal primate
112. Nova Scotia place: Garden of _____
113. "Night Moves" singer Bob
114. Angers
115. Like some wines

DOWN

1. All lathered up
2. It can be filthy?
3. English racecourse attire?
4. Lowly employee
5. Bout, say
6. Hates
7. Lecherous looks
8. Action film staple
9. Paddlers' sticks
10. **Fired up staffer?**
11. Purple plant (var.)
12. Miss Universe Canada headgear
13. 1989 Tom Selleck romcom: _____ *Alibi*
14. Big bird
15. "It's _____ Way to Tipperary"
16. Go to the office, say
17. Places
18. Canadian Mikita who played for Chicago's Black Hawks
24. Chastise
30. Pre-birth
33. Snitch
34. Type of spice
35. Ornamental tree in Osaka?
36. It's adjacent to Victoria: Oak _____
38. Sorvino who won an Oscar
39. Abbr. on an invitation
40. Source of eye redness
41. Restaurant entree offerings
42. Kilns
43. Alter clothing again
44. Book jacket's promo statement
45. Klutz
46. Even if, in brief
47. _____ *Misérables*
48. Restroom door sign
50. Warm alpine wind
51. Prods
54. Linear units, in printing
55. Fathers, in Frontenac
56. United States Marine _____
58. Like battle plans, say
59. Graph line
60. Bait into bad behaviour?
62. Western movie
63. Religious

64. European songbird

65. Canadian movie theatre chain: Cineplex _____

66. Christopher who titled his autobiography *Still Me*

70. "Let it stand," in proofreading

71. Perry Como hit: "_____ Loves Mambo"

72. Somewhat

73. Canadian Parsons who won plaudits for her WWII resistance work

74. Infected tissue liquid

75. Have creditors at your door

76. Bottle sealer

79. And others abbr.

80. Sunbather's goal

81. Long-eared dogs

83. Chinese religion adherents

84. Blink of an eye, say

85. Spill over

88. Meandering metal mender?

89. Bottles for Beethoven?

90. Obama's VP Joe

91. Space shuttle part

92. Land feature at Elora ON

93. Taste quality

94. Shut the door

95. Rude look

96. Chilling

97. Lovers' assignation

98. Old Rick Mercer show: _____ *in Canada*

99. "Good grief!"

100. Remove, from a MS

102. Pilgrim at Mecca (var.)

103. Flat-bottomed boat

106. Go quickly

Canada Cornucopia 6

ACROSS

1. Herring's kin
5. Judy Collins might send one in?
10. Corn on the _____
13. By way of, old style
17. Roll down the runway
18. Chinese fruit (var.)
19. Org. for Perry Mason?
20. Concrete
21. Roman Forum hails
22. Be part of a play
23. 1960s Chinese militant group
25. *Bill & _____ Excellent Adventure*
26. New Mexico or North Carolina
27. Sewing machines components
28. Passé
31. Eye in a rakish way
32. More drugged out
35. Moving quickly, archaically
37. At the acme
41. Orientals and trumpets
42. 1899–1902 war participants
43. Fabric for gloves
44. Rose-scented oil
45. Thespian's role
46. Siberian city
49. _____ *judicata*
50. Pace of 98-A
51. National athletic award: Lou _____ Trophy
52. Pacific Northwest tribe member, perhaps
54. Minister of Canadian Heritage Joly as of November 2015
56. Escaped
57. Rules over the courtroom
59. Some high-schoolers
60. Back of the neck
63. Granola bar morsel
64. Touched a fabric?
65. December 24 and 31
66. Canadian territory

67. Script section
69. Loads of land?
71. Former Canadian television award
72. 2013 Arcade Fire song: "_____ Comes the Night Time"
73. Alberta national park
75. Lauded
76. Trounce
78. History chronicler
80. Prop designer's milieu
84. Capital of Jordan
85. Pushpin
89. Salsa substance
90. Lower oneself
91. Tehran's land
92. Miners' egress
93. Critical care facility (abbr.)
94. Invest with authority
95. Hawaiian goose
96. Computing memory unit
97. Kook
98. Jouster's animal
99. Golden _____ Bridge

DOWN

1. Right away, in the ER
2. Possess
3. Let go a logger?
4. Breaks with
5. U of T lectures
6. Old Roman bodyguard
7. Of base eight
8. Capital of 66-A
9. Octogenarian's decade
10. Shopping _____
11. Silver screen leading lady Merle
12. Nefarious chicken farmer?
13. See 73-D
14. Cure
15. How some like their steak
16. Town north of Calgary
24. Lady

29. Coffin stand
30. All the time, in olden days
32. Smeltery detritus
33. Pocket for hummus
34. Aircraft instrument
36. Some atoms
38. Japanese marinades
39. Percy Bysshe Shelley verses
40. Ant or gnat
42. Some Starbucks Canada staffers
43. Throw off results, say
45. Sinclair, Kennedy and Berton, on *Front Page Challenge*
47. Nocturnal insects
48. Union in Toronto, et al. (abbr.)
51. Created
53. Freeing from slavery
55. Existence
56. _____ of Canada
57. Like a swanky Spice Girl?
58. Newfoundland lighthouse locale: Cape _____
59. Woos with ballads
61. Southern US cornbread
62. Oklahoma city
66. Some cheers
68. Old and infamous London prison
70. Accounting pro, for short
71. Smiled
73. Canada's 23rd prime minister (with 13-D)
74. Quick glance, in France?
75. Black Death, for example
77. Egg producer
79. Chemical compound
80. Lesion crust
81. Neat
82. Went to ground?
83. Promote one's wares
86. Room
87. "I _____ Stop Loving You"
88. Leg joint

13 Destination: Hamilton

All about Steeltown

ACROSS

1. Discharge a stun gun
5. Farm fodder
10. Canadian summer and winter Olympian Hughes
15. Withdraw from mother's milk
19. Singer Turner, and others
20. Abbot's assistant, earlier?
21. Dog-_____
22. Indy 500 winner Luyendyk
23. 19th-C. queen's collection?
25. Iconic franchise that opened its doors in '64
27. It borders this lake
28. Earring style
30. *The Comedy of Errors* setting
31. Kids play it
32. Suffers a defeat
34. Faun's relative
35. Desert pack animal
38. Exhausts
39. _____ out
40. Homeopathic condition, old style
44. Music group minus Benny?
45. Wallop, old style
47. Not false
49. Tailor's tool
50. Trails the leaders
52. Matures
53. 2011 documentary: *Sarah Palin: You _____!*
55. Clean cut?
56. University since 1887
58. Twist out of shape
59. More foggy
61. National athletics association: _____ Canada
62. Like ideal urban transit?
64. Old Italian language
66. Opposite of sis
67. Made into law
69. Brandenburg capital

71. Jim Carrey cinematic character: _____ Ventura
74. Character blot
75. Canadian actress/director Polley
76. Asian perennial
80. Under-the-hood car part
82. Poses in an artist's studio
84. Hamilton Harbour area park
86. "_____ you would think"
87. Aim for
89. Mythological Muse
90. Perfume resin
91. Soft palate parts (var.)
93. Geometric shape
94. Alberta oil strike town, circa 1947
96. "Stairway to Heaven" band: _____ Zeppelin
97. West Yorkshire city
98. Adversary
99. Tibet's capital city
101. Give a speech
103. Bran muffin benefit (var.)
105. Favourite Halloween hangout?
106. Rap star: Dr. _____
107. Machine that polishes
110. Former federal cabinet minister Dhaliwal
111. Castle on York Boulevard
115. Niagara Escarpment hikers' path
117. Where some Canadians become stars
120. Lessen physical discomfort
121. 2015 Adele hit
122. Haughty
123. "Electric Avenue" singer Grant
124. Like a grumpy golfer: _____ off
125. Supporting pole
126. Juno-winning New Brunswick native Gallant
127. Trials or tribulations

DOWN

1. Digital video recorder brand name
2. Linked to, like family?
3. Dissenting religious group
4. Long-time CBC program: *The Fifth _____*
5. Parsley bit
6. Group of three
7. Estuary
8. British-based insurance company
9. Thick-lipped fish
10. Whale constellation
11. Placed
12. Bicep locale
13. Microwave leftovers, say
14. Take in an orphan
15. Most diluted
16. God of love
17. Hokkaido people
18. Lawman Eliot
24. Spoken exams
26. Write like Dr. Seuss
29. Mattress factory proving ground?
32. They're well-read
33. Assayers examine these
34. Design detail, for short
35. Settles down?
36. Take _____ seat to
37. It's under a volcano
38. CFL team name
39. Not inside
41. Speak off-the-cuff
42. More cunning (var.)
43. Montréal subway system
46. Area rug
48. *The _____ & Stimpy Show*
49. She's a water babe?
51. Appease an appetite
54. National Historic Site ship museum
57. Common touch?

58. "No trump," for example
60. Wolf down dinner, say
63. Musing deeply
65. Least tippy
68. Rand McNally publication
69. Some parents
70. Pharmacy stalwart: Shoppers Drug _____
71. Fall _____ of
72. Create a totem pole, say
73. Come after
75. Outstanding, in outer space?
77. Cabbage or clams (var.)
78. Nunavut hamlet: Rankin _____
79. Piece for a pianist's practice

81. Like some lies
83. *Deathtrap* playwright Levin
85. Bachman-Turner Overdrive hit: "_____ Ain't Seen Nothing Yet"
88. Impecunious
89. Extended family, say
92. Thespian's comment to the audience
95. French horn alternate name
98. Rummage around for a weasel?
100. Car wheel cover
102. Changed boundaries, for example
104. Hebrew letters for Liz?
105. Serf's kin

106. Journalist-turned-senator Mike
107. It goes with "aid"
108. Hillside in the Highlands
109. Deceit
110. "Sometimes When We Touch" singer Dan
111. "Vaya Con _____"
112. Open a parcel
113. Take a spin on a cycle
114. Some Senate votes
116. _____ *Baba and the Forty Thieves*
118. Miss. neighbour
119. Auction grouping

14 Canada Cornucopia 7

ACROSS

1. Austen heroine
5. Pillow cover
9. Reason to take Advil
13. Despise
17. Menial worker
18. Scarlett O'Hara's home
19. First album from Victoria's Furtado: _____, *Nelly!*
20. Extremely keen
21. Vacationers' lodgings
22. Tiptop?
23. Sensed
24. Alberta-born singer k.d.
25. Models strut their stuff on these
27. African Mediterranean Sea city
28. *Winnipeg _____ Press*
29. Dress _____
31. Fire a young female?
33. Genre for New Brunswick's Measha Brueggergosman
35. Hammerhead's kin
36. Tapioca source
37. Lacking lustre?
38. _____-Cola
39. Crowbar star Kelly
40. Lake Erie sand spit: Long _____
43. English poet and novelist Walter
45. *Seinfeld* stalwart: Elaine _____
47. He built an ark
48. Eye part
49. Pleasing to the ear, musically
51. American Native
52. You use this to indent
55. Alice Munro classic: *Lives of _____ and Women*
56. Type of plum
58. Dude, in the 'hood
59. Female choir member
61. Egotistical actress, say
62. NHLers Daniel and Henrik Sedin, for short
64. It might be white
65. Some sacraments
69. Indiana NBA player
71. Some appliances, for short
72. Crow
73. Independent U.N.C.L.E. agent?
74. Not digital
76. Many millennia (var.)
77. Destructive weapon
78. Grass cutting blades
80. Little bit of sewing?
82. Book part
83. In any way
85. Like a loosening levee
88. Undo
89. MasterCard rival
90. Family business successor, say
91. Long-running TVOntario kids' show: *Polka Dot _____*
92. Gator's African kin
93. Authentic, in Oppenheim
94. "Beware the _____ of March"
95. _____ by the wayside
96. Cows, old style
97. Hebrides island
98. Furtive letters?
99. Makes every bit count

DOWN

1. Hollywood's *The Ten Commandments*, for example
2. Actress Suvari
3. Expo 67 city
4. Reply in writing, say
5. Trite
6. Headgear for a horse
7. Superpowers' competition?
8. *My Little Chickadee* actress West
9. Horrible
10. CBC Ontario radio host Wei
11. Took a vacation
12. Dines at home
13. Shape in the night sky
14. Greedy
15. Pitchfork points
16. Rims
26. Cry of triumph
27. Confucian ideal
30. Jamaican musical genre
32. Opposite of guzzle
33. Weird
34. _____-board
36. Javier's hands
38. BC Rockies landmark: Marble _____
39. Jiggly gelatin brand
41. Canada joined this org. in 1949
42. Christie mystery: *And_____ There Were None*
44. Canadian golfer Norman, et al.
45. Swiss city
46. It clads a house
49. Western Russia city
50. Spanish wine
52. Baker's spoonful (abbr.)
53. Solo at the Met
54. 2000 Juno Awards single of the year
55. Norwegian composer Edvard
57. Long-time CBC news personality Peter
60. Toy that bounces
61. Church officials' lodgings
63. Prisoner's punishment
65. Gate take
66. Publication from Canada's Podleski sisters
67. Stately tree
68. Cry
70. Cheer segment
72. Honey producer
75. These fall in the fall
76. Garlic bulb
77. Mason's box
78. *Star Trek* Vulcan
79. Ladies' pants style

80. Annual Woodbine event: Queen's _____

81. Best's opposite

84. Covered in soot

86. Like an unaccompanied ranger?

87. 1974 Top Ten song: "_____ tu"

90. Band of 54-D: The Tragically _____

15 How Swede It Is

Scandinavian stuff

ACROSS

1. Order of Canada writer Gallant
6. Overawes
10. Glance over
14. It gives you a sense of direction?
17. Cut from the same cloth
18. Somewhat
19. Mythological goddess of youth
20. It comes before beauty
21. **Prestigious international award**
23. Not to mention
24. Terry Fox _____
25. Prepared broccoli, say
26. Northern Portuguese wine city
28. No longer pristine
29. "Yeah, right!"
31. Unusable crops
33. Shapes with curves
37. Céline Dion song: "Let's _____ About Love"
39. Using a flat iron, say
42. Word repeated twice in Ontario's motto
44. Cornerstone (var.)
46. Tip Top employee?
47. Slowly, on a musical score
49. Groom's "ring toss" at his reception
52. Strait in Newfoundland: _____ Isle
53. Ottawa NHL player
55. Buenos _____
57. Bank (on)
58. **Outdoor power products producer**
61. Altar platform
65. 1988 Olympics city
66. Analyze intensely
72. Love, in Laval
74. Garden clippers
77. Great Canadian _____ Store
78. Fuel derived from organic waste
80. Banish to Elba, say
82. Fine hosiery thread
83. One who gives it the old college try?
86. Light source
88. Internet image that multiplies
89. Bundles of joy for Navajo families
91. Stable mama
93. Any minute now, old style
95. Fish for a tank
96. *Guernica* painter Pablo
101. Garland for a luau
102. They make you scratch your head
103. **Photography supply company**
106. Greek god of cookware?
107. You might worship from here?
108. Opposite of busy
109. Diminish in intensity
110. Decide upon
111. Deceives in a transaction
112. Frobisher and Resolute, in Nunavut
113. Disciplines a wild dog

DOWN

1. Takes charge of the guys?
2. Bucketloads
3. Feeling, colloquially
4. **Home furnishings giant**
5. Canadian actress Diamond of *Night Court* fame
6. Heart-related
7. It keeps a kimono closed
8. Michael Jackson movie: *The _____*
9. Stairs
10. Long-time Canadian children's entertainers: _____, Lois and Bram
11. Glasgow football club
12. **Premium vodka brand**
13. Prefix with con or Gothic
14. French coastal city
15. Chills illness
16. Await resolution
22. Annoying insect?
27. Prickly pear, for example
28. Not as pretty
30. Whup
32. Omani or Saudi
33. Sorrowful interjection, old style
34. Went for a gallop
35. One of the primary colours
36. Fictional genre that spans generations
38. Soul Hybrid carmaker
40. Former Pittsburgh Steelers coach Chuck
41. CFL's coveted prize: _____ Cup
43. Fired up
45. Nordic raw salmon serving
48. Circus spectators' outcries?
50. To do this is human
51. Tear apart
54. Streets, in Châteauguay
56. Made a statement
59. In a scale, it follows "fah"
60. More strange
61. Middle Eastern dish: _____ ghanouj
62. Let off light
63. It's debatable?
64. Hercules cleaned these stables
67. Spanish region: Costa del _____
68. Slender
69. 2011 Toby Keith single: "Somewhere _____"
70. Not at all stressed
71. Balsam fir or birch
73. Slope for a skateboarder
75. Needle
76. Area of urban blight

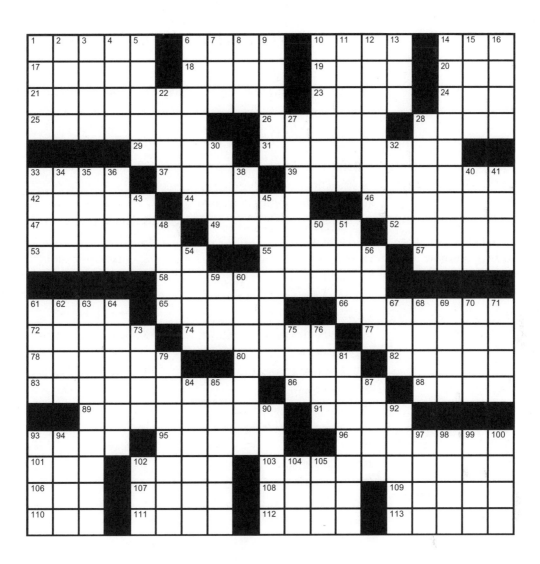

79. **Music streaming service**
81. Slips by, like the sands of time
84. End of a construction worker's boot
85. Some organic compounds
87. Cheese tray item
90. Old Colonial India title

92. Fame, and perhaps fortune, too
93. Dog's dinner brand
94. _____ tide
97. **Musical export extraordinaire**
98. Criticize a bridge player?
99. Fill up
100. Creations of Keats

102. Trail behind the pack
104. 1969 novel by Vladimir Nabokov
105. On the _____

Four-Square 1

Use mini grids to solve a CanCon phrase

ACROSS

1. _____ Gallery of Greater Victoria
4. Greek letter
7. Day's good fortune?
10. Beatles hit: "_____ Loves You"
13. Girl's opposite
14. Mythological bird
15. Ontario Court of Appeal (abbr.)
16. Hankering in Honshu?
17. Just scratching the surface
19. See 4-A
20. Awesome room warmer?
21. Appetizers, in Ibiza
22. Not out playing
24. Minor detail
26. Summer annual
27. Poker table action
28. Diana Rigg TV role
29. Email or text
30. Corporate combos?
31. Have an inkling about a criminal?
38. "Great Lash" cosmetic
45. Japanese monarch
46. Immune system stimulator
47. In an unadorned manner
48. Most inexperienced
49. Wind chime sound
50. Ontario university
51. Joule unit
52. Rideau Hall city (abbr.)
54. McGill uni scholar
56. Israeli city: _____ Aviv
57. To the _____ degree
58. Flightless bird
59. Jackie's second spouse
60. Compass pt.
61. "Goodness me!"
62. Swindle
63. Retired Newfoundland band: Great Big _____

DOWN

1. *Dancing with the Stars* network
2. Gymnast's floor performance
3. Autocrats
4. Zagreb nation
5. Providing with ponies?
6. Winter sidewalks description
7. Quick flight, say
8. Attain one's goals
9. She might work with oils or acrylics
10. Nurse's needle
11. More exotic
12. Makes oneself beloved
18. Expels (var.)
23. Performed, vocally
24. Mother, in Manchester
25. Grow
26. Country songstress Tillis
31. Poets' stanzas
32. Rogers Centre officials
33. Sequin on a US banner?
34. Staffer's reward
35. By and by, old style
36. French scribe of *Gigi*
37. 1987 Blue Rodeo song
38. 1990s Dan Aykroyd sitcom: *Soul _____*
39. Long-running TV drama: *Grey's _____*
40. Causes controversy, say
41. Wild cat species
42. Day planners
43. Refurbish
44. Insect army insect
53. Hot beverage in Québec
54. Identify a Steely Dan song?
55. US org. for international intelligence

To solve the CanCon phrase:

Decode a four-word Tom Cochrane & Red Rider song title by using:

• One horizontal word from Square 1.

• One horizontal word from Square 2.

• One vertical word from Square 3.

• One vertical word from Square 4.

Answer: _____ _____
_____ _____

SQUARE 1

1	2	3	■	4	5	6
13			■	14		
17			18			
■	21					■
24					25	
27						
29						

SQUARE 2

7	8	9	■	10	11	12
15			■	16		
19			■	20		
■	22		23			
26						
28						
30						

SQUARE 3

31	32	33	34	35	36	37
45						
47						
49						■
51			■	52		53
56			■	57		
60			■	61		

SQUARE 4

38	39	40	41	42	43	44
46						
48						
■	50					■
54						55
58			■	59		
62			■	63		

17 Yes, Sirs!

Say "good knight" to these titled Canadians

ACROSS

1. Turn sharply
4. Use a drill
8. Cut like a knife?
12. Sudden rush of liquid
17. Like much Petro-Canada gas
19. Star in Cetus
20. *Mr. Dressup* personality Coombs
21. **Alberta politician James Alexander**
22. "And others" abbr.
23. Innocent in the ways of the world
24. "For _____ us a child is born"
25. Petite pistol?
27. Chaise kin
28. British verb ending
29. Forearm bone
30. Bird kingdom dippers (var.)
31. Downtown Vancouver, say
36. **1896 prime minister Charles**
38. _____ bill of goods
39. Raccoons' meals?
42. Some consonants, in Greek
43. Robert W. Service poem: "The Cremation of _____ McGee"
46. Less consistent
48. Farthest orbital point
50. Animal's pen
51. **Poet Charles G.D.**
52. Nose, colloquially
53. Cooley whose servitude led to Upper Canada's Act Against Slavery
54. Canadian pop star: Carly _____ Jepsen
55. **Businessman John Craig**
56. Boxing icon Muhammad
57. You might count these before sleeping
60. 67-A, for example

61. **Standard time inventor Sandford**
65. Hang around?
66. Small bird
67. Compromise, for Caesar
68. _____ de Triomphe
69. When repeated three times, a Beach Boys hit
70. Average Joe: Ham-and-_____
72. Put up a building
73. **Seventh Ontario premier William Howard**
76. PC logins, say
78. Headgear for a horse
80. Pied Piper's disappointed expression?
83. Except
84. Kindled again
85. African desert
87. *Dallas Buyers Club* Oscar winner Jared
91. Die down in intensity
92. Québec city
93. **Father of Confederation Hector-Louis**
95. Perspiration, old style
96. Not in control
97. With surreptitious intent
98. Ryans Gosling and Reynolds
99. Thumbs-down House of Commons votes
100. Unusual opportunities?
101. Law, in Latin

DOWN

1. Natal Native
2. Before long, to a bard
3. Too much on the market, say
4. Interjection for Scrooge
5. Black Sea port city
6. Appears again
7. Icelandic epic
8. Common sense?

9. Big mythological god?
10. Biblical mountain
11. Garden bloomer: Bee _____
12. Spoofs
13. Laud
14. All around the world?
15. Competitor
16. Adolescents
18. A narcissist has a big one
26. Molokai feast
28. "Suspicious Minds" lyric: "We're caught _____"
30. Composer's output
31. 1970s Canada hockey rival
32. Seizure from a delinquent bill payer
33. 1958 sci-fi flick: *The _____*
34. Made revisions
35. Flubbed file extension letters?
37. Military squad
40. **Insulin pioneer Frederick**
41. Eating utensil
44. Way back then
45. Canadian hip hop pioneer Michie
47. Suffix with Samson or social
49. Mark Howe, to Gordie
50. Monster of myth
52. Classical composer Erik
53. Harper government health minister Tony
55. _____-splitting
56. Mobile state (abbr.)
57. Luxurious place to spend a day
58. Beatles song: "_____ Majesty"
59. A whole Mexican meal?
60. Microscope component
61. Incendiary troublemaker?
62. The same, to Octavia
63. Pleasant
64. Gangsters' weapons
66. Certain
67. Visual Effects Society (abbr.)

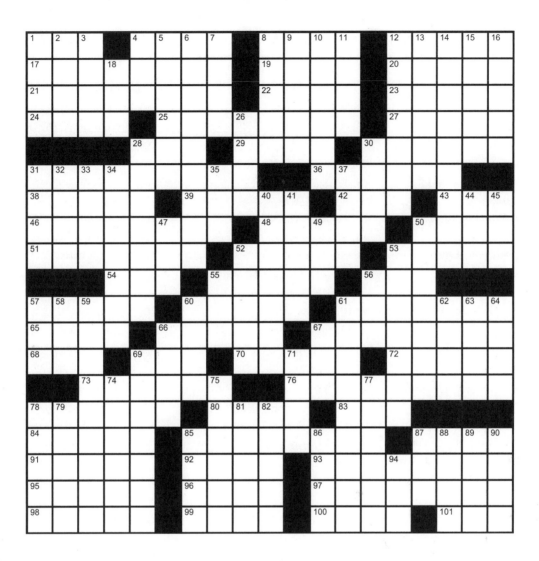

69. Hesitates

71. See 12-A

74. She makes words worthy

75. Shock to the system?

77. Destroyed

78. Famed musical quintet: Canadian _____

79. Prove to be false

81. Mixed metal

82. Speaks

85. Genghis _____

86. To boot

87. Tirana currency

88. It's vile?

89. Small ceramic square

90. Black stone

94. It's a natural resource

ACROSS

1. Eat quickly, colloquially
6. Some Louisiana land
11. Tweaks
18. Abalone
19. Governor General's award-winning writer Shields
20. RCMP employee, colloquially
21. Hockey great Hull
22. City in Ghana
23. Unappreciative person
24. Ethics
27. Middle Eastern royal
28. Large Japanese city
29. Transmits an email
30. Yodeller's acme?
31. Cat Stevens song: "Morning _____ Broken"
33. Lisa LaFlamme delivers this
35. Drumstick
36. Sheep's wool
39. "So _____ written"
41. Without, in Shawinigan
43. The rest
45. Orkney Island landmark: _____ Flow
47. Canadian-grown apple
49. Carson's Severinsen
50. NU or NT
51. Soothing words
53. Greek letter
55. Decks out in dresses?
57. Prince Edward Island capital
60. 1991 movie starring Canada's Neve Campbell: _____ Tango
63. Heap
64. Motley collection of cleaning cloths?
68. Reckon
69. Medium's special sense
71. MGs and Miatas
73. Replay speed
74. Relating to a branch of math
77. Upper layer of Earth's crust
79. Village People hit
80. Nike competitor
81. Summa _____ laude
83. Shed some light on?
85. Physique, slangily
86. Spanish hero: El _____
87. Wolves, to a Spaniard
89. News service: Canadian _____
91. Cleaning product: _____ and Span
93. "O Canada," for example
97. Verified an accountant's account?
99. Canadian channel that airs Project Runway
100. Chef's strainer
101. Canadian Shield igneous rock
102. South American ungulate
103. Feminine pronouns, in Pointe-Claire
104. Chooses
105. Backyard buildings
106. Markets

DOWN

1. Bawls
2. Half a pair of comfy clogs?
3. Like gods' grub?
4. Symbolic crossword?
5. Component of a kitchen set
6. Scoundrel
7. Texas Brazos River city
8. Roll-shaped cloud
9. Ort
10. 2001 romcom: The Wedding _____
11. Out of alignment, say
12. Hockey commentator Cherry, et al.
13. Ewer
14. Without any abatement
15. Calgary CFL player
16. Monkey type
17. He envisions the future?
25. Luau guitars, for short
26. Sharpened a knife, say
30. 2001 boxing film
31. Snake's warning
32. Alberta-based energy company
34. Slow moving gastropod
36. Important mathematical component?
37. Prepare for interment, old style
38. Goes off track
40. NASA doctors' specialty
42. Sailing vessel
44. Castle's defensive ditch
46. Tooth trouble
48. Lofty storage area?
52. Foodies
54. Mythological strongman
56. "Jabberwocky" opening contraction
58. Italian garden bloomer
59. Like discomfiting mysteries
60. Texting acronym for "This Day And Age"
61. Had title, say
62. Like the murder of a monarch
65. Nancy Grace's nightly explosion?
66. Airport Management Council of Ontario (abbr.)
67. Prod
70. Loop of lace
72. Needleworkers' practice pieces
75. Spoiled rotten?
76. Picasso, et al.
78. Old Italian currency
82. Dough or bread
84. Past and present
87. Fills the hold
88. Take verbal potshots
90. Subway entrance
91. Droops

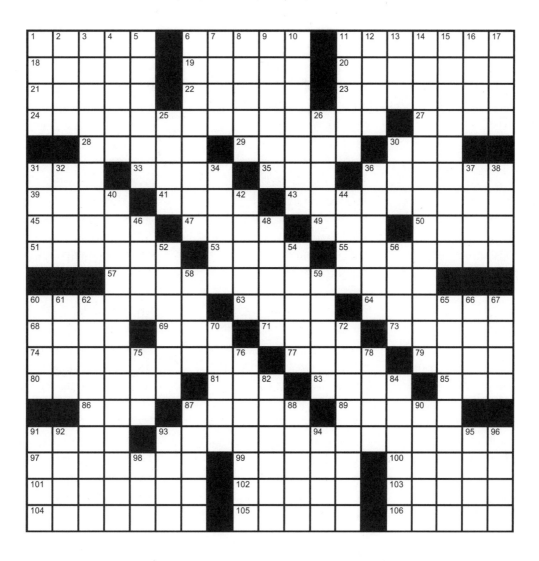

92. Free of pollutants

93. Bottom line, in Birmingham

94. Etcher's fluid

95. First name in motorcycle daredevilry

96. Pigsty, perhaps

98. Twitching motion

Repetitious

Play with a letter pattern

ACROSS

1. Pen name of Canadian cartoonist Gregory Gallant
5. Play guitar, say
10. Mail pickup bldg.
13. European coin in former times
18. Sicken with excess
19. Boxing venue
20. Face parts
22. Lively, in music
23. Some people put on these?
24. Overnights in the great outdoors
25. *Olympic* or *Titanic*
27. Peat product
28. Federal agency: _____ Canada
29. Assegai-wielding South African
30. Airmanship experts
31. Brownstone porch, say
33. Before, before
34. Descendants of Persians
35. Canadian _____
36. **Place to eat pie**
39. Cage
40. Barenaked Ladies hit: "_____ Week"
43. Casual shirt
44. *Exodus* role
45. Anti-fur grp.
47. Nine and 19 (abbr.)
50. Tell all?
52. Soak
55. Notched, like a saw
57. Architectural feature at Anne's place?
58. Painted onto plaster
60. It clings?
61. Lead a movement, say
63. Former Montréal MLBer moniker
64. Steno pool employee
65. Canada's John McCrae wrote a very famous one
66. Greek cheer
67. Aerobics move
69. Daytona 500 racers' grp.
73. King Tut's cross
75. Ship that places explosives
80. Looks forward to
81. Loud and clear?
83. Belittle
84. Some governmental groups
86. Losing colour
87. Not musical to the ear?
88. +
89. Netherlands cheese
91. Tony Randall played this Dr. in a movie
92. Compass point in Québec
93. Ex-Canadien Lafleur who wore #10
94. Predatory fish
96. **Employee filled with ennui**
101. Sew socks
103. Multi-vehicle collision
104. 2015 film: _____-*Man*
105. Like a royal highness?
109. Freudian concerns
110. Gathers one's rewards?
111. Autoimmune illness
113. Successfully treat a disease
114. Everything's better with this on it
116. "Theme From Shaft" singer Hayes
117. Weight allowance, in shipping
118. Contemporary of Edison
119. Jackson or Puente
120. Bones in the pelvis
121. Not under
122. Stalks
123. Setting of *Platoon*, for short
124. Adhesives resin
125. Dump scavengers

DOWN

1. Pyramid schemes, for example
2. Writers T.S. or George
3. Large part of the body
4. Aromatic herb
5. Anatomical pouches
6. Circus acrobat's swing
7. Fish that freeloads?
8. Not ready
9. Pole on a ship
10. Dawna Friesen anchors for this national network
11. Scoundrel, in Seville
12. Unlocks one's emotions?
13. Sri Lankan lentil
14. Eastern Europe Christian church member
15. Reds MLB city
16. Mideast chieftain (var.)
17. Opposite of verbose
21. Literary send-ups
26. Some fraternity members
32. **Little feet make this sound**
34. **Sleeping Beauty beau**
37. Letter unique to the US
38. God of war in mythology
39. **Social gathering goodies tray**
40. CBA and CLC, for short
41. Tide word
42. Dresden's river
46. Rorschach procedure recipient
48. *The Andy Griffith Show* character
49. Shakers or Amish
51. It connects pie and mode
52. CBC's *Heartland* and *Murdoch Mysteries*
53. See 120-A
54. In the know
56. Blame, colloquially
58. Attorney's retainer, say
59. Treating with medication
62. Got riders ready

66. Mucilaginous vegetable pod
68. It makes a big bang noise
69. Canada's Chris Hadfield soared with this grp.
70. Blew away?
71. Bird found in Asia and Africa
72. It gathers US intel
74. Network Time Protocol (abbr.)
75. Past child-bearing age
76. Blood-typing system letters
77. Yin-_____

78. Jacob's twin, in the Bible
79. Be dependent upon
82. Old alarm clock face
85. Perceptive
87. Cigar detritus
90. It protects skin from UVB radiation
92. Mouth of a river
95. He founded Scholasticism
97. Catnip plant, for example
98. Like special order cabinetry

99. Empty a suitcase
100. Religious service officiant
101. Amounts owing
102. End of a drawstring
103. NBA athlete, for example
106. Tropical yellow fruit
107. Saguenay street sign
108. Looks lecherously
111. *Friends* star Kudrow
112. Bunch
115. Some Dalhousie degs.

ACROSS

1. Barrie OHL team
6. Vacuum filter type
10. Electrostatic Discharge (abbr.)
13. Place to store skis
17. Inuit water craft
18. Highest point
19. And not
20. Dash of panache
21. Self-control, say
23. African animal
24. Like pre-stereo recordings
25. Intensely emotional
26. Most lank, like hair
29. John who explored the Arctic in the 1840s
31. Prisoner who won't be parolled
33. Maurice Richard nickname (with "The")
34. Has possession of
36. Station, in Saguenay
37. Completely necessary
41. Canadian tennis star Pospisil
43. Holidays in Dec.
45. San Bernadino County city
46. Heather family shrubs
48. Ridges in the mountains
50. She wrote *Middlemarch*
51. Landlord's list
53. Manitoba Stampede & Exhibition, for one
55. Single digit number, in Québec
56. Piggy
57. Cdn. retirees' plan
58. Cheerleader's encouraging word
60. Stairs leading to the Ganges
64. Ping-Pong playing surface
66. It contains legal precedents
71. Like a Supreme Court of Canada justice
73. ASAP
75. Radio-Canada TV medical drama
76. Lacy fabric
78. Misbehaves on the set?
80. Change
81. Barge into a backyard party?
83. Farmer's field size
85. Theatre box
86. Hairstyling foam
87. Actress Perlman, and others
89. Ottawa Redblacks booster
90. 1973 Harvard-set movie (with "*The*")
94. President Gerald's Ford?
96. Depart
97. Cassis-flavoured aperitif
98. Survive to the end
102. Ultimatum word
103. Guided
104. Keen on
105. Signal receiver
106. Fruit tree type
107. Speech hesitation sounds
108. Observed
109. Appears to be

DOWN

1. Ruminant's regurgitation
2. Jamaican "Cheerleader" singer
3. Eavesdrops
4. Crunchy Mexican shell serving
5. Bagpipe sound
6. Eastern province capital
7. Description of the body's outer layer
8. It can be mightier than the sword
9. Chops
10. Rapt
11. Former Seattle NBA team
12. More intoxicated
13. Payments
14. Succulent plant
15. Waste receptacles
16. Lovers' entanglement?
22. Bluenose
27. Forest canopy component
28. Former Canadian film award prize
29. Irish band member?
30. In on the dirt
32. Stern end, say
35. Small denomination?
38. 1970s tennis star Nastase
39. At the summit, say
40. Former US senator Trent
42. Small racing machine (var.)
44. Garden of Eden snake
47. Chimney substance
49. Transfusion substance
52. We do this every four years?
54. Brewery kiln
57. Some women's hats
59. Goddess in *The Iliad*
60. 21st Manitoba premier Selinger
61. Boxer Oscar De La
62. Aid's partner in crime?
63. Transmit data readings by radio
65. Canadian athletes Derick and Jean-Luc
66. European train car compartment
67. Dwight who became Newfoundland's premier in 2015
68. Not in synch, in the orchestra pit
69. Psi follower
70. 1970s Canadian figure skater Magnussen
72. HGTV Canada specialty
74. Old Russian royal
77. Flatter to gain favour
79. Manning of Reform Party renown
82. More pallid
84. Per
88. Catalogues
90. Coop chirp

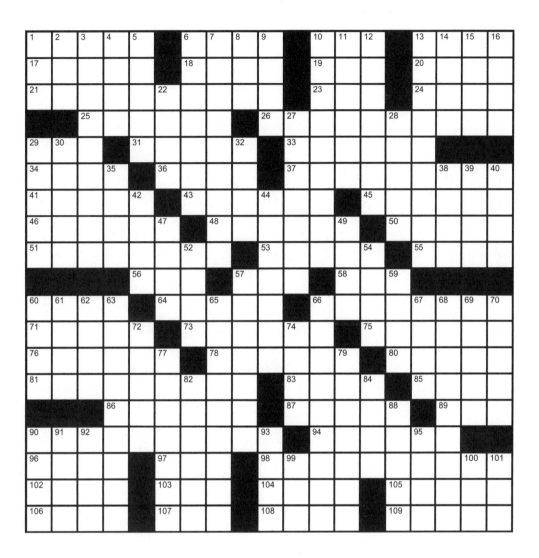

91. Car part

92. Tuscany tourist town

93. Protection (var.)

95. Romantic rascal

99. Ship's heading, sometimes (abbr.)

100. Onyx or opal

101. Time units (abbr.)

21 Either/Or

Canadian style

ACROSS

1. Kids' clique
5. Work at U of T
10. Baker's measurement unit (abbr.)
13. 1983 "Hosers" movie: *Strange* _____
17. "Three men walk into _____ . . ."
18. Domed dwelling in the North
19. Imperial _____
20. Split apart
21. Actor Richard
22. Callisto and Carpo
23. Middle Eastern domains
25. "_____ pinch of salt"
26. Irk
27. Rising to the top
28. More convoluted
31. Spoken aloud
32. Toronto Blue Jays won this in '92 and '93
35. Pretenses
37. Petite amphibians
41. Willow trees
42. Ill-tempered
43. Tune's text
44. Maudlin
45. Annual bike race since 1909: _____ d'Italia
46. Wedding day transport
49. Bird that doesn't get off the ground
50. Rear end
51. Feet, to a zoologist
52. Mountain or former premier
54. Brought home a paycheque
56. It calls soldiers to their quarters
57. Seasonal traveller or Anne Murray hit
60. Capital near Casablanca
61. Great Barrier formation
65. Scuttle

66. Salacious stare
67. Feels sick
68. Sarcastic
69. Burrard Inlet community: Port _____
71. Handy-dandy
73. Envision anger?
74. Gumbo recipe ingredient
75. It's a fruit and a vegetable
77. Old coins of Athens
78. *Your Show of Shows* star Reiner
80. Gathers US law enforcers together?
82. 1970s sitcom family
86. Comportment
87. Ontario-born hockey star Rick
91. Maple Leafs match in the States, for example
92. Properly prepared, to Muslims
93. 1996 Rush single: "Test for _____"
94. OFF! mosquito repelling spiral
95. 1952 Rock Hudson comedy: *Has Anybody Seen My _____?*
96. Idolize
97. It separates the knee from the foot
98. Bends in pipes
99. Emergency Notification System (abbr.)
100. Untidy
101. Ilk

DOWN

1. "Poker Face" vocalist: Lady _____
2. Still sleeping
3. Salve, old style
4. Your niece's son, to you
5. Ontario city or Cowboy Junkies vocalist
6. Narcissistic person
7. Soaring

8. Set up a computer, say
9. Santa's sounds
10. Puts a piggy in the water?
11. Lake or former Governor General
12. Gripping tools
13. Premier Wall's full first name
14. Singer MacNeil from Cape Breton
15. Tied
16. Compass point
24. Hospital worker (abbr.)
27. Rail anagram
29. On your guard
30. You can spend these in France
32. *National* _____
33. Genesis twin
34. Puppies' bites
36. Word component
38. Adjective for the True North
39. Canada's Fleming invented this: Standard _____
40. Gulf War weapon
42. Tom-tom, for example
43. Bestseller from Montrealer Naomi Klein: *No* _____
45. Romance or science fiction
47. Bits of Greek?
48. Shania's ex Lange
51. _____-dieu
53. You don't want to stir up this
55. Adroitly done, say
56. Like some men's clothing?
57. Jerk (var.)
58. Kitchen cranny?
59. Scent, in San Francisco
60. Dip for naan
62. Land for a Dubliner
63. German river
64. Government workers, colloquially
68. Annual Canadian commercial enterprise: _____ hunt

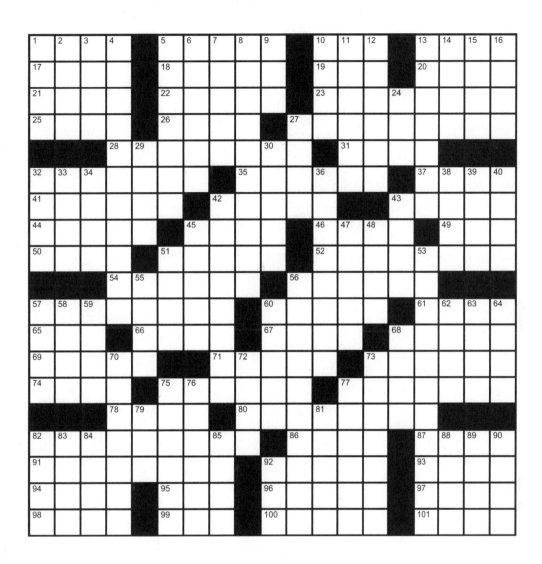

70. Three-syllable metrical feet
72. Not at all racy
73. **Cup or Park**
75. Medics do this
76. **Alberta river or Neil Young song**
77. Removes a ram's coat

79. Buenos Aires country (abbr.)
81. They house missiles
82. Walk to and fro
83. Missing from the military
84. Former name of a Canadian company: CP _____
85. Goos for dos

88. Sore and stiff
89. HMCS *Regina*, for example
90. Fine-tune skills
92. Black Forest _____

Canada Cornucopia 10

ACROSS

1. Stopper
5. "Take on Me" '80s band
8. Former CBC revue: *The _____ in the Hall*
12. Martin Luther King quote: "Let no man pull you _____ as to hate him"
17. Pathway
18. German
20. North American Free _____ Agreement
21. German grandmas
22. Ontario university city
23. Canadian-born cosmetics queen Elizabeth
24. Experimental airplane flyer
26. Tiny insect
27. Old CBC kids' show: *The Friendly _____*
28. Grab a cab during a summer storm?
29. Pungent meat adjective
31. Some sheep
33. National women's magazine since 1928
36. Too decorous
37. U of A advanced deg.
40. Coating of frost
41. You might hold this if you're resentful
43. Accept a dare, say
45. That is, to Tiberius
47. Prepped a violin bow
49. Sheer curtains fabric
50. 33-D, for example
51. Traditional body of poetry
53. Exaggerated depiction in a political cartoon
55. Shade of raw silk
56. Reins adjunct
57. Hounds
58. Canada's "Intrepid" spy William

62. *Goin' Down the Road* character
63. Afternoon meal, in Manchester
66. _____ kitchen
67. French philosopher Denis
69. Canadian clothing and shoes retailer
71. Serene
73. Command, old style
74. White _____ BC
75. It precedes Aviv, in Israel
76. Signals
78. Consequences of calculus?
81. Diatribe
82. At the apex
83. To _____ his own
84. Genesis tower location
87. Eats an entree
89. NYC brownstones, say
93. It puts you away from the scene of a crime
94. Sleeping trouble
96. 2003 Alice Munro offering: *No _____ Lost*
97. Find a new tenant
98. Makes more abrasive
99. "Praise the Lord!"
100. Field who won an acting Oscar
101. Pother or bother
102. Kids' crafting substance: Play-_____
103. Tear

DOWN

1. Novel story?
2. Hobbled
3. Brazen
4. Has a bun in the oven
5. Without any restrictions
6. "Physician, _____ thyself"
7. Rotorcrafts (var.)
8. Setting for *M*A*S*H* (abbr.)
9. Dental filling

10. Singer Céline
11. Black duck
12. Leader in theatrical circles?
13. Iris
14. Russian car brand
15. Japanese broth-based dish
16. Departed
19. Nervous system infection
25. Pizza or pecan unit
30. Southern Alberta city
32. Jokester
33. Nursery furniture piece
34. Conceal
35. Run _____
36. Look at a Lady in London?
37. Drop-down list on a computer
38. Cad
39. L.M. Montgomery created this Shirley
42. See 26-A
44. Model airplane packages
46. Insignificant detail
48. Kitchen nook
52. Before 1492: _____-Columbian
54. Manx or Maine Coon
55. "Beowulf," for example
56. Foreshadow
58. Labour Day month (abbr.)
59. Margaret Atwood novel: *The Handmaid's _____*
60. And others, on a list
61. They're part of the family
62. Put off
63. Delicious, to the dentist?
64. Carve with acid
65. Questions
68. Changes a Conservative party?
70. Prophetic, at Delphi?
72. Greyish-brown horse
77. Canadian parliamentary post: _____ Commissioner
79. Go over again
80. Long-time leader of China

81. Resist authority

82. Very, musically

84. Prisoners' pubs?

85. _____ *iacta est*

86. Québec law: _____ 101

88. Presently, in old poetry

90. Big tippler

91. Tied up?

92. Transmit

95. Morsel

23 Once Upon a Time . . .

These ladies ruled

ACROSS

1. Middle ear bonelet
6. Afternoon social events
10. High school math subj.
14. Jewish theologian
19. Not a person
20. Provide assistance
21. Herman Melville novel
22. Canada's involved with this Asian economic org.
23. She lived happily ever after?
25. Juno-winning rock group
26. Mooring spots for Morgan?
27. *The Sun _____ Rises*
28. European river
29. She suffered from arachnophobia?
31. Busy, say
33. Pad for a Japanese pad
36. 2,000 pounds, in America
37. Most full of wisdom
39. Sticks in the mud?
40. Bright bloom
45. There was no room at this place
46. Set up
48. Canadian rockers: The Tragically _____
51. Redacts
52. Coral's location
54. Eagles' home
55. Lindbergh's craft, et al.
57. Some apples
59. Dirty rats?
60. Montréal mother
61. Hawaiian's patio
62. Like a Greek philosophy
64. Tiny bug
65. Market kiosk
68. She loved winter?
70. Grimm baddies
72. Long-time Canadian paint retailer
73. Beverage first produced in Canada in 1906
75. Produce a magazine?
77. Ovule covering
79. Vegetable you might want to stick with?
80. Loser's position
84. Like a Colón citizen
86. Rome's river
87. Walked (on)
88. Puffiness condition
89. Catch some rays
90. Betrays a conspirator
92. Immature sheep
93. Former CBC kids' show: _____ *Park*
95. Door, in Rivière-du-Loup
96. Right next to
98. Ortiz of *Ugly Betty*
100. Latches onto
101. Free from
102. She hitched a ride?
107. Fast friend
108. It follows *decree*, in court
111. Nickname for actor Humphrey
112. Many parking places?
113. She had great hair?
116. Taco chip topping
117. The same, in Saguenay
118. Plastics component
119. Stompin' Tom song: "_____ Canadian Girl"
120. Comedian Richard
121. They can take a yoke?
122. Getting warm?
123. Chef's list

DOWN

1. Copacati worshipper
2. Shred of fibre
3. Recipient of a delivery
4. Not yet completed
5. Understand
6. Topic
7. Some seafood entrees
8. The entire enchilada
9. Marienbad, for example
10. Sagan's favourite flowers?
11. Full speed ahead, at sea
12. Foresters' journals?
13. It follows East, in Canada
14. She was witty with words?
15. "Sure . . ."
16. Filet mignon, for example
17. Denuded
18. Workplace for researchers (abbr.)
24. Hold oneself back
30. Bygone flightless bird
32. Canada's neighbour to the south, for short
33. The last word you'll read?
34. Instinctive drive
35. Start of a par 5
37. Banting and Borden
38. Once more
39. Reviewer's manuscript notes
41. Toronto-born Hockey Hall of Fame inductee Oates
42. One-dimensional
43. Forever, poetically
44. Personal holdings
47. Becoming popular again
48. Islamic afterlife companion
49. Like a thirst that can't be quenched?
50. Canada's Anne Michaels and Gwendolyn MacEwen
53. Tumbled off the wagon
55. Latte flavouring
56. Greek consonant
58. After-bath powder
59. Menial
62. Like some statements
63. French politician's ouster?

65. John Constable works
66. Angry outburst
67. Mrs. Chrétien's skirt styles?
69. It separates continents
71. Moolah
74. Source of citrusy salad leaves
76. Plant parts
78. Priest from the East
80. Jaunty airs
81. Craftsman
82. Like most schools
83. *Bridget Jones: The _____ of Reason*
85. She was overly protective?
86. School session
90. Besides
91. Toronto's Hanlan's Point was named after this rower
94. It's not WSW
95. Typewriter roller
97. Mexican state
99. San Antonio tourist attraction
100. Travelocity mascot
101. It traps speeders
102. Recipe amt.
103. Wintry coating
104. Unprepossessing
105. Soybean paste
106. Shrub with berries
107. A defendant enters one
109. German card game
110. Capri or Catalina
113. Former national program: Long-_____ Registry
114. Swedish currency of old
115. Saskatchewan place: Fond-du-_____

ACROSS

1. Baked Alaska, for example
6. Half of Tenzin Gyatso's title
10. Touch on
14. Beam of light
17. Take weapons away
18. "It's _____!"
19. Italian city state ruler
20. Hopi cousin
21. Jasper Avenue or Calgary Trail, in Edmonton
23. Gingerbread ingredient
25. BC beer brand
26. Canada's Eastern provinces
28. Banned insecticide
29. Silk-like fabric
30. Some text messages
33. Squirt
36. Wakes
38. Semitic language group
39. Work on a renovation
42. "Uh-huh"
44. Japanese poetry style
45. Tropical hat (var.)
46. House of Commons chair?
49. *Global National* journalist Eric
51. Aristocrat, perhaps
53. New Brunswick city
55. Contemporary
56. Secure a rope while rock climbing
57. Place next to
63. Can _____
65. First Lady in the 1930s and '40s
66. BC river
71. Steffi Graf achieved this in 1988: Grand _____
73. Vital force, in yoga
74. Two-term US president
75. _____-of-war
77. Footballs
79. Timid, in Tel Aviv?
81. Like itchy eyes
84. Type of 4-D
85. Calm
86. Bonavista-born ex-NHLer Michael
87. Anatomical duct
90. Square dancers' linked turn
92. Dutch domestic scenes artist Johannes
96. Where hospital visitors gather
98. Canvas shoe style
100. *Much _____ About Nothing*
101. Semi-monthly tide
102. Is contrite
103. Not upright
104. Sandefjord country (abbr.)
105. Whirlpool
106. Expectorated
107. Canadian actress Mitchell, et al.

DOWN

1. Play for pay, in the subway
2. 1975 hit: "Holdin' _____ Yesterday"
3. Former Oilers star Messier
4. Sandwich component
5. Improve
6. *The Birdcage* star Nathan
7. Grp. for US lawyers
8. Female parents, informally
9. Response to a captain
10. Kind of asst.
11. Skate component
12. More grotesque, in appearance
13. Gretzky was one to 3-D
14. Canadians beat them in 1972
15. Munched on
16. Affirmative answer
22. Aquarium fish
24. Male matey
27. Like Mrs. Claus' cheeks
29. Reign
31. Have feelings for
32. Medical diagnostic procedure
33. Retailer absorbed by RONA
34. Moulding type
35. Lukewarm
37. Toss out of office
38. _____, skip and a jump
40. Neural network
41. Prince William, vis-à-vis Prince Charles
43. Catch a glimpse of, in olden days
47. Middle Eastern gulf
48. Ceramic squares
50. Authentic
52. See 51-A
54. UK nobility title
56. Steady fellow?
58. Livens (with "up")
59. Alberta landmark: Banff National _____
60. Broadcasting live
61. He starred with Cher
62. Clear a blackboard
64. Substance of an idea
65. Rime anagram
66. Bamboozles
67. Patricia who won rowing silver for Canada in Rio
68. Part of NL
69. Carrot top clusters
70. Principal transportation route
72. Copycat
76. Richard who wrote *The 49th Paradox: Canada in North America*
78. Shackled, old style
80. Ranked, in a tennis tournament
82. Venomous snakes
83. Prepares to drive?
86. Hoarse
88. Tapestry
89. *The Red Green Show* star Steve
91. US anthropologist Margaret

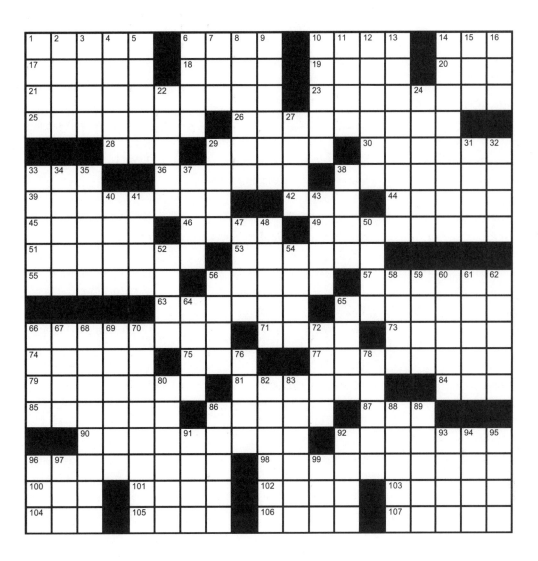

92. Huge in scope

93. Film director Kazan

94. Clampett family daughter: _____ May

95. Soaks flax

96. Outlaw

97. Earned Day Off (abbr.)

99. This veggie vexed a princess

Who Am I? 1

ID this pre-eminent painter

ACROSS

1. Discriminatory type of profiling
7. Cadge
12. Himalayan glacial valley
15. It's near Phoenix
19. It's the new black?
20. Last stanza of an old poem
21. Writer Edgar Allan
22. Ear-related
23. **His *Church and Horse* was featured on this**
25. Utmost
27. It connects to "poly"
28. Lug (var.)
30. End-of-season episodes
31. NL place: _____ Lake
32. Pelletier's ice partner
33. Experiences again
35. Cleans with a Hoover
38. Shifted a filmmaker's focus?
43. Scribe, in Saguenay
46. Poverty, say
48. 1960s singer Shannon
49. Canadian C&W star Clark
50. Chug
52. Inexperienced one
54. "Lucky Man" British band, for short
56. 1980s *Saturday Night Live* actress Nora
57. Eye
58. Long-limbed amphibian
60. Synonym for 6-D
62. It's home to five billion people
64. Understand
65. "_____-Dong! The Witch Is Dead"
66. Slacken a string
68. Playtex baby bottle
69. **His work adorned these in 1967**
72. Spicy sausage
75. Knuckleheads
76. Biblical verb
77. Great happiness
80. Cinematic trailer, say
82. Canadian rail service provider
83. Bop with a billy club
84. Social security cheque, in Chelsea
85. Stringed instrument
86. Long-time Toronto store: _____ the Record Man
88. Like Canada's Rush
90. Arranged in rows and columns
92. Cancel a NASA mission
94. Tear apart
96. Harsh cry
98. Volkswagen model moniker
99. It's found in tea
102. "We Three Kings" singer (var.)
104. Put into words
106. Give a five-star review
107. Sexually suggestive
111. How your heart might beat?
115. Daughter of Minos
117. Lashes
118. Psychiatry therapeutic process
120. **His artistic style**
122. Uneaten part of an apple
123. Mind reader's ability
124. "Have _____ day!"
125. Interweave
126. Fort _____
127. Messy digs
128. Trans-Canada Highway divisions
129. Cause

DOWN

1. Lassoed, at the Stampede
2. Appeared
3. Societal division
4. Come between combatants, say
5. Culture medium
6. You might not have one to stand on?
7. Salad greens mix
8. Recovering one's health
9. Semi-circular shape
10. Up-and-_____
11. More trendy
12. Computer "brain" (abbr.)
13. **His Annapolis Valley town**
14. Field of expertise
15. **His work hangs in this NYC museum**
16. Abbr. for "Them too"
17. You might Google one
18. Some playing cards
24. Biblical sibling
26. Box on a map
29. Responded in court
32. Close inspections
34. Thought, in Trois-Rivières
36. Penguin's relation
37. Korea Bay adjunct: Yellow _____
39. BC trees: Western red _____
40. Tie up the turkey, say
41. Former NHLers Hicke or Kenny
42. Belgrade spending money
43. Tumults
44. Overwhelming desire
45. Lay down lino
47. Very important person
51. Bridge, in Beaupré
53. As _____ a beached whale
55. _____ by law
59. Ripened, like cheese
61. One-thousandth of a litre (abbr.)
63. Littlest of the litter
65. Actress Moore
66. Lacking illumination
67. Reverberate
69. Bats might hang out here?

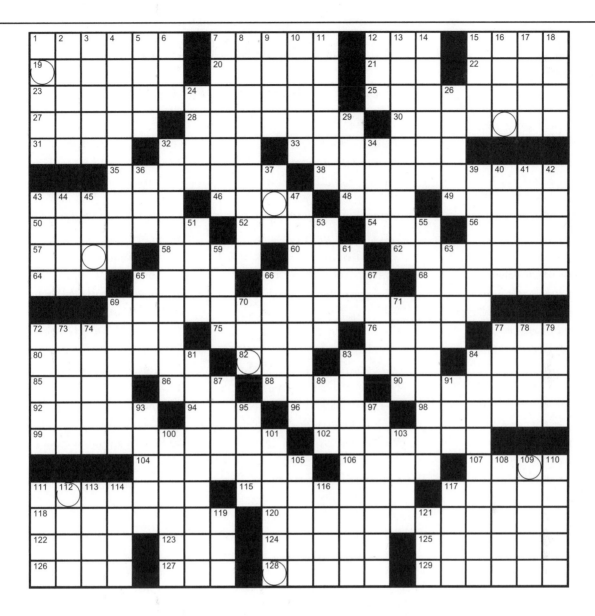

70. Eleventh mo.
71. Kiln for hops
72. Water balloon's impact sound
73. Caribbean island
74. Divulged information
77. Betray one's betrothed at the altar
78. TV preacher Roberts
79. Long ago days, say
81. His WWII role
83. Noel's cold feet?
84. Resistance fighter
87. Muscovite, for example
89. Industry Advisory Council (abbr.)

91. Gathering for quilters
93. Like a dicey dory?
95. Lopsided landmark town
97. Cavorts like a reindeer?
100. Pursues a dream?
101. Skin-related
103. Done
105. BC-born singer Krall
108. 1996 Atwood Giller winner: _____ Grace
109. 1950s TV Western: The _____ Kid
110. Imperial China official
111. Fill a valise
112. Wise to a plan, say

113. Eddo
114. His first name
116. Against, informally
117. Charlie Chaplin's stick
119. Canada's William Stephenson, for example
121. Forever, in old poems

Use the circled letters to unscramble his surname:

_ _ _ _ _ _ _ _ _

Canada Cornucopia 12

ACROSS

1. On the South China, say
6. You might get one of these on the wrist
10. Not as much
14. Costa del _____
17. Alberta tourist mecca
18. Canadian actress Ellen
19. CBC sportscaster Scott
20. It comes after New Year's?
21. Exemplifies
23. _____ acid
24. Guys
25. Hair gel brand
26. Give in to pressure
27. They persuade you
29. Prisoner's telephone type?
30. Ph.Ds
32. Eyelid adjunct
33. _____ and chips
36. Classic fragrance brand
38. Tisane
42. Indian or Atlantic
44. Cajun dish
46. Like northern lights
47. Ford or Fiat
49. Serengeti antelope
51. Unusual
52. Painting and photography
53. Canadian actor Butt
54. Embellishes a lily?
55. Saharan landform
56. Pack rat's pile
57. Orange tuber
58. Ancient Greek plaza
61. 1980 movie: *I _____ Letter to My Love*
62. Slip into sleep
66. Bass or snare
67. Atlantic islands: Cape _____
68. Arboreal symbol of Ontario and Alberta
69. Record collection?
71. Izzy who founded CanWest Global Communications Corp.
73. Alter an alarm clock
74. Halving hairs?
76. Sere
78. Pink, in Palermo
79. Journey to Mecca (var.)
80. Roadside bombs (abbr.)
82. Contracts
84. Thaw
87. Old Testament book
89. Nail polish brand
92. Summerside-born NHLer Steve
93. Climate control sys.
94. Royal pair who visited Canada in 2016
96. Sheltered side
97. It's just a number
98. Equal, in Évian
99. Jewish folklore creature
100. Leary tripped on this
101. Puncture sound
102. Céline's long-time spouse
103. They might be high

DOWN

1. 1969 Braithwaite book: *Never Sleep Three in _____*
2. Scotch _____
3. Barber's action
4. Mini newt
5. Previously, previously
6. Accidental overflows
7. Be idle
8. List of meeting matters, old style
9. Spicy sauce
10. Famous Five member McKinney
11. Net
12. Slip on a pallet?
13. Worldly, as opposed to spiritual
14. Happening every six months
15. Eavesdropped
16. Lorgnette component
22. See 84-A
28. Laboratory heat measuring instruments
29. They might clean the Senate?
31. Gastrointestinal illness
33. 1950s leading lady Nina
34. UN aviation org.
35. Neighbour of a Macedonian
37. Dental office tool (var.)
39. Tirade
40. Pal
41. Molson makes these
43. Nigerian money unit
45. Scolds
48. Beer barrel
50. Multiple Juno winners: Tegan _____ Sara
53. Maugham novel: *Of Human _____*
54. Star watcher
56. Genie Award winner: *Away from _____*
57. Over there, old style
58. Puts on pounds, say
59. Black leads
60. Survived on *Survivor*, say
61. Pharaoh who followed Ramses I
62. Goodyear Blimp, for example
63. Bear, in Bologna
64. Dues
65. Cheese type
67. Dachshund's doc
68. _____ annum
70. Newfoundland city
72. Northwest _____
75. Female kin
77. Close to one's heart
81. Sous-chef's gadget
83. Leg part
84. Ken or Barbie
85. Fifty-seven, to Tiberius
86. Mini vehicles?

88. _____ *for All Seasons*

89. Stare at

90. Open an orange

91. Philosophical tenets

95. Surname for John or Jane

Double Ws

Find the letter pattern

ACROSS

1. Once again
5. Window dressing?
9. When doubled, a fish
13. Shelter for cubs
17. Ecosystem
18. Long-running CBC show: *Front _____ Challenge*
19. Unwraps a gift
21. Additionally
22. Irish vagabond?
23. Perth County ON river
24. Garden climber
25. WWII spy school in Ontario: _____ X
26. Idaho place: Coeur d'_____
27. Health care worker
30. **Frontier outlaw's area**
32. Kung _____ chicken
33. 2016 British Open course: Royal _____
34. Spend too much
36. _____ in "victor"
37. Early Mongolian marauder (var.)
41. Harass
45. Dadaism art movement founder Jean
46. On, like a lamp
47. Treat a lawn
48. Moodily cool
49. Brief memoir?
50. Chinese soup dumplings
52. Storage tote
53. Injure a toe
54. Different from the usual
56. Opt out, in poker
57. Finish up, at the Hamilton Golf and Country Club
59. PST, for example
60. Winter sport: _____ fishing
61. Coagulates
62. Participated in a marathon

63. **Famed English castle**
65. John, to Elton?
66. Exhaust pipe gases, say
69. Successful strike?
70. A Gershwin sibling
71. Some Dell computers
75. End-_____
76. Puppeteers' "people"
79. Gull
80. Fanatic
81. Convention goer's ID
82. It follows George or Richard
83. Viral blemishes
84. Attracted an artist?
86. Irish mythology otherworld: _____-nan-Og
87. Physique, colloquially
88. Patterned tablecloth fabric
89. Bit of parsley
90. Some McGill degs.
91. Pleasing to a musician's ear?
93. Multinational news agency, for short
95. Ocasek of the Cars
96. **Mark's sells it**
101. Employment negotiation at the deli?
106. Famed pilot Post
107. Fairy tale brute
108. Stay abed
109. Lesotho currency unit
110. That is to say, in Paris: *C'est-_____*
111. Hard drive memory units
112. Violin name, for short
113. Creator's notion
114. Abominable snowmen
115. Honey makers
116. Place to fill up in Canada
117. Victoria-born artist Emily
118. Blade in bygone days

DOWN

1. Tangy mayonnaise
2. Atwood's *MaddAddam*, for example
3. Edit
4. **Supernatural creature**
5. Meagre
6. Successive movement at equal intervals, in physics
7. Stunned
8. Tropical fruit tree
9. Very, to Verdi
10. "Four and twenty blackbirds baked in _____"
11. Ticker trouble
12. Dartboard rings
13. Like manuscript gaps
14. Defunct fruit spray
15. Information Security Management System (abbr.)
16. Catch a dogie
17. Awesome, in Aberdeen
20. _____-masochism
28. 2010 Justin Bieber hit: "Never _____ Never"
29. Jots down info
31. She got evicted from Eden
35. Uncomfortable condition for men
36. Overturned criminal conviction, say
38. Not socially acceptable
39. Leaning
40. Ruptures
41. Mixed-up meal?
42. Lady in a choir
43. Heart of your matter?
44. More solemn in tone
46. Horror film actor Chaney
47. Conjunction that connects phrases
49. *Star Wars'* BB-8, say
50. **Crested songbird**

51. Load from a lode

54. Religious order woman

55. Sailor

56. Detritus in the Atlantic

58. Gov. program for retirees

61. Toronto Police Service emp.

63. Some Nixon henchmen

64. Choler

65. _____ Vegas

66. Endows, say

67. Take forcibly

68. Taxi gadget

69. It goes with green eggs

71. Necklace of flowers

72. Mucilaginous mallow family plant

73. Places

74. Old-style prov. abbr.

76. See 74-D

77. Paddle's kin

78. It rolls on shore?

81. Long-time national magazine: *Saturday _____*

83. **Paths**

85. Documentary series hosted by Knowlton Nash

87. Like pastoral areas, in literature

88. Hard, in Hull

90. Paint pigment ingredient

91. Pointed end

92. Leaf-related

94. Long fish

95. Mozart movement

97. Extend in scope

98. Cream of the social crop

99. Falcon's nest

100. Some whiskies

101. Grooming device

102. S-curve, in architecture

103. Strong impulse

104. Narrow estuaries

105. Soft drink

ACROSS

1. Enthralled
5. Canadian world champ pair skater Underhill
9. Chasm
12. _____ mignon
17. Continental currency unit
18. *The Sopranos* actor Robert
19. Par for the course?
21. "It hit me like _____ of bricks"
22. Guinea-Bissau place
23. Japanese entrees
24. Toronto-born painter Bateman
26. Improvised like Ella
28. Cozy lodgings, colloquially
29. Guadalajara goodbye
31. Monarchs' domains
33. Homme who played *The Friendly Giant*
35. Indonesia and Algeria are members of this (abbr.)
37. Dems and Reps
38. Some sandwiches
43. Is unwell
45. Melania Trump, by birth
47. Swiss watchmaker since 1874
48. Rest for the night
50. National magazine that went online only in 2017
51. Small vessel
52. Clothing chain: The _____
54. Like raw text
56. Glove compartment item
57. Pithy saying
61. National magazine that changed from weekly to monthly in 2017
63. Buck in Bucharest
64. Non-union retail outlet?
68. "I saw a mouse!" interjection
69. Canapé quiche
71. Yugoslavian coinage
73. Précis
77. Cream-filled pastry
78. Lounge on *The Canadian*
80. Morley Callaghan novel: _____ *Is My Beloved*
81. Pine secretion
82. Come to a _____
83. Stadium level
85. Flower garden
86. Sounded like a weightlifter
89. Playing card "two"
91. Just about all of it
95. Selected an entree
97. Close at hand
100. Lack of wariness
102. ABC drama that starred Canada's Evangeline Lilly
104. Lothario
105. 1970s federal Conservative leader
106. Number of Nickelback members
107. Public survey tool
108. Body part
109. French possessive
110. It comes after 89-A
111. "_____ never work!"

DOWN

1. Raise children
2. Prius or Lexus
3. Likely
4. Sculpted one's muscles
5. Circus performance venues
6. _____ carte
7. Civil War soldiers, colloquially
8. "Wondering Where the Lions Are" singer Cockburn
9. Delayed
10. Not at all helpful
11. They accepts bets
12. Elfin
13. It used to be Persia
14. Erie or Ontario
15. Auspices (var.)
16. Band from Winnipeg: Crash _____ Dummies
20. *Quod* _____
25. Canadian wrestler Wiebe won gold here in 2016
27. Electrical current unit
30. I or me
32. Con artist
33. _____-relief
34. Hibernia resource
36. Op-ed essay in 61-A
39. Jogged
40. African lizard
41. SW US tree type
42. Instructions, say
44. Lily type
46. BC port city (abbr.)
47. Part of a pizza
49. Releasing from Sing Sing
51. School fundraising grp.
53. SK-born wrestler Rowdy Roddy _____
55. MLS team in Montréal
57. Modify
58. Buffalo–Fort Erie bridge
59. Throws, forcibly
60. Director's collection?
62. Barely manages, with "out"
65. Sign of hair damage
66. Removals specialist
67. Monarch's sphere
70. Rival of 5-A Babilonia
72. Spoke
74. One-third power, in math
75. Low card
76. U of A deg.
78. Provide solace
79. Space shuttle return stage
82. Inters
84. Candy *SCTV* character: Johnny La_____
87. _____ *de boeuf*

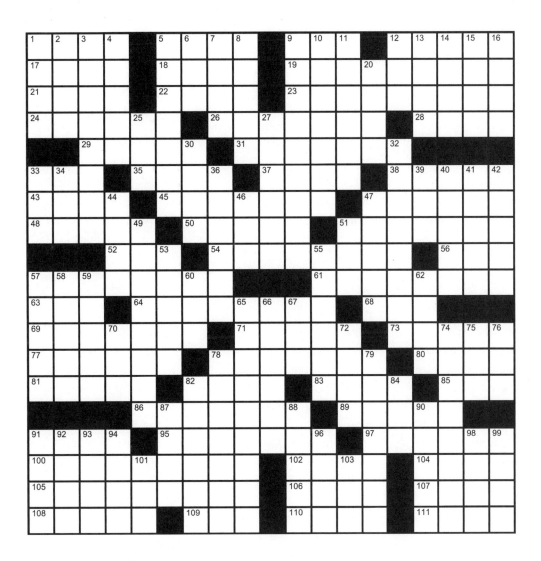

88. Netherlands city known for its pottery
90. Wrist bones
91. Atomizer spray
92. Able to see through obfuscation

93. Mark of Zorro?
94. Cures a hide
96. Sliding _____
98. Male elephant
99. Scream

101. Aliens' transport
103. Cash classic: "A Boy Named _____"

Half and Half

Serious versus humorous, Canadian style

ACROSS

1. *60 Minutes* broadcaster
4. Composer Carl
8. Children's building blocks
13. Portable warehouse platform
19. Frazier foe, in the ring
20. Stir sediment
21. Pending, at Rogers Arena?
22. For each person
23. Dance step
24. _____ buggy
25. It's a terrible waste?
26. Kijiji transaction, often
27. Like cloisonné jewellery (var.)
29. King Cole, et al.
30. High-level programming language
31. Corneal membranes
32. Pantry cans
33. They stick out in the military?
34. **Canada's royal anthem**
37. Stuffs with foodstuffs?
40. Undeveloped seeds
41. Multinational financial services firm
44. Popular Hondas
45. "Caught ya!"
47. Canadians Avison and Atwood
48. ACL locale
49. Inner self, to Jung
50. March with leaden feet
52. Canadian fantasy fiction writer: Guy Gavriel _____
53. Urgently needed
54. Neighbour of Ger.
55. Maiden name marker
57. Small mammal
59. Cuts corners? (var.)
60. Serious shows?
63. Female sheep
64. Canadian women won 2016 Olympic bronze in this
66. Coop groups

68. Pre-popped piece of corn
71. Smart jokester?
72. Taxi for Calloway?
75. Yogurt and cucumber side dish, in India
76. That chap
77. Mass of yarn
79. It follows psi
81. Home Hardware ad personality Olson
82. Hawaiian dances
84. Not happy
85. More sere
86. Rare Fabergé piece
87. Aromatic cooking bulb
88. See-through sleepwear
90. **Fabric of our lives?**
93. Pinched pennies
96. Offspring of Agrippina
97. Dangerous electrical current
101. Move awkwardly
102. Die down
103. Rejecting
104. Share allowance
105. Femme fatale's warning?
106. It separates Indiana from Pennsylvania
107. Canadian singer Roberts
108. Get your eye for an eye
109. Of the pelvis
110. Fail to observe
111. Rideau Canal city (abbr.)
112. United
113. Wade through water
114. Shakespearean play divisions
115. Place to live at U of C

DOWN

1. Race and Ray, in Newfoundland
2. Québec ski resort: Mont _____
3. Carpet type
4. **Government directive to successful citizens?**

5. Rolled meat entrees
6. Tactful manoeuvring
7. Ran away
8. **Our crazy currency?**
9. Baby, in Bécancour
10. Souvenir purchaser's store
11. Edible tubers
12. Salt, in Saguenay
13. Freed felons
14. Mimics' behaviours
15. Pay attention
16. Take in knowledge
17. Acclaim
18. Bieber fans, often
28. Severe headache, old style
30. Defective
32. *The Amazing Race Canada,* for example
33. Howls like a hog?
35. It comes after Shevat
36. Conjure up
37. Ontario Coalition Against Poverty (abbr.)
38. Trattoria drink
39. Nasty piece of work?
41. Step in to mediate
42. _____ and dear
43. Comes together, at the salon?
46. Important Middle Eastern personage (var.)
48. Toy for a breezy day
50. You can buy this at Murchie's in Victoria
51. A chess board has 16, to start
53. **Canada's highest honour for bravery**
56. Paramedics often work for this (abbr.)
58. Searches for
59. 1,101, Roman style
61. Duty roster
62. Adept

65. Burton Cummings song: "My _____ Way to Rock"

66. Hillside, in the Hebrides

67. Called on the phone

69. BlackBerry message

70. Slanting shed?

73. US Pulitzer-winning author James

74. Prisoners are kept behind these

76. Pitcher or caber tosser

78. Inkling

80. Filet _____

82. Occurred

83. Hypothetical situation

85. Good deed doer

87. Saffron-coloured pigment

89. Artist's occupation: _____ design

90. Playing charades, say

91. Son of Venus

92. One official language

93. "Git!"

94. Half of a percussionist's sticks set

95. Critic

98. Motorcycle helmet part

99. Related maternally

100. Some mil. grps.

102. Comedic Canadian writer Ferguson

103. Drug in *Brave New World*

105. _____-boom-bah

ACROSS

1. Muffin fibre
5. Lock, _____ and barrel
10. Our, in Outremont
13. 1990s Russian skating star Kulik
17. Des Moines state
18. Pang
19. Turning topsy-turvy
21. Starting from
22. Gordon Lightfoot hit: "_____ Morning Rain"
23. Like many Sherpas
24. Deposit in the desert
26. Big store sections
28. Pertaining to hearing
30. Prima donnas
31. Banking transaction (abbr.)
34. Icon of industry
36. Greek letters
37. Former Red Chamber speaker Kinsella, et al.
42. School reunion attendee, for short
44. Fruit containing milk
46. Boy, in Edinburgh
47. Remnant from the past
49. Purse part
50. *Titanic* theme: "_____ Will Go On"
51. Manitoba river
53. CIBC machine (abbr.)
54. Not yet final, legally
55. Pas' mates
56. Operating room procedure (var.)
60. Shopper's satchel
63. Bouquet display jug
64. Dachshund or Dalmatian
65. Grab, like a weightlifter?
69. Graphics machines
71. Burdened with
73. Habituate to

74. Canadian a cappella group (with "The")
75. Vancouver "Eyes of a Stranger" band
77. Steffi of tennis renown
78. Helot or serf
79. Val-d'Or vote option
80. More devious (var.)
82. Cdn. terr.
83. Some minerals
85. Predecessor of Sonar
87. Eastern North America mountain range
93. She's living in a material world
97. It used to be Ceylon
98. On the up and up, in law
100. Ramble through an Italian city?
101. Verdi or Dvorak
102. Ham it up, on stage
103. Average, for Canadian comedian Macdonald?
104. "Stupid _____ stupid does"
105. Olden days, old style
106. Sweater consumers?
107. Cancel out

DOWN

1. Prejudice
2. *From Russia With Love* character Klebb
3. On the lam from the military
4. Continental trade pact (abbr.)
5. Fatty acid type
6. Erebus offspring
7. Office of Rail Regulation (abbr.)
8. Freezing
9. Excited, with "up"
10. Territory named for "our land" in Inuktitut
11. *Carmen* and *Aida*
12. Autumn mos.
13. Dawdle

14. Claim by a creditor
15. Research org.
16. Eons and eras
20. *China Beach* country, for short
25. Place
27. Famous Fawcett poster, say
29. Produce mother's milk
31. Take in income
32. Run from the law
33. British band: Jethro _____
35. Top of the country transporter: Canadian _____
37. UNESCO world heritage site (in 82-A)
38. Keats poem
39. Netherlands dairy export
40. Former currency in Italy
41. Collections
43. Canadian non-profit org.: Municipal Information Systems Association (abbr.)
45. Annual celebration for a saint
46. Cell membrane breakdown
48. Meet
50. Broadway show, for short: *Les _____*
52. Gets close to
54. British cookbook queen Lawson
57. US draft org.
58. Flaps
59. Hoodlums in the 'hood
60. Storage containers
61. Type of nitrite
62. Swanky social event
66. U-ey, say
67. Gullet
68. Bulk
70. Mike Pence was Indiana's this (abbr.)
71. Oahu outdoor living space
72. Canadian-born basketball inventor
75. European duck

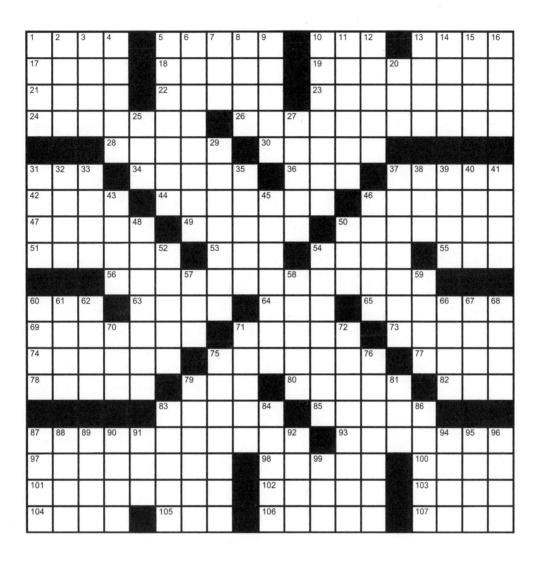

76. Calms with drugs
79. Ours features a beaver
81. Free of
83. Residence for a reverend
84. Place name in Massachusetts and Oregon
86. Horn-shaped object

87. Botany sacs
88. NHLers and MLBers
89. Southern Arizona indigenous people
90. European mountain range
91. Language spoken in southeast Asia

92. Pixar picture: *Finding* _____
94. Sinclair Ross CanLit classic: "The Lamp at _____"
95. Old-style salve
96. Pellets or bullets, for short
99. Came down with

31

Just For the Pun of It

Witty wordplay

ACROSS

1. Overnight outdoors
5. Become bleary
9. *In medias _____*
12. Memoir, for short
15. Napkin's site
18. Follow the rules
19. Type of wolf?
20. German–French artist known for Dadaism
21. Shelf for bric-a-brac
23. Mongrel
24. They can be low or high in card games
25. **Painter's photography technique?**
27. Not more than
29. Two-seater bike type
30. Not completely round
31. You might strike it rich here
32. Bulrush, in Britain
34. 16-year Toronto Maple Leaf Salming, by birth
35. Mix
37. Angry about an injury?
38. Play component
39. Drink created in Calgary: Bloody _____
40. Pot topper
41. North Bay's prov.
43. Former European econ. assn.
45. Windbags may be full of this
47. Mimic
49. Bride's dress fabric
52. Circular band
53. Space between incisors
56. Innkeeper
58. Kennel sound
60. Newfoundland national park site: L'Anse aux _____
62. Biblical son of Joseph
64. Mulroney defence minister Robert

66. Love god, in mythology
67. Crème de _____
69. **Drink at the Round Table?**
71. Circus walker's prop
72. 1957 legislation: Canada Council for the _____ Act
73. Leaf's vein
74. Game invented in Canada: _____ Pursuit
76. Dog for a Dunblane resident?
78. Run _____
80. Old-style ocean travel measurements
83. Big Canadian city (abbr.)
84. Myra who played for WWII troops
86. Study of odes and verses
88. Celebrated California wine region
89. Power usurping military cliques
91. Hawaiian volcano: Mauna _____
92. Eurasian equivalent of 43-A
94. Capture the Grey Cup, say
95. Delights in
98. You might shoot from here
100. Gists
102. Midnight munchies, say
104. Related through mother
105. Moon of Jupiter
107. Tarot card reader
108. Medical troubles?
109. Like Kia cars
110. Canadian Cancer Society description
114. **Fruit for an admiral?**
116. Case for Chantelle
117. Pop tins
118. Frozen dessert item
119. Large-capped mushroom
120. Edge of a window ledge
121. Vancouver Canucks jersey mammal

122. Homer's neighbour on *The Simpsons*
123. Manitoba community: The _____
124. Compass point in Charlemagne
125. Unload shares
126. _____ miss

DOWN

1. 1977 Robin Cook thriller
2. Be adjacent
3. **It measures your level of courage?**
4. Monty _____
5. Accusation of wrongdoing
6. Nuts, in Nicaragua
7. International org. with 195 member states
8. You might stop here along Alberta's QE2
9. Whitewater sport transports
10. Lists of printer's gaffes
11. Leafy green
12. Chisel's sloped edge
13. Dating couple, say
14. Clod
15. Goes out to rake?
16. Group of ships
17. Potato paring gadget
22. Cultivation pro
26. Doris Anderson was *Chatelaine*'s for 20 years
28. Starchy tuber
33. Wee
34. Goat-like Asian antelope
35. Lacklustre
36. Cosmetic surgery technique, for short
37. Like bacon with the most marbling
39. Weaves with rattan
42. Black, in *la belle province*

44. Prague's preferred form of diplomacy?

46. Watches and clocks

48. Leftovers?

50. Mill coffee beans

51. Plenty

53. Battle for the Planet of the Apes?

54. Acronym for a roll call absentee

55. Whisperer's word

57. Kennedy's killer, for short

59. Canada–US agreement until 2001: Auto _____

61. Keep in the clink

63. Sorvino's star in Cetus?

65. Ankle bones

67. Cirque du Soleil ensemble, for example

68. Verdi opera: "Giovanna d'_____"

70. Decorative upholstery trim

71. 1951 Scrooge portrayer Alastair

73. Appearances or airs

75. Urn

77. Norway, to ancient Greeks

79. Laments, loudly

81. *Ben-Hur*, for example

82. Dropped to the floor of the sea

85. Libyan desert

87. Lack of give

89. Stuff thrown off a ship

90. Peaceful sound?

93. Consumer

95. Hold your horses?

96. Twist ribbons together

97. Like trumpets and tubas

99. Beaches, in Nice

101. Baby's footwear

103. Right winger, for short

105. Puts a stopper in it?

106. Not competent

107. Slop

109. Rainforest nut tree (var.)

111. Void's partner

112. Quipu user

113. Former royal autocrat

115. You might gloss over this?

Solution on page 215

32

Four-Square 2

Use mini grids to solve a CanCon phrase

ACROSS

1. Fast serve, on the court
4. Singing cowboy Ritter
7. Beatles moniker: The _____ Four
10. Santa _____ winds
13. Something that's asked often? (abbr.)
14. Santana hit: "_____ Como Va"
15. Poetic work
16. Tim Hortons event: Roll Up the _____ to Win
17. Bested The Donald?
19. Duster
20. Common Italian question: "*Come* _____?"
21. Attain one's goals
22. Tippet-Richardson, et al.
24. Use the AC, for example
26. Apes' fruit
27. Shreddies and Rice Krispies
28. Draw a cartoon?
29. Met in secret
30. Fastens papers together
31. Meredith who played Rocky's trainer
38. More morally pure
45. Like Kennedy's flame
46. Wayne Gretzky's model daughter
47. In an acceptable manner
48. Make notes?
49. Medical services office
50. Feather, to an ornithologist
51. Like a cool Canadian band?
52. Moodie CanCon classic: *Roughing It in* _____ *Bush*
54. Like Prince Edward Island
56. It follows *printemps*
57. Hollywood Myrna
58. Treatment for dehydration (abbr.)
59. Previous name for Tokyo
60. The "S" in CBS

61. Merino mama
62. Employ
63. Agt.

DOWN

1. Where you might encounter an ensign
2. WestJet or Air Canada
3. Royal attendant
4. Manicurist's final step
5. Mask opening for a Cyclops?
6. Crossed out, for short
7. In favour of
8. Inflexible in opinion
9. Glossy plant
10. London-based Premier League club
11. Saltpetre component
12. Gets more congregants?
18. Ceremonial staffs
23. Seductress or siren
24. Youth Criminal Justice _____
25. Hit in the '60s?
26. Some York University degs.
31. Burps
32. Water or power, say
33. Cookbook contents
34. Smile
35. License a lord?
36. Ulrich's eponymous figure skating jump
37. Scheming
38. Canadian Payroll Association (abbr.)
39. Stephen and Laureen
40. Golden hued
41. Talk on the street?
42. More metallic, in sound
43. Fencer's phrase
44. Former premier of Ontario Bob
53. Hook's partner
54. Pittance, in old Paris?
55. Sweatshirt or sweater

To solve the CanCon phrase:

Decode a four-word, long-running CBC show title:

• One horizontal word from Square 1.

• One vertical word from Square 2.

• One horizontal word from Square 3.

• One vertical word from Square 4.

Answer: _____ _____
_____ _____

SQUARE 1

1	2	3	■	4	5	6
13			■	14		
17			18			
■	21					■
24						25
27						
29						

SQUARE 2

7	8	9	■	10	11	12
15			■	16		
19			■	20		
■	22		23			
26						
28						
30						

SQUARE 3

31	32	33	34	35	36	37
45						
47						
49						■
51			■	52		53
56			■	57		
60			■	61		

SQUARE 4

38	39	40	41	42	43	44
46						
48						
■	50					■
54						55
58			■	59		
62			■	63		

33

Witty Women

Canadian comediennes

ACROSS

1. Sitcom starring Canada's Eric McCormack: *Will &* _____
6. Saturate
10. Gyro flatbread
14. Easily pass a tennis test?
17. Mr. Bean portrayer Atkinson
18. Robert Goulet song: "If _____ I Would Leave You"
19. Not odd
20. Pre-teen fellow
21. Aids an arsonist?
22. Six of Cups, for example
24. "_____ Maria"
25. Crazy, at the kibbutz?
27. Somebody
28. Word seen in footnotes
29. They're made in Japan?
30. Small cases, in Calais
31. **Gemini Award winner Shamas**
33. Old Turkish title
36. Not in the bow
38. Atlantic sport fish
39. *Full Frontal* **host Bee**
42. General Services Administration (abbr.)
44. Former NHLers Dryden and Daneyko
45. Canadian pasta and sauce products producer
46. Ski-Doo model (1971–96)
49. Forcibly seize
51. Rock type description
53. Yellow fruit
55. Fleur-de-_____ (var.)
58. Hoosegows
59. Four-door vehicle
60. Idiot _____
63. "Just a _____"
64. Panacea potion
66. Part of a fugue, in music
67. Cocky walk
69. _____ Canadian Superstore

71. Assumed, say
72. Camembert cousin
74. Lay money on
76. **Comedienne/actress Rhea**
78. New Zealand lizard
80. Drink up
83. Total up
84. **CBC Radio 1 *Q* "Cultural Hall of Shame" contributor Kurt**
85. Composed
86. Knee ligament (abbr.)
89. *M*A*S*H* actor Alda
90. Artisans' associations
92. Famous Players promo
96. Russian fighter jet
97. Antiques fair aficionado
99. Loot, old style
100. Reform Party's senate goal (abbr.)
101. Street kid
102. Solo at La Scala
103. Permissible
104. Dental office surgeon (abbr.)
105. Remain behind
106. Technical institute, for short
107. Parolee's bracelet type

DOWN

1. Nana's measurement?
2. 1991 Canada/Australia film: *Black* _____
3. Elicits oohs?
4. *This Hour Has 22 Minutes* **star Jones**
5. Result from
6. _____ good example
7. Fertility clinic supply
8. Poke holes in the lawn
9. Reykjavik spending money
10. Folklore cowboy: _____ Bill
11. Men's tennis great Lendl
12. Canadian opera singer Stratas

13. Common conjunction
14. *Arabian Nights* boy
15. Spelunkers' locales
16. Bodily swellings
23. Securing with twine
26. Minute bug
28. Nunavut tourism destination: Bathurst _____
30. And others, in Lat.
32. Biblical boats
33. Savoury jellies
34. Rinse with mouthwash
35. Like some acids
37. 1964 Zombies hit: "_____ Not There"
38. **CODCO co-founder Walsh**
40. Randy Travis hit: "Forever and Ever, _____"
41. Every _____ and cranny
43. Whooper or trumpeter
47. Pinnacle
48. Opposite of 47-D
50. Québec, directionally from Ontario
52. Manipulator
54. Cut down on, say
55. It's south of Estonia
56. Have in mind
57. High, like a hippie
59. Land for a new build
61. Toronto CFL team member
62. Bride's lacy covering
65. *Royal Canadian Air Farce* **star Goy**
66. Cake type for a crowd
67. 1960s civil disobedience action
68. Rip
70. Pink Floyd genre: _____ rock
72. Persecuted, on the playground
73. Takes a toll on over time
75. Marquis or madam
77. Hitchcock classic: _____ *Window*

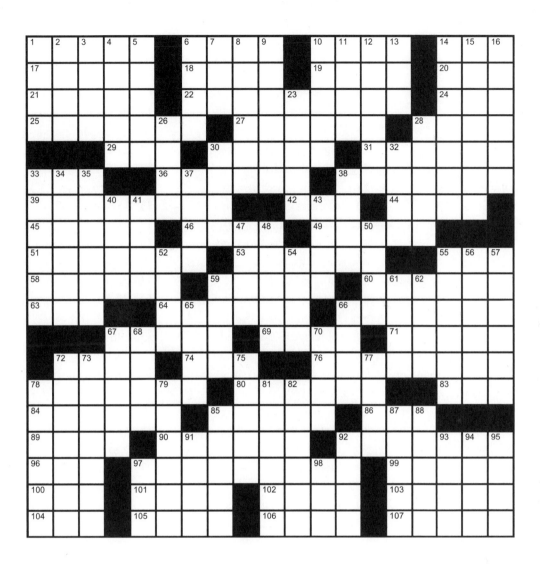

78. Grouped players: _____ up
79. Stewed beef dish
81. Like Marx Brothers comedies
82. Café
85. Like some terriers?

87. **Canada's "Queen of Comedy"**
    Collins
88. Sleep late
91. Radius neighbour
92. Waiter's load
93. Dearth

94. Agatha Christie mystery: _____
    Under the Sun
95. Network of nerves
97. Cowtown cops' org.
98. Western Canada resource

ACROSS

1. Special occasions, for short
6. *On Golden* _____
10. Officiates a match, for short
14. Saw
17. Woodturning machine
18. Frosty covering
19. VP or CFO
20. Former MP Adams
21. Fielder's flub
22. Akron state
23. Ethical principles
25. Omission of a vowel in pronunciation
27. Predetermine, to a priest?
29. Like a little leaguer?
31. Golden Canadian Olympic swimmer Oleksiak
32. _____ care in the world
34. Major US network
36. Injured arm support
38. Pitches and promos, say
39. Phony
40. Bouncy beat
42. Trap setters
44. Mrs. Secord, et al.
45. Pasted
47. Bamboozles
48. Say again
49. Even though, old style
51. Spoonful of medicine (abbr.)
52. Thematic narrative poem
53. Ran into
54. BC's Judith Forst, et al.
58. It follows cul-de-
61. "I'm Gonna Wash That Man Right Outa My _____"
62. Small, to a Scot
63. Ms. Grégoire Trudeau
67. Parlour serving piece
69. Skin layer
71. Impoverished
72. Knights' suits (var.)
73. Getting the truth out of a helminthologist?
75. Chip's cartoon cohort
76. Yoho National Park town
77. _____ and nicotine
78. Remains of a corset?
80. Delicious apple colour?
81. Central Yukon town
82. City on the St. Lawrence
84. Off the mark, like a hockey pass
86. Grand criminals?
89. French diacritical mark
92. Form improperly
93. Golden state for Canadian Olympian Le May Doan
95. An Ontario university is named for this Brock
96. _____ Wednesday
97. Egyptian goddess
98. Lucy's TV love
99. Common _____
100. Home for a hog
101. Fraction of a dollar
102. Work plan detail
103. Held over?

DOWN

1. Run from a crime scene, say
2. Rank below marquis
3. Place to take it all off
4. Plural demonstrative pronoun
5. 64-D, for example
6. Some CBC Radio shows
7. "_____ la la!"
8. Babe in the woods
9. Sag
10. Emails again
11. Previous prisoners?
12. BC waters transport
13. Cold War missile name
14. Mirror message transmitted via the sun's rays
15. Result in, in time?
16. Horror film director Craven
24. Succeed, to a prospector?
26. Farley Mowat book: _____ *in the Family*
28. Parents
30. Legislator, say
33. CSB or RRSP
34. Water surface substance
35. Justin Trudeau government finance minister Morneau
37. Weed
39. Double reed instrument
41. Pour
43. Authorize spending at Alberta's ENMAX?
44. Canadian home furnishings store
46. Bruce Willis movies franchise
48. Real Property Administrator (abbr.)
50. Russian monarchs (var.)
52. Cloistered Christian figure
55. Pimple
56. Curly dos
57. Drove too fast
58. Group of employees
59. Cirque du Soleil performer
60. Afraid of being shot?
64. CBC TV drama that debuted in 2007
65. Like some talk?
66. Checked out?
68. Purples and pinks, in Pennsylvania
69. 1960s movie star Day
70. Like a lawless society
73. Most undulating
74. Circulatory ocean current
77. Bowling alley target
79. Brute
82. Landlord's document
83. Good-looking house framers?
85. Japanese–Canadian

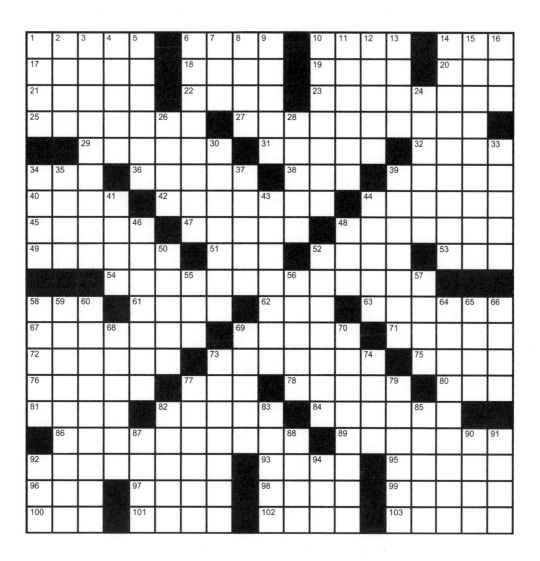

87. Smart, stylistically
88. Armstrong's mark on the moon?
90. Perform eye surgery

91. Passed an exam easily
92. Students' advanced degrees
(abbr.)

94. *Peer Gynt* mother

35 | Rank and Guile

Get in line for these military puns

ACROSS

1. *CSI* franchise network
4. _____ welding
7. Navigator's guide
10. Commotion
14. 24th Québec premier: Pierre-_____ Johnson
18. Alberta place: Medicine _____
19. Prefix with Georgian
20. Grp. for US docs
21. Perry Mason scribe: _____ Stanley Gardner
22. Formerly used orchard spray
23. Ally of CDA
24. Nevertheless, briefly
25. Baie-Comeau citrus drink
26. 1950s Canadian pop group: The Four _____
27. Phoenician queen who founded Carthage
28. **Place to pick up mail?**
33. 59-D, for short
34. Apply by smearing
35. Nymph, in Greek mythology
36. Common street name around YYC
38. This wakes you in the morning
40. New Year's song word
41. Stretched-out rectangles
43. Norse goddess of fate
44. You might draw one in the sand
45. Blow one's own horn
46. Portray
50. Modicum
51. Crone
53. Turkic language (var.)
55. Bird extinct in New Zealand
56. Saturated
58. Iniquity to the elderly (var.)
60. Confederate States Army soldier, for short
61. On the _____ of the moment
62. Compass pt.

63. Equation signs (var.)
65. Sax type
67. They have risers and treads
70. Hypnotic performers?
72. Hairspray type
73. Ladies of Léon
75. Sycophant's usual answer
76. Later
77. *West Side Story* actor Glass
79. Condescend
80. Programmer's task
83. Ump's utterance: "_____ out!"
84. Lots of lots?
86. Canadian Forces base in Ontario
88. Ghost's contemptuous cry?
89. Enlarge or minimize
91. Speaks like Simon?
93. Affirmatives, at sea
94. Property claim
95. Alberta lake formerly featured on Canada's $20 bill
97. Itty-bitty bug
98. *Beauty and the Beast* character
99. Remnants
102. Leans
104. French novelist Pierre
105. Hockey great Bobby
106. **Potential post-military position?**
111. Bakery product
113. Neet marketplace rival
114. US gov. agency since 1908
115. 84-D, for example
116. Debtor's acronym
117. Poi source
118. Metallic sound
119. They come after dos
120. Choose
121. Home extension
122. Renfrew County ON town: _____ River
123. Consequently, to Caesar

124. Tree type
125. Dissenting vote
126. Supremes song: "Come _____ About Me"

DOWN

1. Drink without pausing
2. Baseball diamond corner
3. Military parade leaders
4. Sinus cavity
5. Betty Ford Center program
6. Lose warmth
7. **Preferred sports event broadcasts?**
8. Tickled a fancy, say
9. Fusilli or farfalle
10. Narcissist's favourite?
11. London landmark: _____ Square
12. Popular classical singing quartet
13. Capable of being withdrawn
14. Crazy
15. Person of interest's excuse
16. CBC milieu
17. Softly sing like Bing?
29. Garner gelt
30. Units of force, in physics
31. Aroma, in Atlanta
32. Enthusiastic
37. Spoonful of sugar (abbr.)
38. See 125-A
39. Nutrient-rich soil
40. Feel sick
42. Nocturnal mammal
44. Headed
45. Porgy's partner
47. No goes
48. British Columbia _____ of Appeal
49. Little lakes in the mountains
51. Molson Canadian, et al.
52. Didn't catch a cue
54. Raptors and Blue Jays

57. Annual presidential address: State of the _____
59. Chrétien's *My Years as Prime Minister*, for example
61. Pulled back from
63. Less ruddy
64. Aquarium pet?
66. Get a feel for size?
67. Faun's brethren
68. Little laugh (var.)
69. 17th-C. orchestral composition
71. Hindu mendicant
74. Seines
78. Stopping

80. Caesar salad lettuce
81. Christmas synonym
82. 1993 Blue Rodeo single: "Already _____"
84. Pre-life geological period
85. _____ Francisco
87. Holiday in Hanoi
90. Independent Medical Review (abbr.)
92. "Abominable" Himalayan creature
94. Rents out
96. Household helper in Hull?

97. They show you around the world?
98. Literary mutiny ship
99. Handed out pineapple?
100. Wear away, like a levee
101. Exchange
103. _____ dig
104. Drug for Parkinson's patients
107. Jason's ship
108. Gas with an orange glow
109. This can earn an actor an Oscar
110. See 81-D
112. Dandy dresser?

ACROSS

1. Most vigorous
7. Forerunner of the CIA
10. Game to play on the phone?
13. Hit with an open hand
17. Iago's spouse
18. Instrument for Tiny Tim
19. Archer's ability
20. Upward Facing Dog exercise
21. Maritime province
23. Fresh out of the package
25. Habitual doubters
26. Mannerly conduct
28. Burrow for badgers
29. Roused
30. Moray
31. Free deal, say
34. Cricket match components
36. Straightening up
40. Competed
41. Sudden gush (var.)
42. But, in Baie-Comeau
43. Suffix for sonnet
44. Ancient Roman greeting
45. Lush
46. South American monkey
47. Imperial Oil station name
48. Bottom line books
50. Ontario premier Kathleen
52. Actress Naomi
53. Give authorization to rent?
54. Baloney
55. Karaoke locale
56. Plant in a garden?
59. Canadian nature photographer Courtney
60. Paddler's fulcrum
64. Egotistical
65. Young seal
66. Send a payment
68. Luau dish
69. Atwood short story collection: *Bluebeard's* _____

70. Blue Jay's diamond manoeuvre
71. Risk
72. Singe
73. Montréal Canadiens icon Maurice
75. Chicoutimi chapeau?
76. Transported by coach
77. Attila the _____
78. Unwraps
80. Chairlift alternative
82. Traced using a pattern
85. Governance by the people
89. South African city
90. Not well delineated
92. Military order: At _____
93. African National Congress (abbr.)
94. Nickel oxide (abbr.)
95. Finding a spot to build on
96. Changed the colour of
97. Born as (Fr.)
98. Demo a kitchen, say
99. Conceited

DOWN

1. Coop queens
2. Frenziedly
3. Exist
4. Ticked away, like time
5. Female relative
6. Like an unspoken understanding
7. Rogers Centre inning enders
8. Schuss
9. Vancouver, for example
10. It can follow coffee or end
11. Engine duct
12. Business school admission test (abbr.)
13. City in 21-A
14. Most in need of friends
15. Eras
16. Quadruped's "feet"
22. Tentacled cephalopod

24. Requires
27. Short agreements?
29. Michael J. Fox played a teen one in 1985
31. Sort of round
32. Canadian "Signs" singers: _____ Man Electrical Band
33. Cater to?
35. Sixes, to Tiberius
37. Richard _____
38. One flew over this in the movies
39. NL national park: _____ Morne
41. Put into categories
42. Oodles
45. Caraway pip
46. They deride
47. 2000 Dixie Chicks hit: "Goodbye _____"
49. Former BC premier Clark
51. Thither
52. Disfiguring mark
54. Sword handle
55. Opt out, colloquially
56. Endless time period?
57. O. Henry offering: "The Gift of the _____"
58. Head honcho at a Saputo dairy?
59. Veggie slicing device
60. Left out
61. Creator's big work
62. CANDU reactor component
63. Pleasant
65. Rotter
67. Shortly, before?
70. Financial institution, in Firenze
71. Not yet approved
72. Tex-Mex wrap
74. Pursued big game
75. Busy bug?
76. Largest Canadian island
79. Edmonton arena: Rogers _____
81. Sanction, in the sanctuary

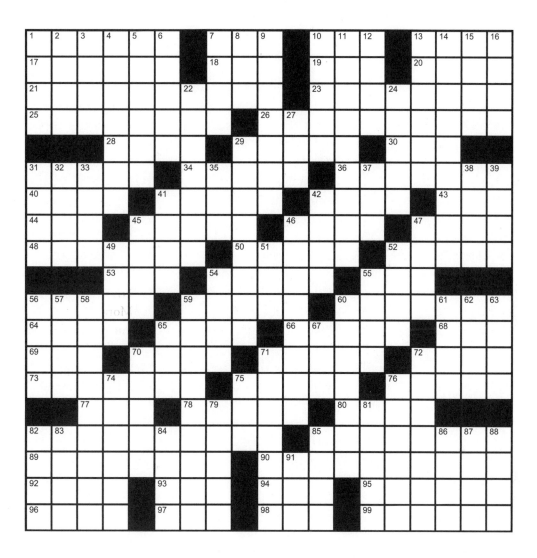

82. Hied
83. Cafeteria salver
84. Mashhad country

85. Token-taking opening
86. Part of ICU
87. Gave to, temporarily

88. Irritable
91. TV *Elementary* star Lucy

Happy Birthday to Us!

Celebrating Canada's 150th

ACROSS

1. Egyptian snakes
5. Traditional dance performed by Maori
9. Parlour piece
14. Identical
19. RBI, for one
20. Super server, on the court
21. Ouzo flavouring
22. Muslim woman's garment
23. UN org. for which Canada has been a non-permanent member six times
26. Start
27. Disentangle yarn, say
28. Eschew
29. Burton Cummings hit: "Stand _____"
31. Southern Ontario locale: Grand _____
32. Chowed down
33. Sound quality problem
36. "(_____ Got a Gal In) Kalamazoo"
38. Moorland shrub
40. Many ages
41. _____ *Miniver*
42. Hit hard
46. Seer anagram
47. Without, in Québec
48. Sushi fish
49. Hotter, in cuisine
50. Western Canada Sedimentary Basin gas type
52. Acronym embraced by Trump supporters
53. Class of serfs in Sparta
54. European nobleman's rank
57. Initiation ceremony
58. Police cruiser's cacophony
59. In the vicinity
60. Suggest, indirectly
61. Garden tools

62. TV's Daniel Boone, _____ Parker
66. Fired up again
67. Our 1867 prime minister
69. Merrymaking
70. Powdery silicate
71. QB Drew traded from Stamps to Redblacks in 2017
72. Move slowly, like lava
73. Waive a privilege
74. Obliterate information
76. Blue Jay's hit: _____ drive
77. Person in penury
78. Bartenders' gadgets
81. Prescription amount
82. Witches' assembly
83. Manitoba city: _____ la Prairie
84. _____ bran
85. Give in to the spelunker?
86. Nickelback member Kroeger
90. Raglan _____
91. Energy amount in volts (abbr.)
92. Guess Who musician Jim
93. Crystalline stone
94. Domain for a goalie
95. How your gut might react
98. Pipe type (abbr.)
99. Complain
102. Knee–ankle connector
104. Juice a lemon
105. Loss of willpower, in psychological speak
107. Freezing cold
109. Vet's personal charm?
112. Showed again, on cable
113. Ice cream parlour dollop
114. Large Ontario lake
115. Perched on
116. Down Under animal
117. Tubular pasta
118. Rims
119. Monogrammed towel word

DOWN

1. Take the edge off
2. Speaker not in need of a mic
3. Green Bay grocery store workers?
4. Overpower
5. Governor General Jean was born here
6. 1987 hit from Canada's Luba: "_____ of Mercy"
7. Pipeline that runs from Alberta to the Gulf Coast
8. Old Athenians magistrates
9. Intimidate
10. Vacation destination
11. Our monarch in 1867
12. Thais and South Koreans
13. *Gimme a Break!* star Carter
14. Subside, at the sea?
15. 1864 meeting to discuss confederation
16. Strongly suggest
17. Related?
18. Set foot on shore
24. Took the passenger seat
25. Possessive pronoun for a duo
30. Daffy Duck, et al.
34. Canadian charity: Easter _____
35. Public relations concern
37. Sheer fabric
39. Our 150th birthday is this
43. Hobby shop purchase
44. Always, in an old verse
45. Like hands in winter
47. Expressed verbally
48. Artist who uses ink
49. Backed away from
51. Stalk game
52. Gordon Lightfoot classic: "If You Could Read My _____"
54. Retailer's workplace
55. Spatial calculation
56. Casino throw

57. Bush secretary of state Condoleezza

58. Seafood selection

60. Malicious kind of mail

61. Atmospheric condition on a humid Toronto day

63. Bet in roulette

64. State flower of 106-D

65. Make time in your calendar (with "in")

67. Mulroney cabinet communications minister Marcel

68. Zero

69. Wander aimlessly

71. Archers shoot at these

73. Preferred thing, colloquially

75. Plunder, in olden days

76. Dallies at the bakery?

77. Shack

78. Ontario Public Service (abbr.)

79. Warsaw country (abbr.)

80. Old-style "before"

81. Canada, as of 1867

82. Squid appetizer

85. Stick-to-your-teeth candy

87. Peloponnesian soldier

88. Financial consultant, for example

89. Leaves a caravan?

91. Convey emotions

92. On an even _____

93. Shift, at sea

96. Shrub type: _____ myrtle

97. Highway 401 has 18 of these in places

99. Former Bank of Canada governor Carney

100. Yellow spread

101. Taj Mahal location

103. Metal hinge

106. Beehive State

108. Crime lab test substance

110. Labour Day day, for short

111. Swindle (var.)

ACROSS

1. Per person
5. Andy's radio show partner
9. *Lord of the Rings* soldiers
13. Hobbled
17. Pierre Trudeau-era cabinet minister Herb
18. Our fleet: Royal Canadian _____
19. Origin of a word?
20. States of choler
21. Tragically Hip singer (with 70-A)
22. Graph component
23. Canadian financial institution
25. Hospital dept.
26. Christopher Columbus ship
28. Public transport vehicle
29. Decorative wall board
30. Middle Eastern magnates (var.)
32. Tipple too much
33. Calliope or Clio
35. Scant, in Scranton
37. Pitchfork point
41. Verify
44. Aussie wild dog
45. GPS, for example
47. Young pig (var.)
48. Marrakesh marketplaces
50. Door component
51. 2016 HGTV Canada show: _____ to Win
52. Lauds
53. Hockey is Canada's this
55. Scull
56. Plundered
58. Clay craft
60. Dashboard letters.
61. Cut
62. Murmured like a dove?
63. Uncluttered
65. Sci-fi author Asimov
67. Short-tailed monkey
69. Card sharp's swindle (var.)
70. See 21-A
72. Humdingers
73. Former prime minister Paul
74. Like an octopus' defensive weapon
75. India's most populous city
77. Make footnotes
78. Adele hit: "_____ We Were Young"
80. Trash receptacle
82. Church service
86. Small bird
90. Singer Belafonte
91. Blue-pencil
92. Beyond the pale
94. Turkish currency
95. Aborted mission, in NASA-speak
96. Drunk's disparaging statement?
97. Tab or Coke
98. Ponce de _____
99. Emerson, Lake and Palmer, for one
100. Chinook salmon
101. Smeltery refuse
102. Liberals' pursuits?
103. Old W Network show: *Take This House & _____ It!*

DOWN

1. Encouraged, in the coop?
2. Scent
3. Showed sincere interest
4. Measuring tool for liquid density
5. Poetry foot type
6. 2017 federal Conservative leadership hopeful Bernier
7. Like ewes and rams
8. Brought order to chaos
9. Canadian aviation pioneer Marion
10. Old Canadian kids' show: *Romper* _____
11. Road Runner's not-so-wily nemesis?
12. Turbine components
13. Opera texts
14. Saudi's steed?
15. Remote control button
16. Commonwealth Stadium CFL team, for short
24. See 61-A
27. Venues for sports events
31. Galsworthy trilogy: *The Forsyte* _____
34. Milk, say
36. Beautiful
38. Naive
39. Japanese port city
40. 2010 Kelly Clarkson single: "All I _____ Wanted"
41. Shade of blonde
42. Kamloops river
43. Axe that's a weapon
44. Tropical tree
46. "Excuse me" sound
48. Obscure, old style
49. Wrap for a ranee
52. Girls just want to have this
54. Emmy-winning drama: _____ *Men*
57. Spore enclosures
58. BC's "Highway Thru Hell"
59. Habituations
60. Longish skirt style
62. Horse-drawn carriage
64. Lots, colloquially
66. No place in particular
68. Country involved in a missile crisis
69. Dracula, sometimes
71. Syrup of ipecac, et al.
73. Quorums, at the synagogue
76. Kinda nerdy

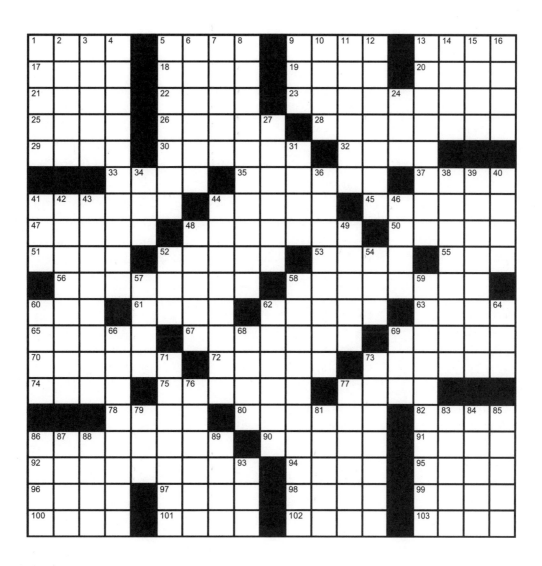

77. Crudités vegetable
79. Ugly old woman
81. Town _____
83. Care deeply for
84. Occult sign

85. Place to put your feet up
86. Birds' lodgings
87. Description of Cinderella's stepsisters
88. Like a loyal friend

89. Luau activity
93. Droop

Yes You Can . . .

Find the letter pattern in these theme clues

ACROSS

1. Cockatoo's cousin
6. *This Gun for* _____
10. _____ de deux
13. Biblical verb
17. Fatuous
18. Yemen city
19. Old-style prov. abbr.
20. Diamond Head island
21. Ridge anagram
22. Even-steven
23. More rigid, like rules
25. Oiler's objective?
26. Military police supervisor
28. Legal right
30. Dined
31. Signalled
32. Bone in the arm
34. Luxurious resorts
38. Indian spice mixture
41. AB-born NHLer Shane, et al.
44. Walk all over the competition?
45. Blackberry segments
46. Trace
47. State of confusion
50. 2002 Canadian romcom: _____ *with Brooms*
51. Foreshadow
54. Snafus
55. Rainbow shapes
57. **2004 Will Ferrell film**
59. Forest undergrowth
61. Not in front
63. 1979 Who rockumentary: *The Kids Are* _____
65. In a family, son of a son of a son
66. Canada's Mike Reno sang on this *Footloose* song: "Almost _____"
68. _____-horse race
69. Lacks, in brief
71. List entries
72. Tragedy or comedy
74. Go back on a promise
75. Papineau parent
76. Heroic tale
78. Spades or clubs
79. Vancouver Canucks mascot name
80. Chauffeur of serfs?
87. A cool summer residence might be this
92. 1958 Leslie Caron movie
93. Plagues
94. Stew over
95. Alice of *Lives of Girls and Women* fame
96. Breech computer security systems
97. Prisoner's breakout, say
98. Make an impression?
99. "Be quiet," on a musical score
100. Oxen harness
101. Navy rank (abbr.)
102. Gaming table tool
103. Fits of pique

DOWN

1. Barbie's best friend
2. Electrolysis particle
3. Precious gem measurement
4. **Protestant**
5. Very small, in Scotland
6. Extreme dislike
7. Colourful language?
8. 1999 Golden Globe nominee Christopher
9. _____ a high note
10. Prairie paper: *Regina Leader-_____*
11. **2015 movie starring 74-D**
12. Geological layers
13. Severinsen and Holliday
14. Witnesses swear one in court
15. Jazz standard: "Take _____ Train"
16. Sling
24. Dander
26. *Nolo contendere* or guilty
27. Flabbergast
29. Annual Ottawa event: Canadian _____ Festival
33. Hippies took trips on this
34. Play a guitar
35. Aquatic mammal
36. Gathering at church?
37. CSIS operative
38. Toddler's early word
39. Embitter
40. More earnest
41. It might be herniated
42. D-Day beach
43. **Luanda resident**
44. Woodwind instrument, for short
46. Advances funds, say
48. Effigy
49. Trig abbr.
52. Sari-clad royal
53. Blue Jay's faux pas
56. Embarrassment
58. Shania Twain hit: "Any Man of _____"
60. Construction zone
62. Fingers a felon
64. Belonging to those people
66. Mark on a playing card
67. Cackleberry
70. **Like West Indies St. John's residents**
73. Alberta, directionally from British Columbia
74. Actor Paul
76. eHarmony user
77. **Like llamas**
78. Get mad
79. Annual event: CIBC Run _____ the Cure
81. Eternal inmate

82. Significant artery
83. Sweater style
84. Leonardo da _____
85. Everglades wading bird
86. Acts of unrest

87. Greyish in colour
88. Since 1947, a UN aviation org.
89. Chrétien-era health minister Allan
90. Raita veggie

91. Doctrines
95. Rushmore and Logan, for short

ACROSS

1. Old-style punitive colony description
6. In the distance
10. They help in emergencies (abbr.)
14. Gusto
17. Stepping lively, say
18. Scrabble player's square
19. Picasso contemporary Joan
20. Internet acronym
21. 1 Sussex Drive, Ottawa
23. Redding or Rush
24. Canadian heptathlete Theisen-Eaton won bronze here in 2016
25. Brooch for a boa?
26. Black Sea city
28. Canadian stand-up comedienne Anthony
29. You might see one on a West Coast boat tour
31. Avow allegiance, say
33. Called to court
38. Shackling
42. Protein particle, in biology
43. Irritated exam taker?
45. Pupil covering
46. Expels
48. Put up artwork
50. Little, in Laval
51. Toothy?
53. Bieber or Trudeau
55. Long-time *Hockey Night in Canada* voice Bob
56. Ladies giving largesse
59. Wolf, in Juárez
63. Sci-fi bots
64. Made nasty Internet comments
69. Catkin
71. German "A"
72. Ontario First Nations group
73. Feudal-era servant
75. Bloor or Yonge, in Toronto
79. Former Ontario premier Peterson
80. Italian appetizer servings
82. Bunches of broccoli
84. Lose light
85. Some indigenous Brazilians
86. CFB word
89. Dreary sounding song
91. Plays in the pool
97. Lode load
98. Noon, in Normandin
99. BC city and band name
101. Lust or sloth
102. Privy to
103. Inlet
104. Milk-producing plant
105. Calendar abbr.
106. Very excited
107. Gets a glimpse
108. Tropical tourist's illness

DOWN

1. Averages
2. Heston picture, for example
3. Not any, in Navarre
4. Tennis whiz
5. Toronto team athlete
6. Parched, old style
7. Bridal shower honoured guest
8. Opposite of nothing
9. Depend upon
10. Skin-soothing substances
11. One of a pair of winter wear
12. Like musical chords
13. 1975 ABBA hit
14. Kitten's contented sound
15. Port Dover is on the north shore of this lake
16. Ruse
22. It follows "Once" in a fairy tale
27. Conciliates
28. Madagascar mammal
30. Commercials
32. Gunk
33. Hurried or scurried
34. Craving
35. Bearing
36. Not quite all
37. Like some pub draft
39. Division word
40. Canadian "Heart of Gold" singer Young
41. Proceeds from a performance
44. Lake Superior city (with "Bay")
47. System Trading and Development (abbr.)
49. The basic idea
52. To be, in Montréal
53. Fitting together, like a carpenter
54. Fiddling Roman emperor
57. Loudly celebrating
58. Weather balloon payload
59. Volcanic output
60. Middle Eastern country
61. Tops
62. Word NHLers like to hear
65. *All in the Family* producer Norman
66. Like a long-running Saturday night show?
67. Modify video footage
68. Pops
70. Finger food, in Seville
74. Adding fatuous details?
76. Baby amphibian
77. Hard to get a handle on?
78. Overthrows an oligarchy
81. Popular Bombardier product
83. Toronto-born actor Arnett
86. Head honcho at the office
87. Opera highlight
88. Remitted
90. Emergency Core Cooling System (abbr.)
92. Abets
93. Exchange stories, say

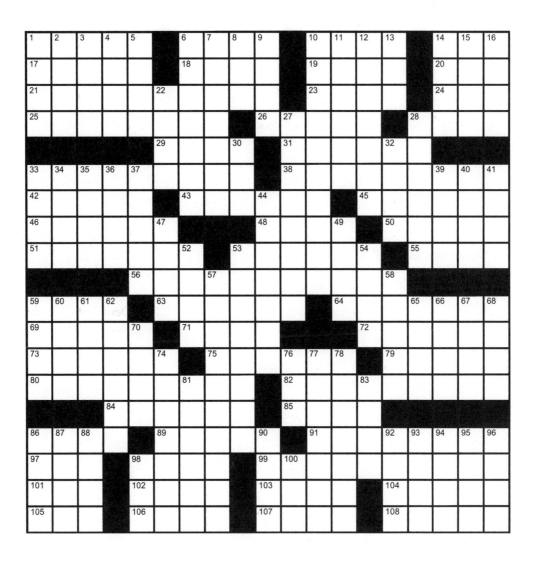

94. 1960s musical
95. Alternative to cream

96. *Return to Babylon* star Ione
98. Actress Farrow

100. Weeding tool

41 Who Are We?

ID this group of Canadian trailblazers

ACROSS

1. Not as much
5. Alternative to nude, in pantyhose
9. Business school admission test (abbr.)
13. Crusty character?
17. Put off?
18. Plummet
19. Pinnacle
20. Canine on a Canadian TV classic
21. Helper
22. Mental keenness
23. Crazy Canucks' gear
24. Comply with instructions
25. Writer's employment type
27. Troubadours
29. Ex-prime minister Joe
30. Scottish noble
32. Dentistry device (var.)
33. _____ Wednesday
35. Opposite of active
37. Bed and breakfast, for example
38. Hamilton landmark: Dundurn _____
41. Wood type
43. Common logic?
45. Bedwetter's condition
47. Indian ethnic group
49. Dental school grad
50. Baby hawk
51. Xavier and Hadrian, to Justin
52. **Irene _____**
54. Canadian visual artist Chris
56. Possessive pronoun
58. Delivered in France?
59. Pachyderm's plant?
63. *Playboy* founder, for short
66. Annex
67. Cronus' mother
68. **Emily _____**
72. Pronto acronym
74. Hippies' digs
76. Hockey's big prize: Stanley _____
78. Thick soup type
79. Hot pepper
81. Rattlesnake's poison
83. Rank between marquis and viscount
84. Stuck out
85. Pool player's signal?
87. Spore holders
89. Pass between mountain peaks
90. Environmental Research and Education (abbr.)
91. Befuddled, on the briny?
93. Public spectacle?
95. Biblical passage
98. Fruit or flowers painting, for example
102. Madison Avenue award
103. Support (var.)
104. African antelope
105. Desktop computer brand
106. She may be sainted?
107. Computer functions list
108. Deep black, to bards
109. *Knocked Up* actress Leslie
110. Pleads
111. School for some teens, for short
112. "Shoot!"
113. Town between Calgary and Red Deer

DOWN

1. Scott Joplin classic: "Maple _____ Rag"
2. Dignitary in Dubai
3. Dining room furniture piece
4. Girder alloy
5. **Henrietta Muir _____**
6. Like ripply chips
7. US university mil. group
8. Tournament participant's trauma?
9. ATCO employee, say
10. **Louise _____**
11. Nitrogen compound
12. Dick Tracy's missus Trueheart
13. Toronto Mendelssohn Choir refrains?
14. Long-time CTV news anchor Lloyd
15. Biblical brother
16. *Trailer Park* _____
26. Chou En-_____
28. Alpine people mover
31. Hurry
33. Over or above?
34. Red Cross supplies
36. Son of Cain
38. Standard practice
39. Queue
40. Latin 101 word
42. Canadian Shewfelt who scored Olympic gold in gymnastics
44. Mutton necks
46. Babe in the woods
48. Equipped to get the job done
50. Inveigle
53. Squealed like a Shih Tzu
55. Santa _____ CA
57. Minestrone or mulligatawny
60. Canada Pension _____
61. Steam bath
62. "_____ North strong and free"
63. Pilgrimage to Mecca
64. Isaac and Rebekah's biblical boy
65. Bumbling or stumbling
69. Utilitarian
70. Protagonist, in fiction
71. Cry out, loudly
73. New England NFL team
75. **Result of their efforts: Living tree _____**

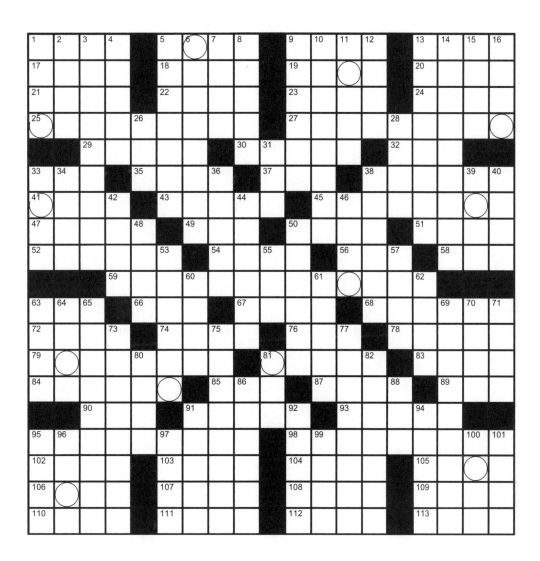

77. God who had an underwater adventure?
80. Coop chirp
81. Neckline shape
82. **Nellie** _____
86. Exhausts one's supplies
88. Woe
91. Ice fishing tool

92. Inquired
94. 1836 Texas revolution battle
95. Crusty skin area
96. Miss Scarlet board game
97. Occasional employee
99. Big brass instrument
100. Provide for oneself?
101. Coastal birds (var.)

Use the circled letters to unscramble their group name:

_ _ _ _ _ _   _ _ _ _

Canada Cornucopia 19

ACROSS

1. US state
5. Shove
9. Did laps
13. Hydrocarbon derivative
17. Canadian poet Phyllis
18. Not fooled by
19. Pasternak heroine
20. Kauai feast
21. Mite anagram
22. Wound with a blade
23. Attributing to essayists?
25. Taking away
27. Long-running CBC show: *Front Page* _____
28. Pomelo, by another name
30. Fashionable brand: Christian _____
31. Cooperative effort between groups
34. City in Germany
36. Big book
40. Coin unique to Canada
41. Copy, genetically
42. Significant UK prime minister?
43. Nips at the finish
44. Worldly, as opposed to spiritual
45. Linked by limbs?
48. Kootenay National Park landmark: Sinclair _____
49. Some conservatory plants
50. First or second
51. Vote of support
52. Volleys
54. Core conviction
56. Device download
59. In stead of
60. Like wild dogs
61. _____ Spumante
65. Raises the stakes?
67. TV character played by Calista
68. Gists
69. Measuring device
70. Arriving prematurely
72. Justin Trudeau cabinet minister Monsef
73. Sign of the future
74. Glass ingredient
76. Points out a perp?
77. Uni social science course
79. La-Z-Boy furniture piece
81. Dry run
85. Waterproof table coverings
89. Tediously repetitive
90. Salacious glance
91. Acid type
92. Pickle
93. Bards' verses
94. See 90-A
95. Half a provincial name
96. Sped
97. Own up, like actor Parker?
98. _____ and crafts
99. Textile tinter

DOWN

1. Needed to pay up
2. Blood pigment
3. Bibliographical note abbr.
4. Inability to understand
5. Stamps, say
6. Messy
7. "We _____ on guard for thee"
8. Folklore creatures
9. Make less taut
10. Do the laundry
11. Montréal-based band: _____ Fire
12. Sport fish
13. Wild Rose province resident
14. Wreck
15. Yin's counterpart
16. Canada has never won an Olympic medal in this (as of 2017)
24. UN working-conditions agcy.
26. Former Canadian astronaut Hadfield
29. Nile reptiles
31. Footfall
32. *Star Wars* franchise character
33. Eggy beverages
35. Sparsely (var.)
37. "Love Train" group member
38. Less is _____
39. Witty writer Bombeck
41. Amusement park ride
42. Muck in a marsh
44. Embankment
46. Canadian men won bronze in this Rio race
47. Canada Post delivery
49. Dart like a dove, say
53. Winged, in biology
54. BC Coast Mountains community
55. Canada National Exhibition location
56. Bubbly Nestlé bar
57. Juicy fruit
58. Legendary Brazilian soccer star
60. Madcap comedy genre
62. Eye irritation cause
63. "_____ she blows!"
64. Schools of thought, for short
66. Layered wood on furniture
68. Group on 27-A
71. In need of ventilation
72. Kitchen gadgets
74. Kinda
75. Not outdoors
76. Boneless steak
78. Calgary Airport Authority (abbr.)
80. Big cat crossbreed
81. Wealthy Canadian impressionist?
82. Ornamental case, in Orléans
83. _____ today, gone tomorrow

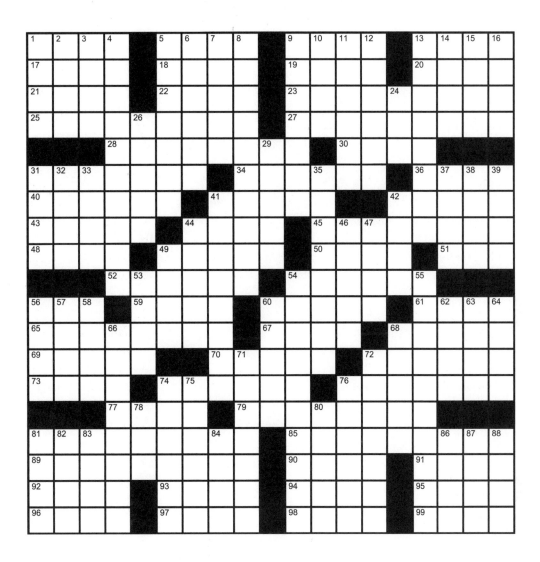

84. Old Roman greetings

86. Town of Helen

87. Bees' domain

88. Simba's uncle, in the movies

43 | Sounds Fishy to Me . . .

And hopefully to you, too!

ACROSS

1. Train track
5. _____ little backbone
10. Former Vancouver Canuck Salo
14. Like a best bet?
19. Teenagers' bane
20. Coffee company founded in BC
21. 2000 Giller Prize short list author Cumyn
22. Make amends for wrongdoing
23. **Fish for an American artist?**
26. Type of congestion that comes with a cold
27. Speedy serve from Vasek Pospisil
28. George Stroumboulopoulos role on some TV shows
29. Sass: _____ off
30. "Ain't That _____"
31. Gave an inkling
33. African capital on the Atlantic
35. Canada's smallest prov., *en français*
37. Crossed paths with
38. Beauty pageant contestant's accessory
39. "Heart and _____"
41. Of consequence
45. Tennis star Djokovic, for one
47. Close in on
49. Eventually
50. Pole for a Swiss shepherd
54. Cedes
56. Ill-fated, old style
58. _____ a bone
60. Platforms for thrones
62. Receive through a will
63. Overused
65. Pith helmet (var.)
66. Queen's Park city (abbr.)
67. Tribal healer?
72. *High Sierra* star Lupino
73. Live

76. Loop of lace edging
77. Slangy handle?
80. Penny-pinchers
82. It causes a buzz in the kitchen?
84. More easygoing
85. Quick and cunning
87. Toured England in a camper
89. Arm-bone related
91. Light bulb unit
92. Fades, like light
95. Nob's sense of style
98. Former employer of Canadians Bondar and Thirsk
100. Bottle toppers
102. Single or double furniture piece
103. It comes after chi
104. Aden's nation
106. Forcefully express one's opinion
108. Breadths
111. Hawaiian island
113. Madonna song: "La _____ Bonita"
115. Common Gateway Interface (abbr.)
116. Previously, in olden days
117. **Fish for a Scottish leader?**
120. More amiable
121. Kidlit author Blyton
122. Selected
123. Assess one's interest?
124. Jamaican fruit
125. Joins together at the altar
126. "A mind is a terrible thing to _____"
127. Long-time Ottawa Rough Rider Jackson

DOWN

1. Royal Indian men (var.)
2. Shrubs with spines
3. Source of fragrant smoke

4. Alexander the Great originally graced this coin
5. Hairnets
6. Fairy tale scribe Christian Andersen
7. B, K or P, when spoken
8. Music style: Doo-_____
9. Mass destruction weapon
10. 1983 Gordon Lightfoot album
11. Frequently
12. *Deus ex* _____
13. It's red when you're indebted?
14. Without (Fr.)
15. Canada won nine Olympic speed skating medals in this state
16. **Fish for a *Gone Girl* actress?**
17. Tooth's surface
18. Locate a new tenant
24. Pronoun for a ship
25. Rich earth
30. Virgil offering (with "*The*")
32. Former Balkans region
34. Old-style interjection of regret
36. Such a shame, really?
40. Nitty Gritty Dirt Band hit: "_____ Over the Line"
42. Fuel hydrocarbon
43. _____ Bear Lake
44. Alternative to an octavo
46. Go out of focus
48. Regional Transportation District (abbr.)
51. Proper's partner
52. Satellite, for example
53. Greenish blue
55. Farmer's planting machine
56. Absence of oxygen
57. **Fish for a Gemini-winning director?**
59. Famed early Mountie Steele
61. Char a steak
62. Big ticket purchase?

64. Expresses grief
68. Morse code symbol
69. It hangs around the house?
70. Medically induced state of sleep
71. Former Scottish islands language
74. Establish a foundation, say
75. 45th US president
78. State of poverty
79. Charge with a crime
81. Brews a cuppa
83. Not refined
84. Devilish practitioners?

86. Flubs
88. Windmill blade
90. Blue jeans dye, for one
93. Famed mime Marcel
94. Taps
95. Like a god
96. Church councils
97. Aquatic mammal
99. Make reference to
101. Book parts
102. Swahili sir
105. Siamese's sound (var.)
107. You might lend one?

109. Catalpa or crabapple
110. Golden Globe-nominated Bryan Adams song: "_____ I Am"
112. Eastern Canada pollution problem: _____ rain
114. Proofreader's manuscript notation
117. _____ Democratic Party
118. Mineral spring
119. Interjection of annoyance

ACROSS

1. Bearded like a bristle
6. Bit of seaweed
10. Tree liquids
14. Lair for lions
17. South American nation
18. Canadian airline founder Max
19. Hill crest, Cambridgeshire
20. Big bird
21. Dessert treat first made in BC
23. Sparkly
25. Fix Fido?
26. Calgary Board of Education employees
27. 1970s TV advertising stalwart: K-_____
28. Toronto and Edmonton newspapers names
30. Authorize to drive
31. Shut down a business
34. Foot, in a poetry syllable
36. Tailor, old style
37. HS reunion attendee
38. United Empire Loyalists, for example
41. Minuscule
42. 2016 event: Labrador Winter _____
44. Legal Aid Ontario (abbr.)
45. Crazies
47. Wanton
50. Brandon-born singer-songwriter Moore
51. Québec town
55. Harper government cabinet minister Bev
56. Oslo nation (abbr.)
57. Payoff
59. "Freedom Tower" locale (abbr.)
61. Map abbr.
62. Movie or song title: *The Way We* _____

64. Ten less seven, in Roman numerals
66. She might move to a new city for her job
69. Calgary equestrian event centre: _____ Meadows
72. Be in the hole
73. Canada's foreign affairs minister (2011–15)
74. Indian class division system
77. Saucy, old style
80. X-ray units
81. Tailors to fit
83. Ingredient in Creole cooking
84. Greek poet
86. Long-_____ shirt
88. Epic story
90. Plumeria necklace
91. Spent July at the lake?
93. Toronto NHLers
98. Cold War competition?
99. Eschewing others
100. Sign of peace
101. Cross between
102. Run in neutral
103. _____ firma
104. Append
105. Like long fish
106. Small islands
107. Portfolio holding

DOWN

1. Skin affliction
2. 1980s George Michael British band
3. Weather system: La _____
4. Synthetic rubber, for example
5. Clears jet wings
6. Missing from the Marines, say
7. Over there, in Trois-Rivières
8. Unnecessary
9. Kind of gland
10. Trick-taking card game
11. Heavenly presence?
12. Versailles, to a Parisian
13. Violinist's technique
14. Lessening of international tension
15. Canadian country band: _____ Drive
16. Gardening centre
22. Uncooperative animals?
24. Post Brexit UK PM May
29. Duck type
31. Two-time Habs coach Julien
32. Related to the lower back
33. State of confusion, mentally
35. Canadian children's entertainers: Sharon, Lois and _____
37. Luminous
39. Confucian concept
40. Photocopiers' kin
43. Wrath, for one
46. Pianos have these
48. Coconut husk fibre
49. Tippler
52. Pop singer Carey
53. Go to extremes
54. Sesame bits
58. Biased publicity
60. Trenton or Petawawa (abbr.)
63. Holds in high regard
65. International Civil Aviation Organization (abbr.)
67. Sense of wonder
68. Component of some hearing aids
70. Contrary to popular opinion?
71. Charitable organization: _____ of Canada
74. Tapioca source
75. Enticed
76. Originated from
78. Old Semitic language

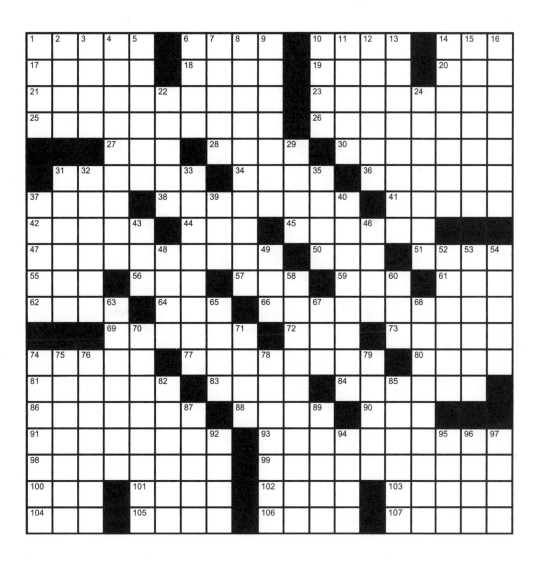

79. Offenbach opera: *The _____ of Hoffmann*

82. Mexican wrap

85. Jai alai, by another name

87. It sticks on glass

89. In an appropriate way

92. Refuse to acknowledge

94. Falsehoods

95. Pretenses

96. Cost of a cab ride

97. Board under a bed

45 They Hail from Vancouver

Born in Gastown, known around the globe

ACROSS

1. The big picture?
5. Angry bird?
9. Animal's shelter
13. 1915 novel by American Winston Churchill: _____ *Country*
17. California city: Santa _____
18. Membrane of the eye
19. _____ 500
20. Central Alberta community: _____ Lake
21. Loud growl
22. Bring in the barley
23. 1950s Canadian prime minister Louis
25. Footwear store gadgets
27. Prom kings and queens
28. Conducted an orchestra
29. Mongolian dwelling
30. Revise
32. 2013 film starring 84-A: *This Is the* _____
34. Taxing Canadian org?
37. Feline food: _____ Mix
39. B&B alternative
40. Put in the picture?
43. Greek coins, old style
45. Former NHL left winger Kariya
47. Food flavouring for everyone?
49. "_____ a Grecian Urn"
50. Hindu god (var.)
51. Self, in Saguenay
52. Painful thing?
53. Ex-BC premier Campbell
55. Taste option for 37-A
57. Famed Canadians Marion or Bobby
59. Goddess of dawn
60. Truck fuel
62. Like some fruit
65. Tent securing stick
68. *Show Boat* song: "Can't Help Lovin' _____ Man"
69. Not totally closed
71. Actress De Carlo
75. Euro forerunner in Italy
77. Some scale notes
79. Canadian media personality Jerry
81. Cyber communication
82. Old-style greenhouse
84. Actor Rogen
85. Horse holders
86. Middle Ages flag
87. Richard Gwyn's *John A*, for example
89. Food Network Canada show: *Carnival* _____
91. *Malcolm X* director Spike
92. Sri Lankan lentil dish
93. Astute
95. Variegated
97. Furious
99. Norwegian inlet
101. Summaries about art?
106. Pub, in Plessisville
108. John Candy comedy: _____ *Runnings*
109. Aspen alternative
110. Politician's assistant
111. You don't want to tempt this
112. See 15-D
113. Insider's scoop
114. Prepaid postal option (abbr.)
115. Skedaddled
116. Barbie's dolls, say
117. Adept

DOWN

1. Transgresses
2. Bear created by A.A. Milne
3. Jack Nicklaus competitor Aoki
4. NHL goalie Price
5. Rage, in Ramsgate
6. Breaches a levee
7. Switch a baby from bottle to cup
8. Slip
9. You might do this to CBC Radio?
10. They receive signals
11. Lazed
12. Actor Reynolds
13. Canadian Cancer Society daffodil mo.
14. Meadow rodents
15. Mother of two British queens (with 112-A)
16. Receiving CPP, say
24. Addicts
26. *Star Trek: TNG*'s Data, for example
31. NHL left winger Lucic
33. California wine-growing area
34. Wooden footwear item
35. Start over again
36. One who emulates an orangutan?
38. Ralph of *The Waltons*
40. Coquettish
41. Canyon reverb
42. Barely passing grades
44. AB-born cartoonist McFarlane
46. Soft palate component
48. Plunder
54. Straighten up
56. Take _____ from
58. Aircraft system: Thrust _____
61. Recipe direction
63. See 97-A
64. Feature of Olympic Stadium in Montréal
65. Alka-Seltzer ad word
66. Alternate name for Ireland
67. Some male relatives
70. Actor Priestley
72. Use a hammer
73. Cardinal number

74. Woody Allen film: *Anything*
_____

76. Winnipeg-born *True Blood* star
Paquin

78. Luxury lover

80. 1978 Burton Cummings hit: "I
Will Play a _____"

83. Plays 18 holes

88. Truly

90. Dames and duchesses

93. Nunavut community: _____
Harbour

94. You might see one in a marina

96. Environmentalist Suzuki

97. Business school degrees (abbr.)

98. "Madamina" from *Don
Giovanni*

100. MLB pitcher Francis

102. Irish lad

103. Sugary stick?

104. Annual Toronto cinematic
event in Sept.

105. _____ machine

107. Song from The Who's *Tommy*:
"____ Me, Feel Me"

ACROSS

1. _____ accordance with
6. Chip type
10. US record label since 1955
14. Doug McKenzie's brother on *SCTV*
17. Toe troubles
18. Great horned avians
19. Sticky stuff
20. Blood classification letters
21. The Queen Charlotte Islands are now called this
23. Make a point?
24. US band: _____ Speedwagon
25. 1967 Montréal fair
26. Nursery _____
27. Good deed doing, say
29. Well-known Canadian poem: "Alligator _____"
30. Warmongering god
32. Angry outburst
33. Civil trial participant
38. Place name in ON, QC and PEI
42. Colorado ski resort
43. Old-style second-person verb
45. Polynesia is part of this
46. You might have a pocket full of these?
48. Raise your glass
50. South African grassland
51. Excited, like Rorschach?
52. Canadian mystery writer Louise
53. Grandma _____
54. Mock horror cry
55. Small songbird
56. 2002 Berton book: *Marching as to _____*
57. James T. Kirk journeys?
60. To-do
61. Rite of contrition
65. Diminish in intensity
66. Parisian river
67. Manual
68. Contract proposer, in law
70. Go in
72. Similar to
73. Promise, conditionally
75. In its original state
77. _____ an ear
78. Some URL endings
80. Female rabbit
81. It's not cheap?
84. Moulded jelly serving
86. _____ Smith NWT
90. "Far out," to the HVAC pro?
91. Gershwin and Levin
92. Saskatchewan CFLer
94. "Our Lips _____ Sealed"
95. Hawaii state bird
96. Groom a moustache
97. Goddess of peace
98. Real estate industry abbr.
99. Mardi _____
100. Nazi war criminal Rudolf
101. Geeky

DOWN

1. 1981 Rosanne Cash hit: "Seven Year _____"
2. Inveigle
3. Excursion
4. _____-Aryan
5. National Security Agency (abbr.)
6. Like a fair-haired boy
7. Not at home
8. The Weather Network topic
9. Willow tree
10. Horrified
11. Hammer or mallet
12. Business agreement
13. Perform surgery
14. Some male singers
15. British charitable service awards (abbr.)
16. Explosive sound
22. Parliament Hill pol, colloquially
28. Boding ill, in Illinois
29. Fruity drinks
31. Northeastern European republic
33. A bit moist
34. Hieroglyphs goddess
35. Active
36. Role for Canada in global conflicts
37. 12 and 20 (abbr.)
39. In the pink?
40. Annoy
41. They have a special day in June
44. Former prime minister Harper
47. Something to spend in Tirana
49. Picnic predator
52. Toronto attraction: Black Creek _____ Village
53. Order from him?
55. Luau serving
56. Cyst
57. Toddlers' terrible times?
58. Water float
59. Groups of interconnected rooms
60. Wife of Zeus
61. Standard examples
62. Film _____
63. Pop brand, for short
64. Got the most from
66. He fuses metal
67. Barnyard bird
69. _____ on empty
71. Asian silkworm (var.)
74. Throws a pigskin
76. _____ Ness
79. Canadian business journalist Turner
81. Wee tipple
82. *SCTV* character: _____ Camembert
83. Capital of Yemen (var.)
85. Then, in Témiscaming

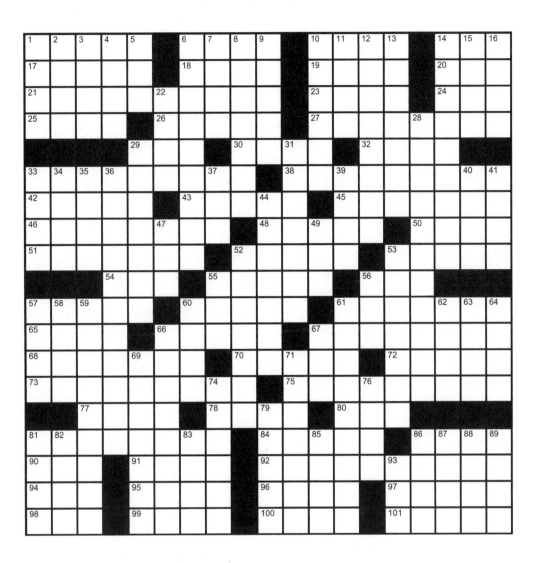

86. Adele hit: "Set _____ to the Rain"

87. German river

88. Rip apart

89. Three on a die

93. _____-Tin-Tin

47 On the Diagonal

Find the fitting nine-letter word hidden here

ACROSS

1. Mites' urge?
5. Shape of a rainbow
8. Fox hunt disruptor, in Oxford
11. Confront
17. BC salmon catch
18. Title for Gandhi
20. TV drama that was set in Toronto: _____ *Blue*
21. George or Charlotte, for short
22. Singer Iggy's flowers?
23. Barbershop ointment
24. Talkative starling
25. They rise and fall, depending on the fashion?
27. Typed, say
28. Islet
30. Geological age
31. *Frasier* actress Gilpin
33. Accurately done
37. Ornamental shrubs
42. Part of Santa's laugh?
43. Station, in Paris
44. Skirt around
45. Where to put a sock?
46. Computer architecture acronym
48. Plant parts
50. Canadian ice dance icon Virtue
51. Québec Christmas visitor: Père _____
52. Friar's do
53. Illegal Irish whisky
54. On
56. Neighbour of CDA
57. 1940s screen queen Turner
58. Confirmed by evidence
61. "Frosty the _____"
63. BC swimmer Cochrane who won Olympic silver and bronze
67. Architectural column type
68. Equitable financial division, in Derby
69. Yesteryear
70. Big bag
71. Petite particle, old style
72. City in Russia
74. Expend resources
75. More conclusively, to Hadrian
77. Plain
79. Release light
80. Barenaked Ladies hit: "_____ All Been Done"
81. _____, borrow or steal
82. Drawn-out attack
86. Impersonal, like a physician?
90. Twelfth Jewish month
93. Like fancy furniture
95. Enrage a Calgary NHLer?
96. Old West gamblers' game
97. Canadian oil field employee
98. Escalate in price
99. Directors do this in a suite
100. Postulate
101. Rocky peak
102. Curling match finale?
103. Some dark loaves

DOWN

1. Nuclear arsenal component (abbr.)
2. Rona Ambrose, colloquially
3. Beijing garden bloomer?
4. Windbags are full of this
5. Asian household helper
6. Completely demolish
7. Richly coloured reptile?
8. American author Gertrude
9. He might take it like this?
10. Denture component
11. Annual Rate of Payment (abbr.)
12. Colloquial question to a chef: "What's _____?"
13. Accept an invitation
14. Sanction
15. Big order of beef
16. Got ready to drive, at Glen Abbey
19. Pewter, for example
26. Pips
29. Two-year-old sheep
32. Sally Field film: *Norma* _____
33. Famed Taber AB product
34. Tenth-longest US river
35. Milk container
36. March with a military unit?
37. Stun
38. Like some food supplements?
39. Massachusetts' motto beginning
40. See 98-A
41. "Northwest Passage" singer Rogers
44. Difficult to grasp
47. Harpsichord, for example
49. Catastrophic natural disaster in 2004
50. "It hit me like a _____ of bricks"
53. Gasped
55. Sam Spade, for short
57. Canadian sweets shop: _____ Secord
58. Hummus pocket
59. Structure topper
60. Catch _____
61. Group of Giller Prize nominees
62. Humans saw this for the first time on 7/20/69
64. Little miss?
65. Bottom, on a Britcom
66. 1971 Sonny and Cher album: *All I Ever _____ Is You*
68. Lacking in emotion
71. Ambition
73. Tennis court shot
76. Balance precariously
77. Effective
78. Stoner's cigarette
80. Establish by deduction

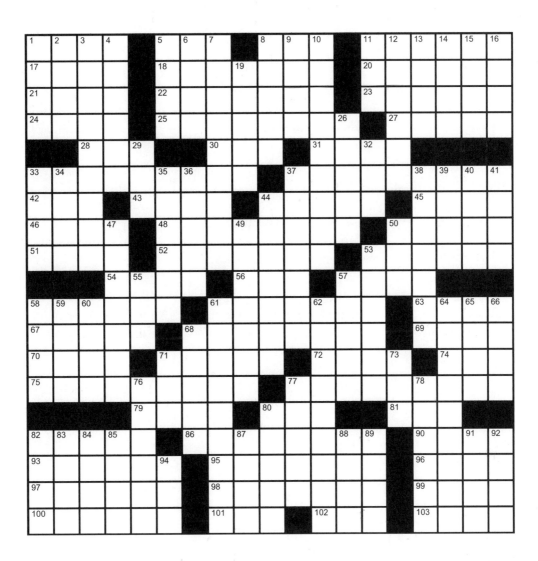

82. Short-billed bird

83. Symbol of Québec: Blue flag

_____

84. Some technical program grads

85. Hamilton ON park

87. Enthusiastic about, colloquially

88. "You said it, preacher!"

89. Give, temporarily

91. _Ugly Betty_ co-star Michael

92. Many auction options?

94. Menopause treatment (abbr.)

48

Four-Square 3

Use mini grids to solve a CanCon phrase

ACROSS

1. Uses Scope, say
8. Tree liquid
11. Film technology software (abbr.)
14. Egg-shaped instrument
15. Iconic NHLer Bobby
16. Aged
17. Relaxed
18. Root you can eat
19. Mordecai Richler novel: *Solomon Gursky _____ Here*
20. A Manx is missing this
21. One and Two, in *The Cat in the Hat*
23. Ocean refuse
26. Saving grace?
28. Balloon filler
29. Eggs
30. African country
31. _____ Moines
32. _____ Westminster BC
33. Cereal grass
34. 1960s hit?
35. Popular 1980s band
38. Canadian Gas Association (abbr.)
41. Grp. for US attorneys
44. The whole shebang
47. Military leader with civil power
49. Nancy Drew's boyfriend Nickerson
50. Canadian national holiday month
51. AWOL prisoner
52. Cause to go crazy
54. Come to pass
55. Roll call response
56. Scotland Yard div.
57. Bride of Lennon
58. Shampoo brand
61. Manipulate
62. Hawaiian necklace
63. Audience's enthusiastic response
64. McGill postgrad deg.
65. Build onto
66. Let go

DOWN

1. State in India
2. Government legislation
3. Toronto NBAers
4. _____ Slave Lake
5. Tryst
6. Gated neighbourhood
7. Hopeful author's enclosure (abbr.)
8. Infant's pacifier
9. Robin Hood's sport
10. Western Canada land description
11. She wields a rope
12. Spectacles
13. Bar servers might ask for these
22. "As if!"
23. Craze
24. Duffer's deception?
25. Mouth
27. Like some scientists?
35. Stun
36. Illicit drug
37. Like an arched walkway
38. Director Francis Ford
39. Groomed putting surfaces?
40. Lymphatic tissue
41. Long-time Canadian entertainers: Wayne _____ Shuster
42. Apiarist's hairdo?
43. Type of endocrine gland
44. Memory loss
45. Hang back in the pack
46. Janitorial-strength cleaner
48. Runner's track circuit
53. Mountain ridge
56. Stanley _____
58. Pro
59. Ship's call for help
60. Charlotte-to-Raleigh dir.

To solve the CanCon phrase:

Decode a four-word slogan for Charlottetown:

• One vertical word from Square 1.

• One horizontal word from Square 2.

• One horizontal word from Square 3.

• One horizontal word from Square 4.

Answer: _____ _____
_____ _____

SQUARE 1

1	2	3	4	5	6	7
14						
17						
■		20				■
23	24					25
28			■	29		
31			■	32		

SQUARE 2

8	9	10	■	11	12	13
15			■	16		
18			■	19		
21		22			■	
26					27	
30			■			
33			■	34		

SQUARE 3

35	36	37	■	38	39	40
47		48				
51						
■	54					
56			■	57		
61			■	62		
64			■	65		

SQUARE 4

41	42	43	■	44	45	46
49			■	50		
52			53			
■	55			■	■	
58					59	60
63						
66						

Solution on page 219

Great Scotts!

Solve their surnames

ACROSS

1. Red Chamber pol.
4. First scale notes
7. European waterway
10. Central points (var.)
14. Go for a stroll
18. Very variable
20. Cosh
21. Any minute now, old style
22. Song for a soprano
23. Like a seismologist's opinions?
25. Songwriter Bacharach
26. Geddy's group
27. Buck or doe
28. Economic grp. created in 1957
29. Genetic material letters
31. **Film and television actor**
33. Solicit
35. Sunnybrook Farm girl
38. Tolkien tale creatures
39. Dormant, say
42. Serving dish
43. Work mate of 13-D (abbr.)
44. Uris novel: *The _____*
47. **Ex-NHL Devil and Duck**
49. Snobbish school chum?
52. Garden of Eden mother
53. Did an usher's job
54. Stairway to the Ganges
55. Engenders heartache
56. Gobs
58. Ship's docking spot
59. Gambler's "Absolutely!"?
61. Blue reading material, say
62. Challenging
64. Mammal not found on Vancouver Island
65. Olefin
67. Rwandan capital
70. Divorce settlement outcome: _____ support
72. Kitchen storage space
73. _____ band

74. Equine hybrid
75. Pooch's pest
76. Helicopter blade noise
77. Saharan nomad
79. Pork or beef
81. Some computer keys
85. Deck of 78 cards, often
87. Julia Roberts film: *Eat _____ Love*
88. Photographic tints
90. Gershwin of lyrical fame
91. Natural essential oil
93. ***Income Property* host**
95. Calendar abbr.
96. Treatment for dehydration (abbr.)
97. Commotions
99. Knights' protective plates (var.)
100. Skyrocket, like prices
101. Like slightly underdone pasta
103. Jackrabbit's jump
104. **The Kids in the Hall troupe member**
108. _____ sum
109. *Bloodletting and Miraculous Cures* Giller winner Vincent
111. 1814 Niagara Falls event: Battle of Lundy's _____
114. Rant
115. Hawaiian stringed instruments, for short
117. Without any exceptions
120. Spoken
121. Not fake
122. Shoshonean
123. *Born Free*'s Elsa
124. Muscle type, for short
125. Glimpse
126. Margaret Atwood novel: *Life Before _____*
127. Old poetic preposition
128. Third-person pronoun

DOWN

1. Nickname for a Yukon Gold
2. Seabird
3. Nasal gusher
4. US drug enforcement grp.
5. **Gemini-winning sportscaster**
6. Disdainful expression
7. Diminish in intensity
8. Rotted (var.)
9. Charles' first fiancée: Lady Diana _____
10. Great, in slang
11. Cross to bear, say
12. Big business description
13. Some ER employees
14. Municipal districts
15. Jack-in-the-pulpit, for example
16. *Top Chef Canada* host Ray
17. *Blazing Saddles* actress Madeline
19. Glasses type for some movie viewers
24. Transparency
30. Serena often serves one
32. Cyber money
34. Disco popsters: The Bee _____
36. _____ beware
37. Blue-flowered plant
39. From the start
40. Brahma and Vishnu companion (var.)
41. Draft science journal paper
44. Caused injury
45. Harmonize
46. Court cut-up?
48. Janitorial employee
50. Recording artist's tag?
51. Aquatic mammal
54. Like a foolish bird? (var.)
57. Pert or Prell
59. **Long-time sports journalist and author**
60. Stilt walker's story?
63. _____ mode

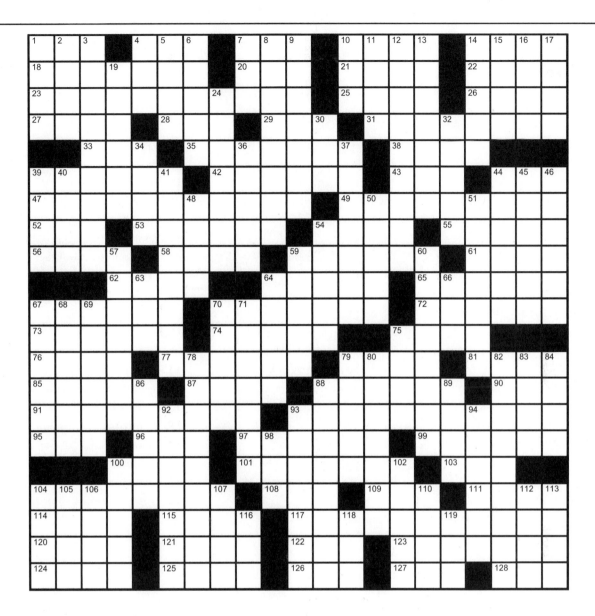

64. Canadian Tire _____
66. Local Area Emergency (abbr.)
67. Old-style Chinese gesture
68. Breathe
69. Prepared (with "up")
70. Lamb Chop's puppeteer Lewis
71. Fishy 1978 horror film?
75. Flunk a course
78. Calligrapher's movements
79. Follows who portrayed Anne of Green Gables
80. Long letter
82. Where WestJet jets fly

83. Slope in the Highlands
84. Articulates
86. Scouts Canada pack
88. Organizational plan
89. Ah of relief
92. File deletion
93. Token amount
94. Instrument for Canada's James Ehnes
98. Saskatchewan hamlet: _____ Wives
100. Petite fish
102. Golfer's great score

104. Stepped
105. Contestant in an Aesop fable
106. White House room: _____ Office
107. Type of tide
110. 2010 Olympics ice dance gold medallist
112. He preceded Mansbridge
113. "What _____ can I say?"
116. Nickname for Stallone
118. _____ Mile Lake BC
119. Delicacy from a beluga

ACROSS

1. Canadian-born '40s film star June, et al.
7. Understands a concept
13. _____ nova
18. Breakfast serving (var.)
19. Leased abode
20. Put in a stake
21. Bounce baby on your knee
22. Eight-legged underwater creatures (var.)
23. Canadian sports news provider: the_____
24. Genie- and Gemini-winning actress McCarthy
25. Prairie province
27. Ardour
28. Pitch
29. Tailor pants, say
30. Annual shot type for many
32. *Michael Collins* actor Stephen
34. Pay-_____-view
35. Rice dish
39. Wales emblem
41. Stairway part
43. Photo
44. Hind end
45. Lewd gawker
47. Purge of
48. Frequency measurement
50. Come together, say
52. Dance music style
53. *CTV National News* reporter: John Vennavally-_____
54. Baby carriages, in Britain
57. It airs *Survivor*
60. Row of potential perps
61. Cuts apart, in biology class
65. Nickname for BC
67. Romaine
68. Popular Internet search engine
69. Valhalla god
70. They plug products
71. Value
73. 1982 Disney film
74. _____ *non grata*
76. It succeeded the USSR
77. Weep
79. Bryan Adams hit: "_____ Only Love"
80. Institute for Public Knowledge (abbr.)
81. Nestling noise
83. Bering and Beaufort
85. Hybrid language
89. Facts
92. Removes wrinkles
93. Ethnic
94. _____ fibrillation
95. Ranee's wrap
96. Canada won 12 Olympic medals here
97. Enter
98. Watches a flock
99. Like some dough
100. Protect under glass

DOWN

1. Bricklayers' boxes
2. Nursemaid in Nanking
3. South American country
4. It might be a goodie?
5. Basement
6. Ballpark thief?
7. Canadian Paul who starred in *Due South*
8. Summarized
9. More jittery, like the entomologist?
10. Worker on the *Titanic*
11. Like Vatican decrees
12. Open an envelope
13. Noisy parties
14. Again
15. Pack away
16. Blood fluids
17. Yemen place
26. Some Mexican–Americans
30. Group of particles
31. Big name in little building?
33. National flyer founded in 1937
35. Conservatives, say
36. YK or NU
37. "Bye-bye," to a Brit
38. Pasta type
40. Seaweed
42. Electrical conductance unit
43. Bullfight participant
46. Spools in an old cinema
48. Toothpaste consistency
49. Equine (var.)
51. Colombo country
52. Adult sheep
55. Stompin' Tom Connors song: "_____ the Spud"
56. Fly by the _____ of one's pants
57. Horse hoof sound
58. Portend
59. Recipe instruction
62. Given name of BC premier Clark
63. Beep
64. Marty and Mark, to Gordie Howe
66. Like anonymous artwork
67. Trigonometry function
71. Frankfurters (var.)
72. Person held for ransom
75. Some composers' works
76. Ballroom dance
78. Canadian author Pierre
81. Shipping box
82. Bell's _____
84. Goldfinger's first name
85. Tilt, like a ship
86. Dies _____

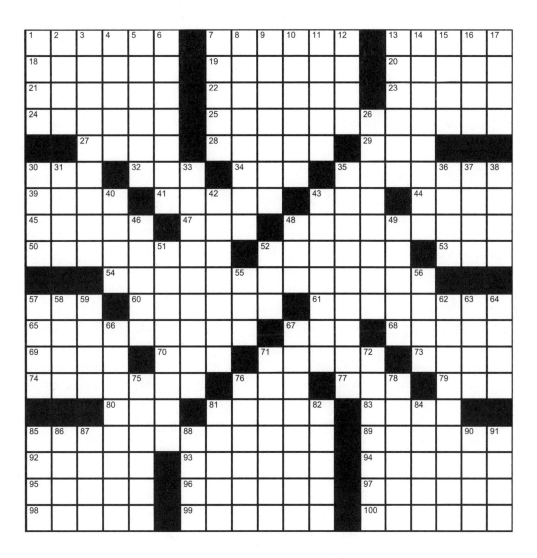

87. Wagnerian goddess
88. Come apart at the seams?

90. Derbies and bowlers
91. Blackthorn

51   Loud Enough For Ya?

Not the sounds of silence . . .

ACROSS

1. Knee ligament (abbr.)
4. Halifax-born *Prince Valiant* comic strip creator Foster
10. US natural gas utility org.
13. Sylvester's pronunciation problem
17. Early '80s Harlequin hit: "Thinking of _____"
18. Tied the score
19. Aries, in the '80s
20. He beat Connors to win Wimbledon in 1975
21. **Noisy place to ride, in olden days?**
23. Food scrap for Spot
24. Indian bakery offering
25. Harper did this to senators 59 times
26. **Strident repressive measure?**
28. Aggressively curious (var.)
29. Plug-in software protection devices
30. Landlocked West African country
33. Tree secretion
35. It might have multiple piercings
39. 2009 blockbuster directed by Canada's James Cameron
42. Vertebrae layers
44. Military marksman
45. Suckerfish
47. Summarily appoints
49. Mend a sock
50. **Loud place to snooze?**
52. Slope, in Scotland
53. They steer ships
54. Alias
57. Sister's addiction?
61. Traditional PEI recipe: _____ Island Biscuits
62. **Basketballer's boisterous victory?**

67. Its capital is Muscat
68. It protects a pupil
70. Learn?
71. Clan's check
73. Grab forty winks
75. Take _____ of absence
76. Buford T. Justice, for example
78. Ancient Peru resident
80. Ed Sullivan had a really big one
81. Lavender sachet, for example
83. Rocks formed by volcanic activity
86. **Explosive Australian comeback?**
89. Colourful warnings?
93. Grapefruit/tangerine hybrid
94. Director's holler
95. **Cacophonous southern Asia country?**
96. Defrost
97. Always, old style
98. Affirm to be true
99. Dunblane denial
100. They grow in pods
101. It's often obtained by swabbing
102. Neon and argon (var.)
103. Workplaces for some residents (abbr.)

DOWN

1. Famed British pianist Hess
2. _____ d'état
3. Coal or sugar piece
4. Sunny prefix?
5. Garden bloomer: Chilean _____
6. To remain, in Rivière-du-Loup
7. Like a Cyclops
8. Soft metal
9. Pesticide banned in Canada, for short
10. It gets squirreled away?
11. Mechanics' milieu

12. Lesson that draws you in?
13. Overwhelming election victory
14. Former PGA pro Aoki
15. Honoured playwright at Niagara-on-the-Lake
16. *Dead Man Walking* actor Sean
22. They're related to tuna
26. Grape type
27. Musical theatre giant Jerome
29. Like a contrary collie?
30. Vancouver-born Singer of *The Beastmaster*
31. State
32. Tibetan holy man
34. Call on the dogs?
36. Birthstone for a Libra
37. Earthen barrier wall
38. Water birds (var.)
40. "One who is worthy," in Buddhism
41. Emulates Toronto's Drake, say
43. Crosses over to the other side?
46. Lippy
48. Some ducks
51. Swindles
53. Blood related
55. Thinking about Kintyre?
56. Toddler's parent
57. Cinnamon flavoured candies: Red _____
58. Domestic servant, in Asia
59. Denuded?
60. Allows to enter, old style
63. Put on clothes
64. Colorado neighbour
65. Guelph-born *House of Cards* actress Campbell
66. Had an inkling
68. Ruled over the rules?
69. Mo. the first crossword was published in 1913
72. Capitol Hill helper
74. Inventors' certificates

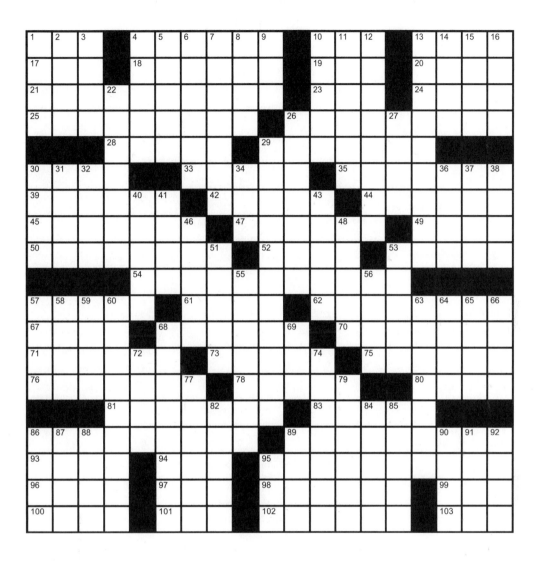

77. Married ladies, in Munich
79. Prods
82. Sinus cavities
84. Untrue
85. Slippers without heels

86. Hit 1970s dance?
87. Architectural moulding style
88. _____ podrida
89. Pro _____
90. Lévesque of Québec

91. Former Bulgarian royal title
92. Hall & Oates hit: "_____ Gone"
95. Shopping tote

Canada Cornucopia 23

ACROSS

1. Font flourish
6. Pendulums' paths
10. Canadian Brass member
18. Toronto lakeshore venue: Ontario _____
19. Fish type, when doubled
20. Milky Way place
21. Poison made from the castor bean
22. "_____ See Clearly Now"
23. Best Great Lake?
24. Grey complected
25. Minor dent
26. It's next to Eritrea (abbr.)
27. Canadian service station name
28. Ph.D. students' works
30. Had brunch
31. Pore on a petal
33. Containers for a condiment
36. Force into servitude
40. Petite
41. Tiny skin openings
43. Number worn by Maple Leafs Bailey and Ellis
44. Canadian Liza who became Iceland's first lady in 2016
48. Meddle
49. Emu, for example
50. Precipice
51. "We stand _____ for thee"
53. Extort funds from, colloquially
54. Rumba or waltz
55. Riding school
56. Grammy-winning Canadian pianist Glenn
57. Set
58. Arcade game: Whac-_____
59. Land depressions
60. They say nay
61. Bird beaks
62. Pens for pooches

63. Boxer's blow
64. Hill near Balmoral, say
65. Patient's woe?
66. Sea floor salvaging aid
67. Canada won 10 medals at this country's Olympic Games
69. Free from micro-organisms
71. Judges' incidental remarks
77. Ecclesiastical council
79. Of the last month (abbr.)
80. Some drums
81. Agile
84. Mixed breed mutt
85. _____-on sunglasses
87. Cuban coins
88. Optional course at U of T
90. Lottery-like casino game
91. Instant, old style
92. Battery terminals
93. Egg on
94. Number of Canadians rowing in some Olympic races
95. Pittsburgh NFLers
96. Hiss that's barely audible
97. Copenhagen folks

DOWN

1. Nursery rhyme duo with dietary concerns?
2. Canadian actress Cuthbert who starred in *Happy Endings*
3. Alberta premier Notley
4. Most slippery
5. African foxes
6. In the centre of
7. How some profiling is done
8. CBC *At Issue* panellist (with 57-D)
9. Céline or Shania
10. Erato and Euterpe
11. Like words not spoken
12. Drew off a liquid

13. "_____ Got You Under My Skin"
14. Frosted Flakes or Froot Loops
15. Part of the eye
16. American Society of Oral Surgeons (abbr.)
17. Hudson Bay island
29. Always, in music
32. Editors edit these (abbr.)
34. Cook's grease
35. Glib presentations
37. Like a broken marriage?
38. Guts
39. Cost
42. Kind of newspaper column
44. Bucharest country
45. Nail varnishes
46. Like a lowly lord?
47. One-on-one sword fights
49. Canadian group: Downchild _____ Band
50. St. Vincent indigenous people: Black _____
52. Bronze follower
53. Jacket style worn by Ravel?
54. Ottawa-born *Ghostbusters* actor Aykroyd
56. Loco about a Lady?
57. See 8-D
59. Gastown
60. Have nerve
62. Concur
63. Notes
66. Farm structure
67. Investigation Discovery channel topic
68. Reworked resources
70. Eros' love
72. Be brave, on a saddle bronc?
73. European peninsula
74. Endorse with another
75. Lozenge

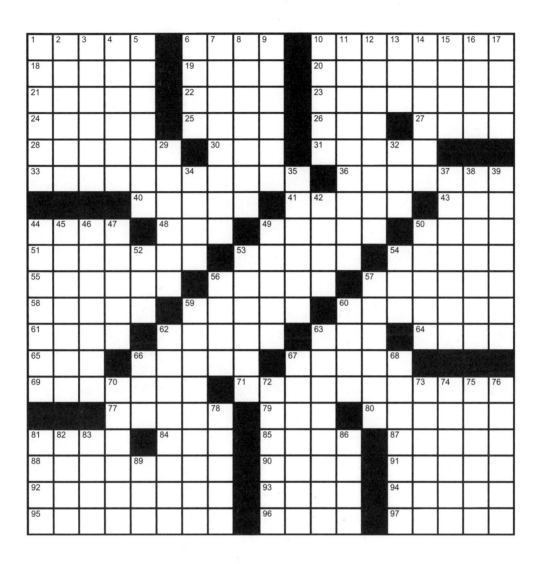

76. Your best qualities, say
78. Sheath or shift
81. Parts of mins.

82. _____ du jour
83. Tree anagram
86. Rhyme writer

89. Ella lyric: "My momma done
_____ me"

ACROSS

1. Edible tuber
4. Eastern philosophy ideal
7. Italian lawn bowling
12. Own
19. Doing well, in a dice game?
21. Pictorial wall hanging
22. Devoid of life, in science
23. Not specific, chronologically
24. Alexander II and Nicholas II
25. Verse form used by Dante
26. One-eighty turn
27. **One of his hobbies**
30. Not hard
31. Late, great boxer
32. Oval or rectangle
33. Bread maker's ingredient
35. Parking place
36. Swampy area
38. Blue Jays domain?
40. Golden Monkey black and Gunpowder green
41. Yemeni's neighbour
43. Basra citizens
45. Halifax, for example
47. Military incursion
48. Leon who wrote *The Haj*
50. Old-style swats
51. Exhaust
52. **Ontario university he attended**
56. Real Estate Exchange (abbr.)
57. French naval vessel
58. Reason to take a pain reliever
59. Order of Canada canocist Cain
61. Churchy choral work
63. Innocent person
67. "_____ Louise!"
68. Jogged along the campaign trail?
69. That woman
70. TV fare: *Come _____ With Me Canada*

71. Osprey kin
72. Giant Greek god
74. *Maid of the Mist*, et al.
76. Slight advantage
77. Bombardier's Dash 8
79. Munich grandma
81. **His Québec birth city**
83. Climbing Mount Rundle?
86. Potato chip, in Chelsea
88. Sound effect at a magician's show
89. Hut by the pool
90. Faces, informally
92. Midmorning meal
96. An Indian language
97. List reference sources
98. Stink to high heaven
100. Canada's first female lawyer: _____ Brett Martin
101. Small sampling
102. More certain
104. Worthless type of talk?
106. B flat or C minor
107. Hot springs spots
109. **He is . . .**
113. Preacher, for short
114. 17th-C. gowns
116. Sheer, silky fabric
117. Pan's home
120. Doomed, old style
121. Big pictures?
122. Pin for a gentleman
123. These fall from pine trees
124. "Socrate" composer Erik
125. Enervate
126. Wine description

DOWN

1. Anne Murray hit: "_____ Needed Me"
2. Ring-shaped
3. Dessert wine
4. Bit of tater?

5. Hebrew letter
6. Not new, to the milliner?
7. Like fish and chips fish
8. Rough estimate phrase
9. Tor
10. Emily _____ University of Art and Design
11. They try to write?
12. Ottoman Empire bigwigs
13. Follows direction
14. Canadian singer Tegan, to Sara
15. Heavy drinkers
16. Stunt a plant's growth
17. Baroque orchestral piece
18. More hair-brained
20. Sunbeam
28. Grand literary work, say
29. _____ moss
31. Friend, in France
32. Bake eggs
34. Honks one's horn
37. **Show he co-hosted on BNN**
39. Tinker Bell, for one
40. Stanley Park pole
42. **His nickname**
44. Window threshold
46. Annual Vancouver expo (abbr.)
47. Hearts, for example
49. Flying high
51. Surpass
52. Minimum _____
53. Laptop brand
54. At that time
55. Speechify
57. Special forces unit
60. Biological molecule (abbr.)
62. Part of Santa's postal code
64. _____-mémoire
65. Swenson of *Benson*
66. Canadian Cancer Society program: Look Good _____ Better
72. Shoe care product company

73. Early visitors to Canada
74. Less couth
75. Hoity-toity one
78. Director Wertmuller, et al.
80. Some scale notes
82. Flashlight
83. Sir John A. Macdonald, by birth
84. Turtle's shell
85. Ability to endure
86. Yellow gemstones
87. Facade
90. Ukrainian city
91. Will be, in Seville
93. _____ the day you were born
94. Rock fissure

95. NT town: _____ River
97. Hilltops
99. Jeweller's measurements
103. Pronouncement from 24-A
105. Canada welcomed refugees from here in 2015/16
108. Virile guy, colloquially
110. Indian palm tree
111. "Let me sleep _____"
112. Centres of activity
113. It's bigger than a mouse
115. Web acronym
118. Mushroom with a big cap
119. US dog pedigree registry (abbr.)

Use the circled letters to unscramble his ABC show:

__ __ __ __ __   __ __ __ __

ACROSS

1. Not very close
5. Quick turn in the pool
8. Hebrew month name
12. Like craft fairs?
17. Song by Shania: "_____ On Over"
18. Epoch, *en français*
19. Canada's Margot Kidder played this Lois
20. Indo–Canadian film director Deepa
21. McMaster University city
23. She said "Thank You" in song
24. 1980s Mr. T series: *The _____*
25. Impassioned
27. Hotel employee
29. Eastern Michigan University (abbr.)
30. Québec place: _____ Saint-Jean
32. Bread for an Indian grandmother?
33. Guy's game pieces?
34. They entrap
38. Cell phones predecessors
40. Growth on a tree trunk
41. Greek letters
42. Seed shell
44. Wet with morning moisture
46. Rework words
47. Kitchen set
49. Copenhagen breakfast treat?
53. Bridle part
55. Apartment style
57. Florida city
58. See 41-A
59. Annual event in Kitchener
62. Seat for a Sunday morning
63. Mistreat
65. Curtain maker's loot?
66. James and John
68. Pilots
70. Irrigated
72. Took a Red Rocket
73. It's similar to STAT
75. Wrap worn in India (var.)
76. Apple beverage
77. Summit Series rival of Canada (abbr.)
80. Frankie Valli's New Jersey hometown
82. Kurt, Elvis and Patrick
84. Scale note (var.)
85. 1974 Streisand classic: "The Way We _____"
86. _____ *Ring des Nibelungen*
88. It follows Christmas?
89. Ecclesiastical organization: Canadian _____ Council
92. Losing influence, say
97. Irritate
98. Iridescent gem
100. More morose
101. Seduced
102. Great, to the drug dealer?
103. Geisha's tie
104. Painful
105. Panache
106. This Yukon town recorded Canada's coldest ever temperature
107. Small, in Dundee
108. St. John's tops Canadian cities for this

DOWN

1. Tummy trouble
2. Froth
3. Bullets, et al.
4. Say again
5. Route around a construction zone
6. Steel substance
7. _____ code
8. English Literacy Development (abbr.)
9. Secular
10. Like loose shoelaces
11. Canadian Cohen who released *You Want It Darker* in 2016
12. At full throttle, at sea
13. Bundle of nerves?
14. Hot prefix?
15. The Stratford Festival has four of these
16. Imperial China bureaucrats
22. Green fruits
26. Inattentive moment
28. Recced, say
31. This keeps Red Angus from roaming
34. Earth tone pigments
35. Without question
36. Panel on CBC's *The National*
37. Skimps on one's assignment?
39. FL reptile
40. Asian starling
43. Gives to one's alma mater, say
45. Light bulb units
47. US terr. that divided into two states
48. Remove traces of
50. Collapse into oneself
51. *Star Wars* bike type
52. Nautical ropes
54. Transvaal settlers
56. Some indigenous dwellings (var.)
60. Raft wood
61. Lay down grass
64. Brown meat
67. Banality
69. More competent, mentally
71. Angry
74. Sentence enders
76. Quibble
77. Normal orders?
78. Shakespearean composition
79. Fracas, colloquially

81. Bayonet, for example
83. Canadian politician Leitch
85. Hockey icon Gretzky
87. Seed again

90. It precedes kit or shed
91. California valley
93. Rubik's favourite shape?
94. Get _____ a good thing

95. Pianist Peter
96. Sprouted
99. Race segment

55 Stately Songs

All-American music

ACROSS

1. Like suspicious glances
7. Come together?
11. Number one Nickelback song: "_____ Away"
14. Canoe, for example
19. Skullcap
20. Expel evil, say
22. Love struck girl's interjection?
23. Her weather system?
24. **Frank Sinatra standard**
26. *Rogue One* female lead Jyn
27. Gator's cousin
29. Bad-mouthed
30. Silent
31. LaFlamme or Mansbridge
33. Thaw out
34. Mature reproductive cells
36. Sister Sledge disco hit: "_____ the Greatest Dancer"
38. Captured again
40. Wannabe's tape, say
41. Like an atheist
43. You can do this cross-country or downhill
45. Gauchos' weapon
50. Scottish squires
51. Paltry payment
55. Foul
56. They practise law (abbr.)
57. Crib, in Britspeak
59. Dip bread in gravy
60. Wide open space
62. Olympic code for an Indian Ocean country
63. Sod
65. Swallow a mouthful
66. Royal LePage employee
67. **"Sound of the '60s" Beach Boys song**
70. Journalist John, inducted into the Canadian Broadcast Hall of Fame

73. Canadian cinema classic: *Goin' Down the* _____
74. Spanish compass point
75. Paving goop
78. Like a deductive conclusion
79. Quick escape
80. Johnny Mathis hit: "Chances _____"
81. Copper exporting country
82. Hit your fingertip while hammering?
83. Amaze
86. Hearts of the matters
88. Plural pronoun
90. Roman mythology goddess
91. Blithe
94. Freebie
97. Former papal palace in Rome
98. Announce in words
99. Like crude callers
103. Tie tie-down device
105. Tax on imported goods
107. Ali's former surname
108. Open a present
110. Long-time CBC program: *Hymn* _____
111. Korbut of gymnastics fame
114. **Patti Page classic**
117. Sign up for classes (var.)
119. Dine at one's abode
120. Ocular issue
121. Recover one's losses
122. Plot
123. Little red bird in a folk tale
124. Canadian painter Paterson
125. Vancouver NHLers Daniel and Henrik

DOWN

1. _____ seaman
2. Burn a bit
3. **Little Willie Littlefield was the first of many to record this**

4. Negatively charged particle
5. Writer with a palindromic surname
6. They might have pets?
7. Synagogue candelabrum
8. Company VIP
9. Sound from 14-D
10. Famed Canadiens goalie Ken
11. Initial
12. Poses the five Ws?
13. Reverse one's word
14. Pasture creature
15. Poet's couplet
16. Up and _____
17. Pianist's talent?
18. Children
21. Spring
25. Party platter item
28. US grp. that drills its members
32. Muck
33. Pacific Blue Cross program: _____-Assist
35. Unruly Mafia members?
36. Hip-swaying dances
37. Related through mother's side of the family
39. Held onto
40. Clangour
42. Store door posting
43. Not emotional
44. Greek letter
46. Semi-circular shapes
47. Laundry fuzz
48. Adverb in a famed Hemingway title
49. Prognosticator
52. Destructive wave disaster
53. Cherry, in Charlemagne
54. Apply one's strength
57. 1970 Québec tragedy: October _____
58. Popular mosquito repellent
61. Like some ale

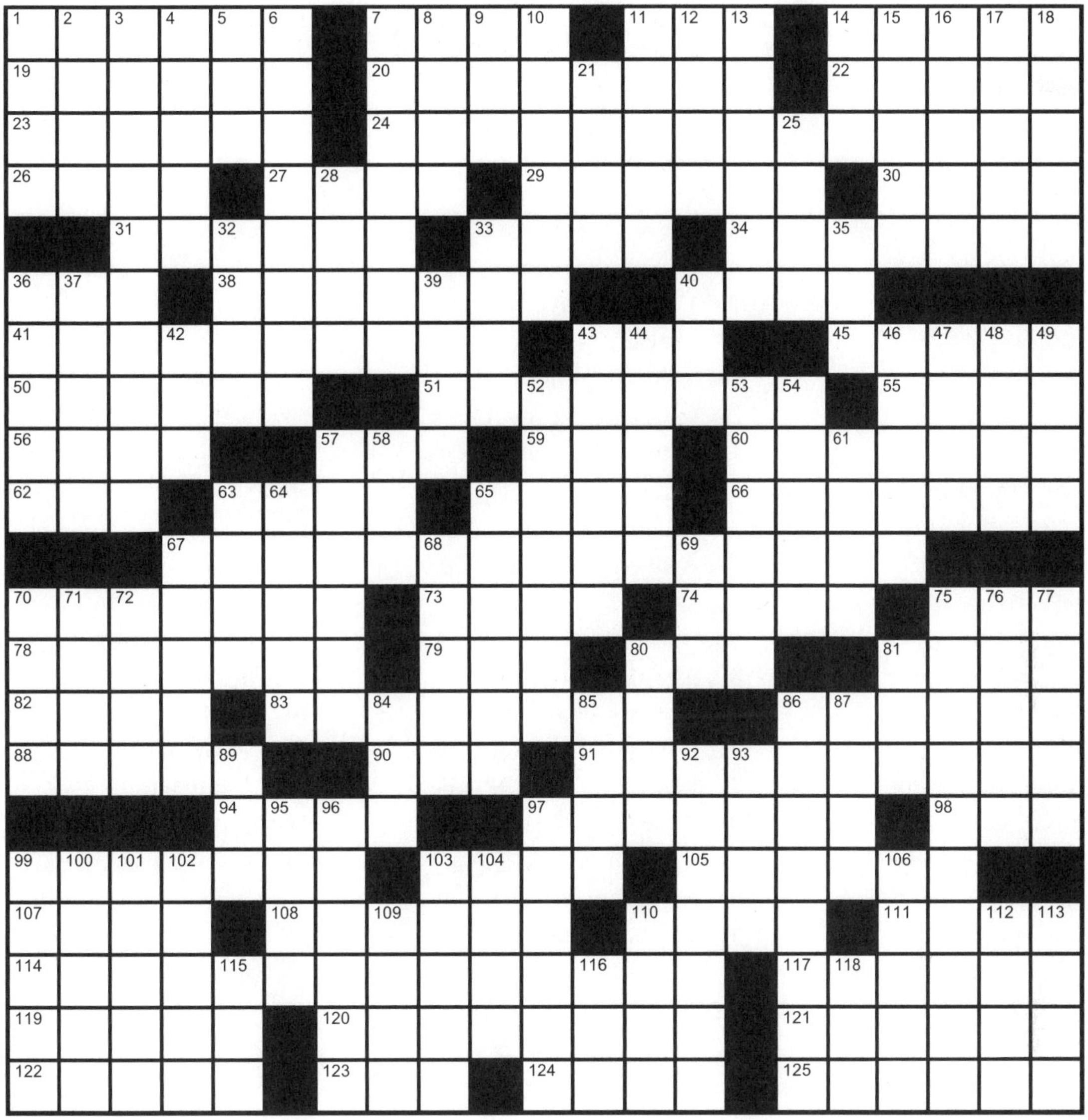

63. Starchy food root
64. Ne plus _____
65. Responses to puns
67. Applies plaster up high, old style
68. Low deck on ship
69. Cologne country (abbr.)
70. Carry on and on
71. Large tropical fish
72. Vigour, in Venice
75. Vintage Stevie Ray Vaughan number
76. Victoria's Save On Foods Memorial Centre, for one
77. Out of practice
80. *Cat on _____ Tin Roof*
81. Currency used in Kabul
84. _____ *Chef Canada*
85. It accompanies crackle and pop
86. Battle horses
87. Royal Indian lady
89. Deg. for a preschool employee
92. Habitual Internet user
93. Ocean Spray drink: _____•Apple juice
95. Encumbrance
96. Good guy, in Yiddish
97. Digestive enzyme
99. Eight of a kind?
100. Go blurry
101. California city: _____ Clarita
102. Doubting Thomas
103. Mythological ruler of Thebes
104. Statutes and acts
106. Royal Canadian Air _____
109. Existed
110. Sebaceous gland problem
112. It holds things together
113. A foehn blows here
115. Treelike *Lord of the Rings* creature
116. Ayres who played Dr. Kildare on the big screen
118. _____ Brunswick

Solution on page 221

ACROSS

1. Canadian actors Moranis and Mercer
6. Creamy cheese
10. Cherry centres
14. Canada lynx, for example
17. Until now
18. Certain mien
19. Iroquoian language
21. Arizona sycamores
23. Striped, like rocks
24. Spike for a camper
25. Method of printing from raised type
27. Pleasantly pastoral
29. Eurasian Economic Commission (abbr.)
30. Urban utility conduit
35. Senior's church job
39. Past, to a poet
40. Stationery shop purchases
42. Old-style British levy
43. _____ de France
44. "American Woman" band (with "The")
46. Trudges
48. Michael Jackson movie: *This _____*
49. Allures
50. _____ and Services Tax
51. Prolonged sleep states
52. Daily grind, say
53. Plate on a door
54. Bon Jovi hit: "You Give Love a _____ Name"
55. Consistency of some soup
58. Doorbell sounds: Ding-_____
59. Slender dagger
63. Currier and _____
64. Stir up passions
65. Saskatoon cinema and performance theatre
66. August astrological sign
67. Flowers for mother?
68. Not accompanied
70. Dive into, say
71. Thefts
74. Sailors' swords
76. Canadian Pointer, for example
77. Catholic diocese administrative office
79. CBC news nightly broadcast
82. Architectural feature between rooms
88. Bird with a big beak
89. Alabama city
91. Not impartial
92. Mine entrance
93. *This Old House* carpenter Norm
94. Winnipeg river
95. Kennedy and Williams
96. Allows
97. Ceremonial displays

DOWN

1. Wholly absorbed
2. Newfoundland strait: Belle _____
3. Primary colour
4. Clark _____
5. Put your foot down?
6. Data display charts
7. Regret
8. Dublin country
9. Lightened a burden
10. Address necessity for mail in Canada
11. Brides-to-be, say
12. Vacuum pressure measurement
13. Sharpshooters
14. Book of religious questions and answers
15. Ripens
16. Youngsters
20. Has courage
22. Alouettes or Argos
26. Cravat
28. "Later," in Lucca
30. They're witty
31. Olden days malady
32. Pigeon-_____
33. Guarantees
34. Save
36. Turn type, on the slopes
37. Hip bones
38. Goldfish and guinea pigs
41. Kitchen sink scrubbers
45. _____ blanket
47. Foresters saw these?
48. Some esters
50. Cotton production machines
51. _____ Pension Plan
53. Families comprise these
54. Displeased spectator's interjection
55. 1995 album from Canada's Alanis Morissette: *Jagged Little _____*
56. Place for an iris
57. Got more supplies
58. Established in an abode
59. Draws out
60. Pointed tools
61. Excellent review
62. Changes colour
64. Trail at Whistler
65. Multiple Juno-winning band: _____ Rodeo
67. Data capacity measurement
69. Block, biologically speaking
72. Actress Didi, et al.
73. _____ Clemente
75. Vega's constellation
78. South African region
79. Norse god
80. Give the edge to?
81. You might wash your clothes with this

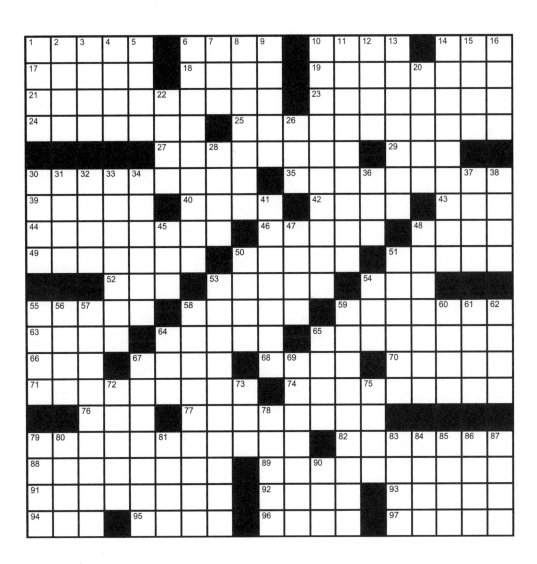

83. 1974 hit from 44-A: "_____ for the Wolfman"

84. Transient

85. Hook bait

86. Quickly, for short

87. Thanksgiving dinner tubers

90. Obedience command to a dog

57 Spice Up Your Life . . .

In Saskatchewan and Alberta

ACROSS

1. Weapon with a blade
6. *Laura* actor Clifton
10. Ph.D.
13. Piece for playing cribbage
16. Carafe volume measurement (var.)
17. Greek mythology goddess
18. "Yuck!"
19. Old-style thermometer description
20. Like a one-sided decision?
22. Red Rose product
23. Roman-like feature?
24. **In Alberta**
25. Person holding professional accreditation
28. Ken Dryden hockey book: *The _____*
29. Early Roman Empire invaders
30. Big bird of myth
31. Singer Fitzgerald, et al.
34. English cottage roofing material
36. Exchange repartee
39. Canadian band: A _____ in Coldwater
40. Extinct New Zealand birds
41. Melliferous
43. Precede
45. Some stock market swings
47. Prolonged geological age
48. Jasper and Whyte, in EDM
49. You can do this at Sunshine
50. Mushroom type
53. Like the most lacklustre links?
55. **In Alberta**
57. Soft Italian cheese
60. Porky Pig's paramour
61. Power Assisted Steering (abbr.)
64. Rood anagram
65. 1950s Oval Office nickname
67. Pride, for one
68. Make

70. Some HGTV Canada stars
73. Sore toe cause
75. Perth County ON river
76. Thai monetary unit
77. Black birds
79. Skulked
80. Canada's pre-Dominion name (abbr.)
81. Juniper bush
82. The real deal, in Dortmund
84. Wile E. Coyote's nemesis
87. **In Saskatchewan**
91. Recessed abbey area
92. Wood fungus result
93. It's west of Mumbai
95. Twosome
96. Lillehammer country (abbr.)
97. Ancient European region
98. Spring flower
99. Montréal CFL players, for short
100. Apple type: Northern _____
101. Leer
102. Lieu

DOWN

1. 2-D might do this with words?
2. Lush
3. Elevator inventor Elisha
4. Reduce in rank
5. Comedies' opposites
6. Cabbie's question
7. Supernatural (var.)
8. Playtex product
9. Voter's chit
10. Amsterdam gardener's implement?
11. S-shaped mouldings
12. Canadian world champion figure skater Patrick
13. Like a take-charge type
14. Campbell River is on this side of Vancouver Island
15. Kind of club

19. **In Saskatchewan**
21. Scottish hat
26. Eczema symptom
27. High chair part
29. Petro-Canada product dispenser
31. Very poor grades
32. Anne Murray hit: "Just One _____"
33. Golden Canadian Olympic cyclist: _____-Ann Muenzer
35. West African ethnic group
36. American Revolutionary War traitor Arnold
37. Makes do
38. Take a breather
40. Climbing Everest?
42. Loser's situation?
44. Sand particles
46. Wild plums
51. Chinese zodiac reptile
52. It builds your immunity
54. Petri dish culture medium
55. **In Saskatchewan**
56. Like some sentences
57. Curtains hang from these
58. "What's the big _____?"
59. Capital gains calculation phrase
61. Smooth a road surface
62. At the peak
63. Posted
66. Knight's pursuit
69. Truffle, for example
71. Kennel snarl
72. Michael Bublé cover: "_____ the Last Dance for Me"
74. Ready for service (var.)
78. Bossy broad
79. Cardsharps
81. Busybody
83. Clinton Global Initiative (abbr.)
84. _____ Nui
85. October birthstone
86. Large vases

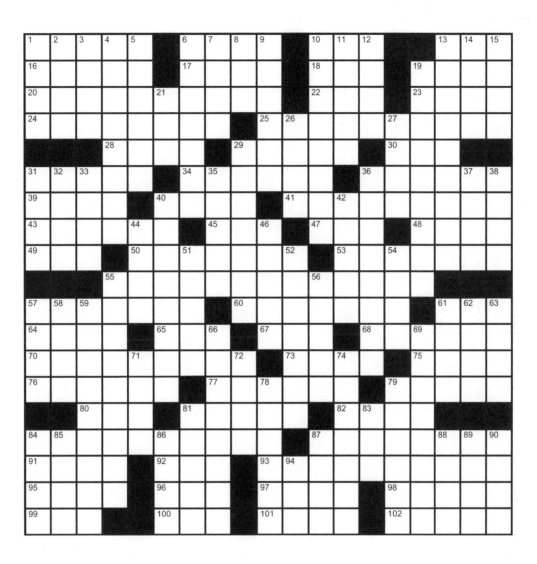

87. Biblical king

88. _____ of Wight

89. *Star Wars* franchise princess

90. Employer of Lt. Columbo

94. Maid's cloth

ACROSS

1. Soft sweatsuit fabric
7. Roses' thorny parts
12. Place name shared by Ontario and Ukraine
18. Conjure up
19. Turn about?
20. Vancouver Island city
21. National fiscal policy setter
23. Prepare to serve wine
24. Dorothy Gale's aunt, et al.
25. Atomic particle
26. Will be, to a Spaniard
28. Prospectors' treasure troves
29. Meat of a matter
30. Emergency care for the injured
32. Native-born Israeli
35. Synthetic textile
37. Hamilton-area feature: _____ Springs Falls
41. Farmer's plot
42. Baeumler HGTV Canada series: _____ Inc.
43. Fashion designer Vera
44. Rap sheet alias letters
45. Parisian putsch?
47. Pub serving
48. Commotion
49. Canadian sports org.: Slo-pitch National
50. Discovery channel offering: How _____ Made
51. Beats badly
53. Jail, colloquially
54. Shaky breath
56. _____ célèbre
57. Dublin lad
58. Mornings that have broken?
60. Spousal co-star on 42-A
61. Canada's Milos Raonic, for example
62. Immediately
65. Bankrupt, say

66. Bryan Adams hit: "Hearts on _____"
67. Immediate ancestry
70. Common abbr.
71. Furtive look
72. Eradicated a disease
73. Building additions
74. Miniature racers
76. Soothes
77. Welcome
78. You might eat one with spaghetti
80. 1970s TV actress: _____ Barbara Allen
82. Chanel, et al.
85. Top-of-the-line
86. 1984 Olympics Canadian gold winner Lori
87. Livestock field
90. Opposite from the mouth
92. Manitoba NHL team
95. _____ à trois
96. _____ a positive note
97. German quantum theory physicist Max
98. Place for a lace to thread through
99. Symbols on a musical staff
100. Tithing amounts

DOWN

1. Ambiance, colloquially
2. Cheese with a red rind
3. A monocle has one
4. Victoria area: _____ Bay
5. Ideal location?
6. Make shipshape again?
7. Breadth
8. Like some ears?
9. Tax cheat's circumvention?
10. MOMA word
11. It tours Canada annually: _____ on Ice

12. Somewhat strange
13. Big Bluegrass hit: "_____ Banjos"
14. Create a cryptogram
15. Fish type
16. Commonsensical
17. Insect world builders
22. Colleagues
27. Souls, in Hinduism
29. Get ready, for short
30. Knives, forks and spoons
31. Cheap Trick hit: "_____ That a Shame"
32. Egg pouches
33. Reynolds/Minnelli movie: Rent-_____
34. New _____
36. Swedish carpet style
38. Reasoning
39. Analogous, like a brother?
40. Yellow-breasted songbird
42. Little Women woman
43. Dry the dishes
46. Pads
47. Like some toddlers' toys
48. Devious
52. Guofeng who succeeded Mao
53. Maine _____
55. Lodgings for a vacationer
56. Complain about the fish?
57. Partner of born
58. Teabag flake
59. Long-time Canadian retailer: Princess _____
60. Afternoon nap
61. Biceps exercise, in England
63. Eye wolfishly
64. Direction of Canada's prairies?
66. Greek cheese
68. BC place: Salmon _____
69. Shore bird
71. Augur

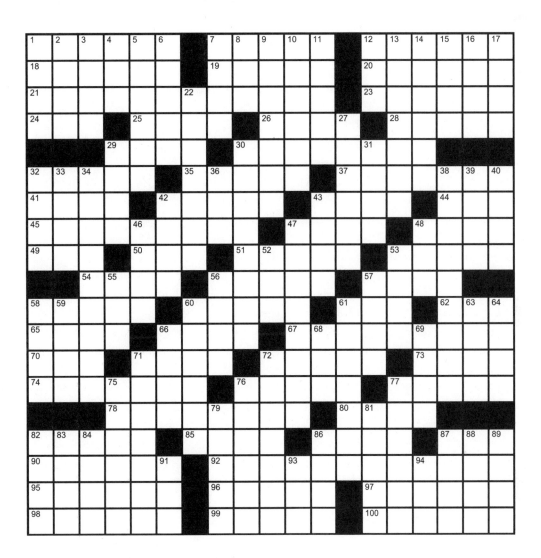

72. First of the month, in ancient Rome
75. Without any ethics
76. Dog or tooth
77. Flock of Canada geese
79. Secluded arbour
81. Clumsy

82. Originated (from)
83. Heed orders
84. Pylon
86. These allow fish to move
87. Period before Easter Sunday
88. _____ A Sketch
89. Queries

91. Canadian Top 40 hit from Luba: "_____ It Go"
93. Negative adverb
94. Alzheimer Awareness mo. in Canada

Called It Macaroni . . .

Well, not quite, but close ☺

ACROSS

1. Parrot
6. Knock to the canvas, colloquially
10. Finely ground liver
14. Moms' pampering place
17. Toughen up (var.)
18. Holly shrub
19. Unbleached linen shade
20. 1986 Alice Cooper song: "_____ Back (The Man Behind the Mask)"
21. Attorney's serving?
23. Salad and soup, for example
25. Snakebite treatment
26. Canadian world pair champs Duhamel and Radford, for example
28. Garden bloomer
29. Compressed gas container
31. Electrician's repast?
32. Window part
35. Lascivious glance
36. Vitamin B3
38. Nabisco sandwich cookies
40. Papa
42. Risk to glassware when moving house
46. Comedian's *bête noire*
49. Gelt thief?
51. Paintings that show all
52. Bone inflammation
54. Everything's bigger here . . .
56. Canada's Dennis Lee, for example
57. Pasta for the person who's "it"?
60. Hearth warming shelves
64. Sets off on the sea
65. Plodding prodder?
70. Like Wrigley Field's outfield wall
72. Reservation abode (var.)
74. Flower-filled table ornament

75. Early generators
77. *Sister Wives* network
79. Québec city: _____-Tracy
80. Meagre
82. Forerunner to formaldehyde?
85. Canada geese fly in these
86. Serving for Chef Boyardee?
89. Enlighten, spiritually
92. Meeting matters list
93. Imitate a primatologist?
94. Male relative
98. Hung around
100. Dish for a celebrant?
102. Samuel's biblical teacher
103. Citrus fruit peel
104. Branch of the family?
105. Canadian Olympian Cockburn who won three medals on the trampoline
106. Duffy or Wallin (abbr.)
107. Jordan who was the Juno's most promising female vocalist in '89
108. Actor Caesar, et al.
109. Cabbage salads

DOWN

1. Baffin Island landform: _____ Incognita
2. Partner of ever
3. Canadian Harnett who won three Olympic cycling medals
4. Edible thistle
5. Like a feeble gardener?
6. Shoe style for a Scot?
7. Estranged, in olden days
8. Geisha's desire?
9. Sunscreen substance: Zinc _____
10. Señor's coin
11. Work on a film set
12. Speak evil of
13. Like Turkey or Thailand
14. Competitor of Petro-Canada

15. Hazardous situation
16. Very, to Varèse
22. Lounge around
24. Use your noodle?
27. Mantel display piece
30. It precedes strip or race
31. World traveller's serving?
32. Big Apple district
33. Greek god of war
34. Clan faction
37. Wild goats with curved horns
39. Buttonhole, for example
41. Spreadsheet information
43. Much fuss about nothing?
44. "Gosh!"
45. Clock setting in some parts of Canada (abbr.)
47. Some Greek letters
48. Supper for an oil field crew?
50. A goalie guards this
53. Most sneaky (var.)
55. Spill over
58. Independent Labour Party (abbr.)
59. Lea ladies
60. That guy
61. Morning meal for Marcus Aurelius?
62. Annual Alberta music event: _____ Valley Jamboree
63. Using one of five?
66. Sole _____
67. Brute, colloquially
68. _____-jerk reaction
69. Fish lacking fins
71. They unscramble electronic transmissions
73. Jewish month
76. Hermes' sandals
78. Like scabby skin
81. Sound from a puppy
83. Shows a lot of feeling
84. Kuril Islands residents

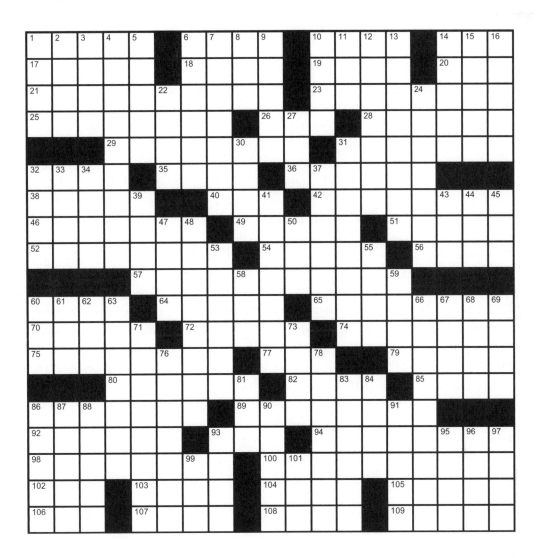

86. Raspy breaths
87. Adjective for acrobats
88. Snake's toxic substance
90. Some turns

91. Canadian-born NHLers
Holden and Schultz
93. Appends
95. Tourists spend these in Turkey
96. From scratch

97. Cysts
99. Rank on the starship *Enterprise* (abbr.)
101. Aria composed by Verdi: "_____ tu"

ACROSS

1. Timmins is named after this mining magnate
5. Players in a play
9. It causes you pain
13. A grand, for short
17. Without any urgency
18. Middle Eastern title
19. Fast pace
20. Prairie oil field structures
21. *General Hospital* genre
23. Qualifying words
25. Disrespectful attitudes
27. Trudeau or Trudeau
28. First three letters
29. Lawyer's files
31. Red Serge, for example
35. Direct to
37. Gardeners' abodes?
38. British network, from 1968–2002 (abbr.)
41. Drug type
43. Anomalous
44. More lewd
46. Tale teller
48. Biblical pronoun
49. BC Fraser Valley district municipality
50. He led The Family Stone
51. Music genre
52. Tropical root
54. Capris and culottes
55. Festival name in Vancouver and Saskatoon
59. Communion disk
62. Gambling or drinking
63. One of 52
64. Conducted
67. Grass skirt dance
68. Hold tightly to
70. A ship might ground here
72. Like a blacksmith's alibi?
74. Grasp a concept
76. Logo or emblem
77. Drivel
78. Canadian illusionist Darcy
79. Stab one's finger
81. Largest portion
82. Text that's tacked on
84. Dodge truck
86. You can only take this?
89. Portrait artist who parodies
95. Protein building molecule
97. Safe to drive through
98. Spring colour in Québec
99. Unacceptable action
100. Fifty-fifty
101. Connections, say
102. Get green-eyed?
103. Pomeranians and poodles
104. Emulated Enya
105. Actor Byrnes, et al.

DOWN

1. Not yet final, in court
2. Scent, in Chicago
3. Spray banned in orchards
4. Over-the-top publicity
5. Rankin Family birthplace
6. Punish, old style
7. Paddock papa
8. Hypnotized
9. High points
10. Union member only workplace
11. Concealed
12. The end of the story
13. Musical threesome
14. Hurried
15. Shrek, for example
16. Chernenko's country (abbr.)
22. Gametes
24. Ceremonial dinner
26. Witty poker player?
30. Margarita fruit
31. Libs' opposition, in the House of Commons
32. Gemstone type
33. Breezy
34. Sticky substance
36. Pro
38. Travis Lulay, for one
39. Sobbed
40. Very, in Verdun
42. Rhino's South American relation
45. Comparative conjunction
47. Select
48. Like the north of Canada?
52. Take a tumble
53. Electrical discharge
54. Bards' works
55. Withdraw gradually
56. Proving
57. Phonograph inventor's initials
58. Rideau Canal winter pastime
59. Use a mixer
60. Ambiance
61. Broadway bomb
64. Western wolf
65. Mythological archer
66. Shoulder muscle, for short
68. Greet, somewhat superficially
69. Fall cleanup implement
70. Honolulu greeting
71. Thinker's sound
73. CBC comedy series (1987–1992)
74. Cowboy boot part
75. Furs fit for royalty
80. Cowardly
82. Female relative (var.)
83. Decorative wall panels
85. Coffee cup
86. Goalie's moment
87. Portent
88. Missile type (abbr.)

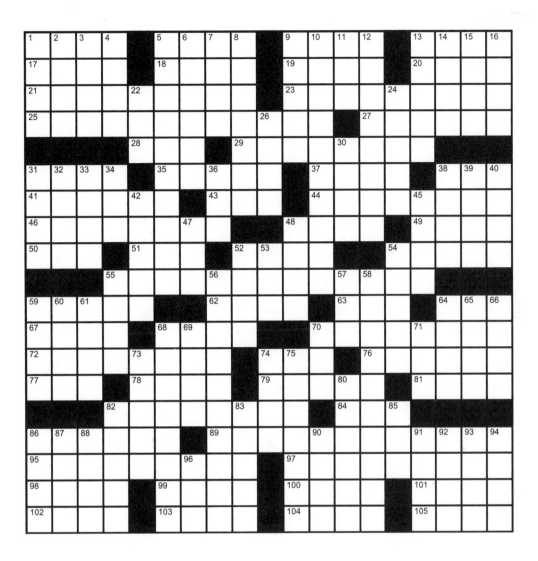

90. Sparkling Spanish wine

91. Appraise

92. Footnote note, for short

93. Huskies' haul

94. Hardy heroine

96. Murmur

Canadian Capes

A geography lesson

ACROSS

1. Wall hanging
6. Uses a shovel
10. "_____ A Small World"
13. Even-steven, to an artist?
17. Rental agreement
18. "I'm working _____!"
19. Ladies' swimsuit type
21. Woodbine Racetrack competitor
22. Fury
23. Burial cloth, to a bard
24. **Cape in New Brunswick**
25. Tenement district
26. Scottish islands
27. Like those who are eternally young?
30. Justin Bieber, when he hit the big time
31. Door knocking onomatopoeia
35. Biblical verb
37. "It Came _____ the Midnight Clear"
41. Grammy-winning singer Keys
42. Went out with an old flame?
45. Official in some provinces
46. "Me as well"
47. Vacuum's pressure measurement
48. Sweet aperitif
51. Gel
52. Northern Canada sea creature
55. RBC and Scotiabank, for example
56. Neighbour of Kan.
58. **Cape in Newfoundland**
60. Our nation's capital (abbr.)
61. Welsh _____
63. Toddler's to-do
65. Gossipy paper, say
67. Secretive
69. It might be fixed, for Freud?
70. Japanese metropolitan area
72. Old distance measurement to a dacha?
73. Dazzling public display
75. Sartorially appropriate?
76. Sibilant summons
77. Second Greek letter
79. Secures the hatches
80. Place
82. Elizabeth II, vis-à-vis Canada
86. Naughty banter?
90. Beatles classic: "_____ Together"
91. **Cape in Prince Edward Island**
96. Gave directions, in Asia?
97. Parka or pea
98. Beatles song: "_____ Day's Night"
99. Covering up (with "over")
100. Word in the golden rule
101. Prepped to paper over plaster
102. Separate into categories
103. Golfer's shirt?
104. Hold onto your horses?
105. Hogwash

DOWN

1. European skiing destination
2. Haul in the harvest
3. **See 58-A**
4. Adrift on the Red?
5. Erose edge
6. **Cape in Nunavut**
7. As a whole
8. Lively classical music composition
9. Stalks of roses
10. Skin irritation
11. Uses social media
12. Iced palate cleanser
13. Gradual decrease in loudness
14. 1960s sitcom star Donna
15. Pimple outbreak
16. Dampens
20. *Garçon's* dad
28. NHL netminder's stat
29. Pronoun for that woman?
31. Room warmers, for short
32. Arouses enmity at Area 51?
33. They giggle
34. Take part in a play
36. Join with others
38. Get through to
39. Passed on the track, say
40. Earns, in the aggregate
42. Not up
43. Buddhist sage
44. Hard labour, in Lachine?
45. Canada's "Man of a Thousand Songs" Hynes
47. Old-style wedding pledge
49. Beyond the norm
50. Handsome, in Huberdeau
53. Slightly
54. Québec-born composer/conductor Bouchard
57. Most animalistic?
59. Leave in, like text
61. Party invitation answer, for short
62. A short-order cook might prep this
64. Scope product
66. Wanders aimlessly
68. 2009 Michael Bublé single: "Haven't Met You _____"
71. Meet, like a board
74. Machinist's disk
75. Cul-de-_____
77. 1983 Michael Jackson hit
78. *SCTV* actor Levy
79. **Cape in Nova Scotia**
81. Hotel alternatives
83. Come to pass
84. Shania sang this song: "_____ Needs to Know"
85. Famed violin maker

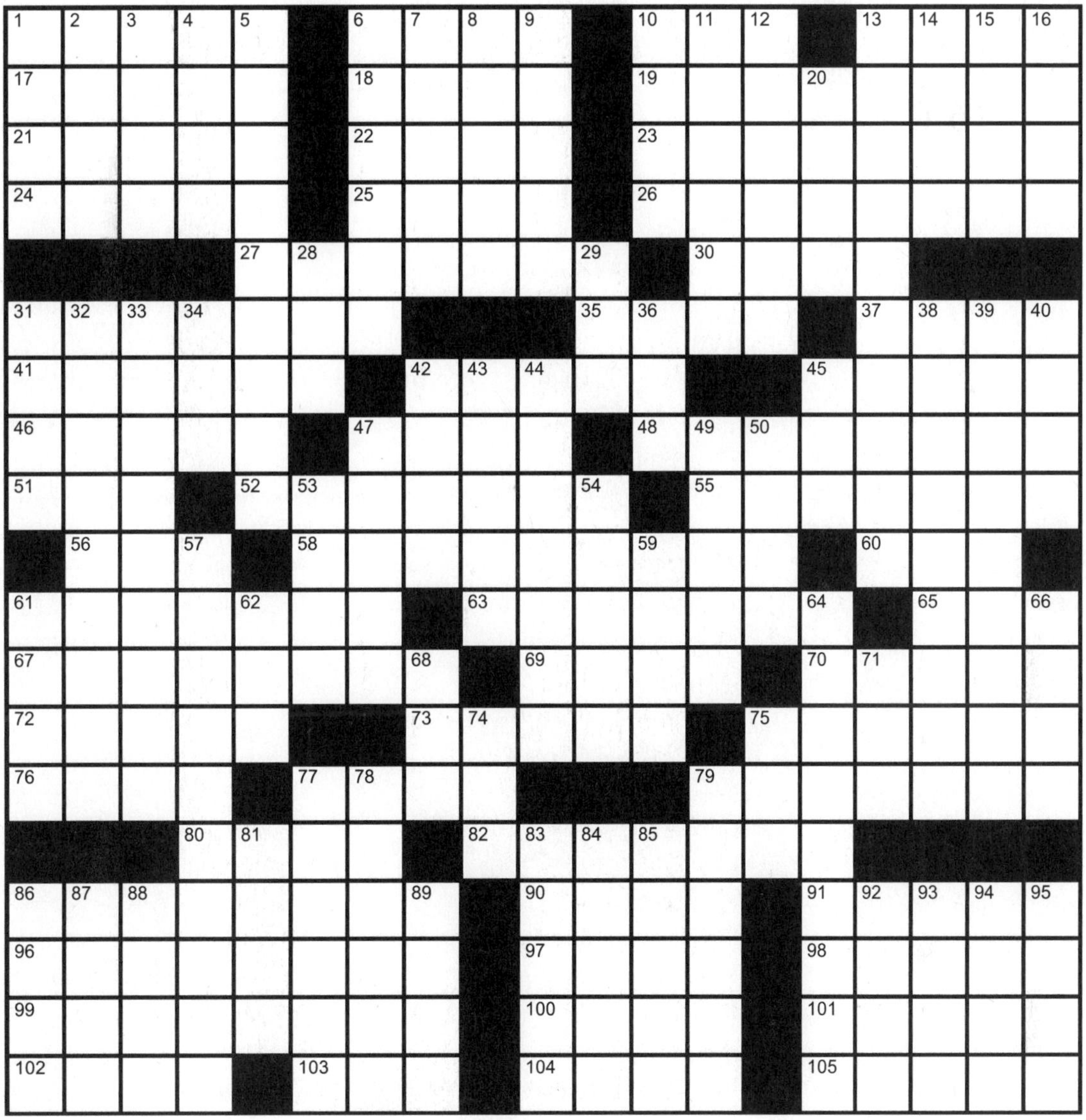

86. Swamps
87. Folksy vocalist Guthrie
88. Fashionable Christian
89. Outer limit?
92. On a clear day you can see this from Ontario
93. Cape in British Columbia
94. Joni Mitchell hit: "_____ Man in Paris"
95. Aquatic vortex

Solution on page 223

ACROSS

1. Spanish artist Salvador
5. Botanist's interest
10. Bawdy
14. Wag's asset
17. Dressmaker's appliance
18. Some kitchen floor coverings
19. Pasture pulling pair
20. Kerfuffle
21. Canadian financial institution
23. Samoan monetary unit
24. Young sheep
25. More attractive
26. Shania Twain song: "You're _____ The One"
28. Mare's nest
29. Grief
31. _____ cuff
33. Aptly named Dalmatian?
36. Farm storage space
37. Took out tangles
40. Automotive service franchise with Canadian shops
42. Heart hit covered by Céline Dion
44. Sneer at
45. _____ Empire Loyalists
47. Highlands daggers
50. St. Catharines-born supermodel Evangelista
51. More than willing to share
54. Pubs serve these
56. Close, as an envelope
57. It joins the Red River in Winnipeg
60. Lettuce type
64. Wedge for under a wheel
65. Casey Jones, for one
70. Coolly, in demeanour
72. Determined to
74. 1985 Madonna hit: "Into the _____"
75. More frilly
77. Bring together
80. Support an academic institution
81. Luxury train section
84. Kitten's cry
86. Blow off steam?
87. Lady of Lecce
88. Floodgate
90. National charitable group: The War _____
92. Heads or _____
94. Debit card user, for example
98. It might be worn with a grass skirt
99. Poses for an artist
100. Sudbury ON region
102. Gallivant
103. _____-deep
104. Bay window
105. End in _____
106. Attention Deficit Syndrome (abbr.)
107. Grows riper
108. Exhausted
109. Manitoba-born actor Cariou, et al.

DOWN

1. It separates two vertebrae
2. US oil company
3. Hover
4. Without a will
5. Talents
6. Monrovia country
7. Winning at Yahtzee?
8. Canadian comedian James
9. Makes a request
10. Balm for chapped skin
11. Glorifies
12. Canal city in Ontario
13. _____ fingerprint
14. Hull marking
15. Fateful day for Caesar
16. Canadian kids' retailer: Bonnie _____
22. Industry Liaison Office (abbr.)
27. Bone attached to the sternum
28. Finicky 9Lives advertising tabby
30. Largest Canadian national park: _____ Buffalo
32. Old Chinese money unit
33. Self-satisfied
34. Long for
35. Norse war god
38. Viking's reading material?
39. Monty Hall show: Let's Make a _____
41. Transfusion fluids
43. Ontario lake
46. Makeshift bed, in Bournemouth
48. Sign of a sore shoulder
49. Waken
52. It delivers Americans' mail (abbr.)
53. Father
55. Small setback
58. In its original state
59. Alternative name for Ireland
60. 1960 legislation: Canadian _____ of Rights
61. Global aviation org.
62. Some teeth
63. Pancakes served with sour cream
66. Like tacit communication
67. Way
68. This cosmetics company came to Canada in 1914
69. _____ Gingrich
71. Burglar, in slang
73. 2008 Jodie Foster movie: _____ Island
76. Alternative to owning
78. Her name means "happy"
79. Lad

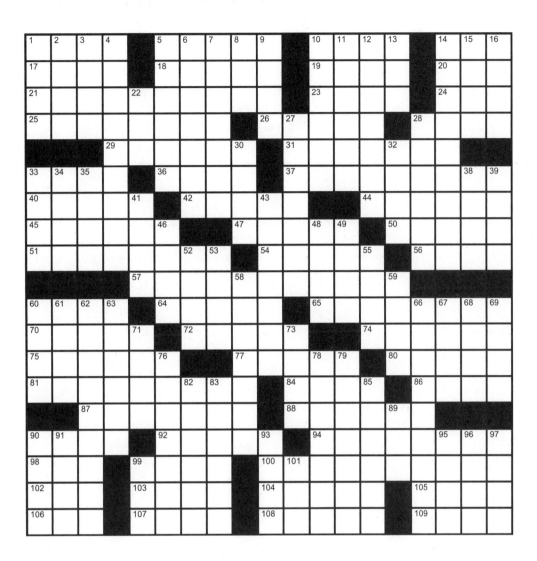

82. Close-fitting military jacket

83. Crops up

85. In a sagacious manner

89. Animation frame

90. Gala anagram

91. Honeyed drink

93. It falls in flakes

95. Head, in Saint-Hyacinthe

96. Tiger Woods' former missus

97. Some rds.

99. Calypso cousin

101. Rage, in Dublin?

63 Soup's On

Eat this one up

ACROSS

1. Canada _____
5. About, for short
11. Excited cries
15. Union defier
19. Edward who abdicated for Wallis
20. Record jacket
21. Dental office picture
22. Biblical "you"
23. **New Englander's entree?**
25. Body of water in the Rockies
26. Engagement gift
27. Happy face emojis
28. Hab to a Leaf, say
30. Top spots
32. Devour
33. Character set for computer code
34. _____ of the devil
35. Adjust an alarm
36. Oxford or espadrille
38. Slip by, like time
40. Northern European country (abbr.)
43. Lyric poems
44. Extra tires
46. Birth country of Giller winner Ondaatje
48. Jersey shore wear?
50. Removes all traces
53. ICU component
54. Tirana is here (abbr.)
57. **Soup for a Scot?**
59. Came up
60. Barrel maker's merchandise
62. Plant pests' genus
63. Ribbon dispensing device
64. AWOL student
65. Jazz combo instrument
67. Cartoon that debuted in 1969: *The _____ and the Aardvark*
68. Presidential forgiveness
70. Comes out on top?
71. Identity thief's name?
73. Feline's favourite tree?
74. Preserves pork, say
75. **See 57-A**
78. Bard's "dusk"
79. Regina's early name: _____ O' Bones
80. Self-sacrificer
81. British sailors, colloquially
83. Collection of written passages (var.)
85. Brings out
87. Last part of a sonata
91. Canadian energy regulation agy.
92. Grand Canal bridge
95. Vexes
96. Summoned singer Patti?
97. *The _____ and the Ecstasy*
99. Killer whales
101. Jews born in Israel
102. Need for a drink
104. Sully a reputation
105. Tuckered out
107. Lighten a load, say
108. Pueblo pot
110. **Cold soup for a Frenchman?**
113. _____ *en scène*
114. Place in Parliament?
115. Sees, in olden day
116. Junkie
117. Begged
118. He wrote *Les Misérables*
119. Built to last
120. Nova Scotia place: _____ Harbour

DOWN

1. Plumber's pipe type, for short
2. Peanut, for one
3. Blue-eyed feline
4. Most reticent
5. Pale
6. Tactic
7. Seats for Sunday sermons
8. One of Canada's official colours
9. Supervise
10. Dry, like a desert
11. **Soup for a cattle farmer?**
12. Exam form
13. Guffaw syllable
14. Fusion of chromosomes during meiosis
15. Groove on a glacier
16. **Poultry producer's favourite?**
17. The best of the best
18. Bothers an entomologist?
24. Stroke cause
29. Compete for
31. British bobbies were named for this Home Secretary
32. To and _____
33. It comes from the heart?
34. Shopper's costly indulgence
36. Like Thai cuisine
37. Listen to the angels sing?
39. Lend a helping hand
41. Blue Mountain trail
42. London art gallery
44. Match attire for Milos Raonic
45. Trickle out
47. Southern Ontario town
49. Play parts
51. Make a meal of leftovers?
52. Similar, to a sister?
54. Statute
55. McAllister of CBC's *Holiday Ranch*
56. **Fishy soup for the French?**
58. Neglect
59. Absence of enthusiasm
61. Subtle shade
63. Outpourings
65. Pelvis-related
66. Buckets or bunches
69. Sister of Bert Bobbsey
72. Gardener's large patch

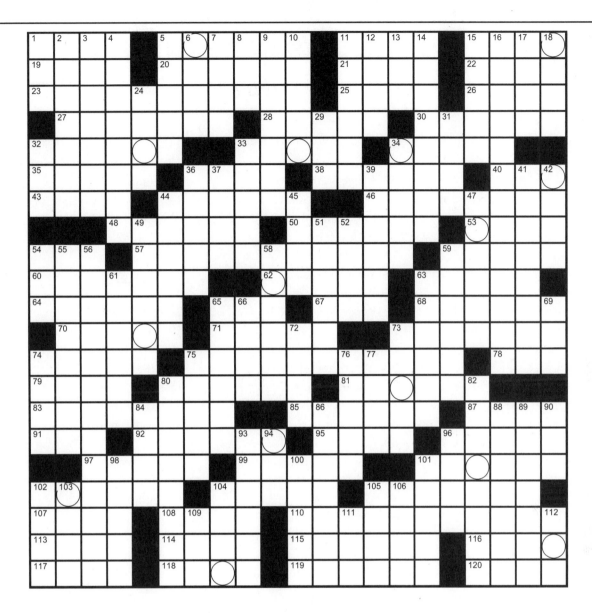

73. 2013 Arcade Fire track: "Here _____ the Night Time"
74. Attention _____
75. Skewered Indonesian serving
76. Goes glassy
77. Canadian funny man Mercer
80. National apple of Canada
82. Pincushion-shaped flowers
84. Loving Greek god?
86. Daily journal writer
88. Like Shrek
89. It separates Jordan and Israel

90. These sometimes pop up?
93. **Preference of a Red Tory?**
94. Rock that's refined
96. Links averages
98. Avarice
100. Spelunkers explore these
101. Pert
102. Occasional staffer
103. Destructive weather event
104. Steel plant waste
105. Blender noise
106. Ogled

109. Romanian currency
111. PC's innards
112. Physics particle

Use the circled letters to
unscramble more types of soup:

1) __ __ __ __ __ __ __

2) __ __ __ __ __

3) __ __ __

ACROSS

1. Curl hair
6. Throw out a line
10. Read Only File System (abbr.)
14. Music genre
17. Actors memorize these
18. Chinese nursemaid
19. *La Bamba* star Morales
20. Speedy serve
21. Gulf of Guinea capital city
22. Canadian PGA pro Weir
23. "Her" city is on Vancouver Island
25. Borsos who won a Genie for directing *The Grey Fox*
27. Pleaded, persistently
29. Discharges from active military duty
31. Canadian construction giant: _____Don
32. Family quarrel?
34. You might get a bunion here
36. Pilot
38. "_____ a Small World"
39. Onion bun
40. Plants' prickly bits
42. Secluded spaces
44. Home for horses
45. *Front Page Challenge* panellist (with 52-D)
47. Stephen who led the Ontario NDP (1970–78)
48. 1970s Robert Blake TV series
49. Declassify documents, say
51. Fitzgerald and Horne cover: "Can't Help Lovin' _____ Man"
52. "You can't _____ kidder"
53. British bachelorette's do: _____ party
54. Passenger ship strolling spot
58. Genetics Society of America (abbr.)
61. Some UK crime investigators
62. Blokes
63. Soup container
67. Male paddler
69. Ovens for potters
71. Canadian "Never Surrender" singer Hart
72. Bone related
73. Soldier's flask
75. Wheel, in Watford
76. Knitter's purchase
77. Sauté
78. _____ Ababa
80. Automaton, for short
81. Bring in an income
82. Swell up
84. Washington state city
86. Close tennis set decider
89. Based on sound reasoning
92. Kind of charm
93. Manger visitors
95. Actresses Falco and Sedgwick
96. Funny texting acronym?
97. A masseuse might soothe this
98. Señor's spending money
99. Small songbirds
100. Single digit
101. Pay attention to advice
102. 1984 Glenn Frey hit: "The Heat _____"
103. W Network show: *Say _____ the Dress Canada*

DOWN

1. Sound of thunder
2. Wealthy
3. Occurrences
4. Country singer Haggard
5. "The Lord is my shepherd," et al.
6. '00s BC premier Gordon
7. Michel's pal
8. H.H. Munro's pen name
9. Movie music?
10. Fills with disgust
11. Egyptian god of the afterlife
12. Truths
13. Undisturbed: In _____
14. 1970 "(I Know) I'm Losing You" band
15. Embitter
16. Green veggie
24. 1974 April Wine hit: "I'm _____ for You Baby"
26. Infinitesimal amount
28. Barre bends
30. Withdraws
33. 2016 Nobel Prize literature winner Bob
34. *Life of Pi* actress
35. *Closer* actor Clive
37. _____ & *Martin's Laugh-In*
39. Derived from a certain mineral salt
41. Jordin Sparks hit: "One _____ at a Time"
43. B or C, say
44. Military trainee
46. Railway employee
48. Bridge table action
50. Pub close to your home?
52. See 45-A
55. Hr. div.
56. British Columbia place name
57. Granny _____
58. Newfoundland place: Happy Valley-_____ Bay
59. South Saskatchewan River city
60. Capillary adjunct
64. Complaining caregivers?
65. Chocolate bar manufactured in Canada
66. Russian refusal
68. Fished with a net
69. Craft for 2004 golden Canadian Olympian Van Koeverden
70. It puts you under?
73. Ribbited

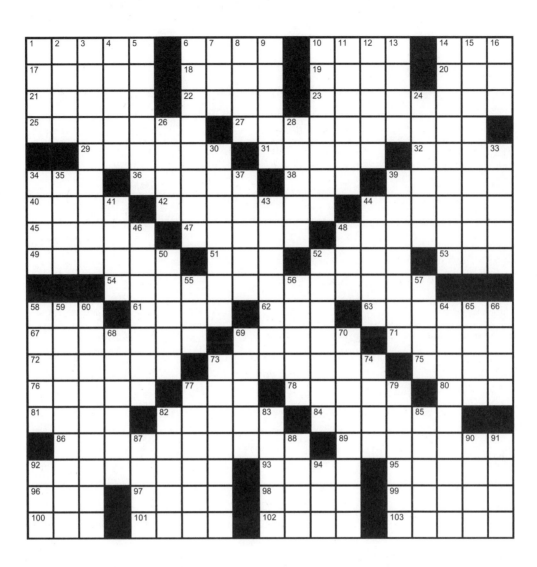

74. Sportswear brand
77. Arrow, in Abitibi
79. Muscular
82. Niagara Escarpment hiking mecca: _____ Trail
83. Adagio and allegro (var.)
85. *The Treasure of the Sierra* _____
87. Boring
88. Politico Bob and explorer John
90. Loaned
91. Rival of Shell, in Canada
92. Hasbro stuffed toy: _____ Worm
94. Guelph Symphony Orchestra (abbr.)

Inundated

In these Canadian places . . .

ACROSS

1. Per person
7. Cover with cleanser
13. Duffer's fib?
16. US DoJ agency (1933–2003)
19. Early eastern Asia marauder
20. Linked units
21. École nationale d'équitation (abbr.)
22. Keanu Reeves role in *The Matrix*
23. **Cape Breton community**
25. Kept in a sheath
27. Change from blonde to brunette
28. Barges
29. Breakfast cereal option
31. Two-time Australian prime minister Kevin
32. Part of the eye
34. Bit of an inch?
35. Throat lozenge
37. Place restaurant patrons at a different table
39. Input data again
41. Snap jacket snaps, say
42. Trim the tree, say
43. Pre-Revolutionary Russian royals
45. Saturated hydrocarbon
47. 0, in soccer
48. Clay court sport
50. **Northern Northwest Territories town**
51. CBS forensics show franchise
54. _____ all come out in the wash
56. Bristol bathrooms
57. Threefold
58. Swerves, like a ship
59. You might break this?
61. Obama's lodgings?
63. Australian sea
64. Old-style light source
68. BC destination: Radium _____ Springs

69. Widespread devastation
71. ABC show that starred Canada's Victor Garber
72. Opposite of passively
77. Possess title to
78. Fine powder
79. a.k.a. rollerblading: _____ skating
80. 113-A does this
82. Surname of Barry, Robin and Maurice
86. Sherbrooke, vis-à-vis Montréal
87. **Community in Manitoba's Rural Municipality of Reynolds**
88. _____ at the wheel
90. Chalk River research reactor, for short
91. Stately old dance
92. Large pane of glass
93. Taut
95. "Goodness gracious!"
98. Marijuana op operator
100. Galloped?
101. Marine's obstreperous offspring?
103. *Mork & Mindy*'s Dawber
104. 1974 hit from Canada's Gino Vannelli: "_____ Gotta Move"
106. Neck scruff
107. Parked at port
109. Tim Hortons menu item
110. 1978 Alice Munro collection: _____ *Do You Think You Are?*
113. Throne stealer, say
115. **Community north of Peggys Cove**
118. EU member country
119. Gallery's goods
120. Convicted criminals
121. Larry, Curly or Moe
122. Before, in olden days

123. You can enjoy this at the Empress
124. Faddish
125. Atlas' daughters

DOWN

1. In the thick of
2. Paddock baby
3. **Town in Oxford County, Ontario**
4. Mind part
5. 1992 k.d. lang song: "_____ Craving"
6. Provoke emotion, say
7. Unaccented vowel
8. Clumsy clods
9. Consumed
10. Allows
11. Like disorderly conduct
12. Quebecer's wages
13. *Futurama* female
14. **Town west of the QEII in Alberta**
15. Common Market letters
16. Offensive remark
17. Sharp stick for a seamstress
18. Soaked
24. Former PEI premier Robert Ghiz, to former PEI premier Joe Ghiz
26. Come to mind
30. Explore a cave
33. Poetic contraction
34. Seas, in France
36. Armoured vehicle
37. Raja's mate
38. Tinker with words
39. Mrs. Gorbachev
40. Kind of attack
43. Trust No One (abbr.)
44. Arrogant aristocrat
46. Fermented Russian brew
49. Gr. 1–6 school
50. Steaming mad

51. Former Canadian Labour Congress head Shirley
52. Illegally obtained drapery?
53. _____ of Man
55. Spring bloomer
57. Treasure _____
58. Juno and Grammy winner Neil
60. Accounting pros (abbr.)
62. Ungulate that can run 50+ km/h
63. Bully a Black Angus?
64. Vancouver span: Lions _____ Bridge
65. Synonym for 95-A
66. Riverbed deposit
67. Mammal loaned to zoos by China
70. Pigeons' shelter
73. Adhere

74. Orange and black wildcat
75. Final competitor to finish
76. Season for carolling
79. **BC vacationers' destination**
81. It might be matched
83. **Town name shared by Ontario and Nova Scotia**
84. Cheese tray item
85. CBC Radio *As It Happens* ex-host Barbara
87. Poet's metrical foot
88. Throat clearer's sound
89. HGTV series: *Income* _____
91. Crowbar user, say
92. Bundle up baby
94. Not well
95. Major river in Europe

96. Pencil end
97. Medicinal capsule (var.)
99. Blue Jays first game of the year: Home _____
100. Saskatchewan export
102. Cardiology artery
104. Coward's flower?
105. Neighbour of Djibouti (abbr.)
108. Fissure
109. Guess Who hit: "Share the _____"
111. Gigantic
112. Miners' find these
114. AB-born former NHL forward Conacher
116. Old Saturn model
117. Snake type

66 Canada Cornucopia 30

ACROSS

1. Cordial
5. Out of control
9. Chemical radical
13. Like a leisurely pace
17. Film format developed in Canada
18. You might do this at Scotiabank?
19. Womanizing man
20. Ontario's Voyageur Hiking Trail passes through here
21. Insect's sensory organ
22. It beats a deuce
23. Maori dance
24. Middle Eastern gulf or city
25. More sycophantic
27. Some tubers
28. 2009 Cotillard/Kidman movie
29. Preferred plant of 47-A?
31. Originality
33. Hug
35. Go on the road
36. Consents or coincides
37. Male singing voice
38. Chile city
40. Trial and _____
43. Description of some mental illness sufferers
45. 1976 film: Welcome _____
47. Jellystone Park cartoon character
48. Baroque era stringed instrument
49. Something to follow at an old board meeting
52. Salem state (abbr.)
53. Like graceful language?
56. Written piece
57. Male gymnast's "horse"
59. British spy novelist Deighton
60. Ontario city
62. Opposite of ruddy
63. Sign over a theatre door

65. Swerve around (var.)
66. Snafus
70. 1970s talk show host Shore
72. Alberta attraction: _____ Provincial Park
75. _____ hoop
76. Lenses sit in these
78. Canadian-born TV actor Raymond
79. Lean, say
80. CTV sitcom (1983–85)
82. Basic principle
84. Whittle
85. American Revolutionary War hero Nathan, et al.
87. Lament writers
90. Top spot
91. Lily type
92. "Don't bet _____!"
93. Porn
94. Hut
95. See 1-A
96. Egyptian president: Abdel Fattah el-____
97. Tresses, colloquially
98. Hip 1960s Brits
99. You might propose on a bended one
100. Tams and toques
101. Click fingers together

DOWN

1. Little bites
2. Mosque VIP
3. "Goodnight Mrs. _____, wherever you are"
4. Emotional
5. Up and about
6. Cloud formation over a pasture?
7. Excessively adoring
8. Door opener
9. Nirvana attainer
10. Serengeti growl

11. Potato created in Canada
12. Renter
13. Where cygnets might be raised
14. Gents don't go here
15. 1936 Olympics sprinting champ Jesse
16. Ebbs
26. Prepare a geographical survey
27. *Spelling It Like It Is* author
30. Word heard at Rogers Centre
32. Teensy, in Troon
33. Columbia Business School (abbr.)
34. _____-Labelle QC
36. Kind of aunt
38. Truths, old style
39. 1980s George Peppard show: *The* _____
41. Beastly brute
42. Louis who led the Red River Rebellion
44. Multivitamin component
46. French nanny?
49. See 62-A
50. Geological Survey of America (abbr.)
51. Some animals do this (var.)
53. Vamoosed
54. *General Hospital* actress Ainsworth
55. Lacking knowledge
56. Sewing cases, in Cannes
58. Appliances' innards, say
61. Red giant in Taurus
62. Person without singular views?
64. Sunflower family plants
66. Fragrant shrub with white flowers
67. Sci-fi trilogy series by Manitoba-born author Douglas Hill
68. Animal with antlers
69. State

71. Uris fictional offering: *The* _____

73. Canadian-based company: _____ Forme

74. Calgary newspaper name

77. Six Nations reserve band member

79. Journey component

80. Muscle throe

81. Tortilla chip

82. Lady of Laval, say

83. 42-D was one

86. Bait

88. Canned fish type

89. _____ aerobics

92. Second-largest Kyrgyzstan city

Suit Yourself

You'll win if you play your cards right

ACROSS

1. Elephant "pet" on TV's *George of the Jungle*
5. Small amounts
10. Canada's largest urban park: _____ Creek (in Calgary)
14. Miles _____ hour
17. Simba's spouse in *The Lion King*
18. Kind of freaky
19. She sings lower than a soprano
20. Western US Native
21. Canada is this to the United States
22. Strident sound
23. Pigs' feed
24. Electronic device light source (abbr.)
25. **Milieu for mirthful singers?**
27. Aardvarks' grub
28. Imbibe excessively
29. UNESCO World Heritage Site in Nova Scotia: Landscape of Grand _____
30. Spot a secret agent?
32. Muslim group of ladies
34. **1989 Blue Rodeo hit**
36. Animation sheet
39. Possessive pronoun for us?
41. Romanced with Riesling?
43. Line in a ledger
44. Apple or Google
47. Fabrics for Levi's and Lees
49. Hot drink for a cold day
50. Fords and Ferraris
52. School day breaks
56. Durango or Cherokee
57. Corporate "wedding"
59. In a senile manner
60. Completed, in Catania
62. Religious scroll
64. Prickly-headed plant (var.)
65. They pass through the Rideau Canal
67. Abnormal growths, in Gainesville
69. Short gumshoe?
70. Held one's ground
72. Muck or guck
73. Aeries
75. Repents
77. Pen or cage
79. Ella Fitzgerald singing style
82. Japanese–American
84. Zagreb citizen
85. Cat's appendage with claws
86. **Top name in fashionable accessories**
88. Canada has one on three coasts
90. Global aviation org. headquartered in Montréal
92. Scottish number, old style
93. Racetrack finish line
95. Not at all nice
97. **It proves you're alive . . .**
101. Aunt of Maria?
102. Scandinavian mythology god of war
103. Holstein or Hereford
105. Oscar-winning director Kazan
106. Rank in the USN
107. Enjoying one's golden years (abbr.)
108. Linen shade
109. Cosmonaut Gagarin
110. Riddle-me-_____
111. Florida area
112. Spread smoke in a sanctuary
113. Stone and Stallone, for short

DOWN

1. Bump in the road, say
2. Canadian comedy show: *The Kids in the* _____
3. She, in Chibougamau
4. Cheque endorser
5. Reform Party's first MP Grey
6. Donovan Bailey and crew won this for Canada at the 1996 Olympics
7. Canadian ambassador Ken Taylor served here
8. Special delivery?
9. Teeter
10. Zipper or snap
11. Doomed to fail
12. Desist
13. **Famous blue gemstone**
14. Preacher's platform
15. Perpetual, in old poetry
16. Cash in a coupon
26. **Drink for a golfer?**
31. There's one at 41-A
33. Remove
35. Gives inaccurate information
36. Network that aired 2-D
37. Shoreline damage
38. Ornamental ceiling panels (var.)
40. Intelligent
42. Daisies, et al., in botany
45. Religious order student
46. Wheat farm fungus
48. Parcel out
51. Truth _____
53. Takes the measure of a man?
54. *Baywatch* beauty Carmen
55. Grandpa of Canadian Olympic hockey medallist Gillian
57. Former Alberta cabinet minister Ted
58. Nettle plant harvested for hemp
60. Federation of British Industries (abbr.)
61. Ink blot examination?
63. Antlers
66. High spot in the pecking order
68. Dads' TV viewing chairs
71. Comes down the mountain
73. **1982 song from Canada's Spoons**

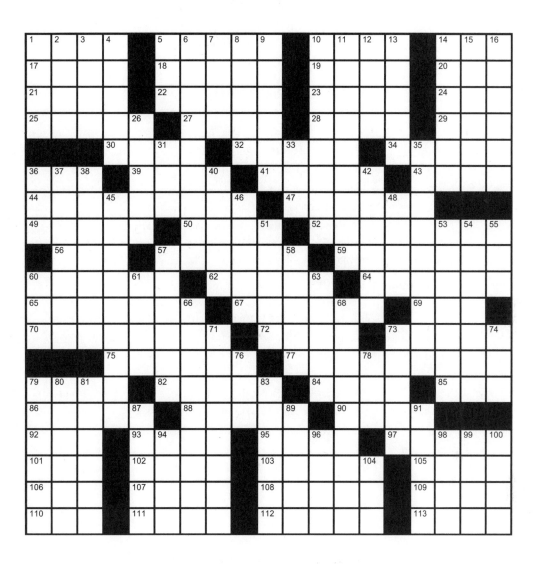

74. Make clothing
76. Glimpse at the poker table?
78. Huron, to a Quebecer
79. Canada's Patrick Chan, for example
80. Dog's fang?
81. Command from a sergeant

83. _____ pentameter
87. **Gardener's chore?**
89. Audacity
91. Is good, like Fido?
94. _____ *fixe*
96. Long time, geologically speaking (var.)

98. Sixth Hebrew month
99. Ethereal
100. Fruity cocktails: Mai _____
104. Colour

ACROSS

1. To any extent
6. Grumpy seafood eater?
10. Toddler's parent
14. Tool for a cobbler
17. Ontario place: Sault Ste. _____
18. Trick
19. CEO or CFO
20. Paltry amount, in old Paris?
21. Jobs for co-op students, say
23. Vulnerable place?
25. Wounded with a sword at Antietam
26. Rat poison, for one
28. _____ General of Canada
30. Blade for a boater
31. Moved quickly, at the cooperage?
36. Third-largest Manitoba city
41. Cineplex _____ Corporation
42. Oil cartel grp.
44. Presses the accelerator aggressively
45. From head to _____
46. Baden-Powell boating group member
48. Well up in years
50. Char, on the barbecue
51. Wins affections
52. _____-four thousand dollar question
53. Actors Adam and Mae
54. Ottoman Empire commander's palindrome
55. Features of bison and lions
56. Canadian history event: _____ of 1812
57. Act melodramatically
60. Canadian river or territory
61. Montréal-born alt-rock bassist Auf der Maur
65. Bird that coos
66. Salk developed a vaccine for this

67. Noted San Francisco transport option
68. Fury
69. Biblical travellers to Bethlehem
70. Kublai or Genghis
72. Squeaky clean persona?
73. Anarchic groups' tactics
76. Repeated musical phrases
78. Scientist's workplace
79. Raised
81. National highway or pipeline name
85. 1984 hit from Canada's Luba
91. Government department: Canadian _____
92. Obituary phrase
94. Petro-Canada product, for short
95. McGuinty's Ontario predecessor
96. Taking action, colloquially
97. _____ Québécois
98. Instrument for Arthur Godfrey
99. Cincinnati _____
100. Small rugs
101. Atlas page box

DOWN

1. Rock concert stage equipment
2. Samoan coin
3. Middle Eastern citizen
4. Some parasites
5. Ogle
6. Naive
7. Annual event: CIBC _____ for the Cure
8. Horse rider's position
9. Stupefy, old style
10. Some WWII soldiers
11. Thread in a nerve cell
12. Skilled
13. Deeds
14. Withdraws via suction
15. Pooh's home: Hundred Acre _____

16. Pear-shaped stringed instrument
22. Brunch or breakfast
24. Crusty skin covering
27. MS-_____
29. Workplace org. div.
31. Audio equipment brand name
32. Arabian Peninsula port
33. Analyze tea leaves, say
34. Purplish-pink
35. Confine
37. Mysterious (var.)
38. Plant that can poison you
39. Layer of paint
40. His and _____
43. Weather phenomenon near the Rockies
47. British singer Rita
49. Yoked beasts
50. South American bird
52. *Tobermory* writer
53. Journalist-turned-senator Pamela
55. Donkey's trait?
56. *Charlotte's* _____
57. Modify text
58. Morley Callaghan novel: _____ *Joy in Heaven*
59. Supersized
60. Baseball great Berra
61. Ladies' short capes, old style
62. "Vamoose!"
63. Powdery starch
64. Child of Zeus
66. _____ for the course
67. Show's stars
69. Mafia member
71. Praiseful cry in church
74. Sari wearer
75. Bloomington shopping mecca, for short
77. The same, to Augustus
80. Linguistic lingo
81. Via (var.)

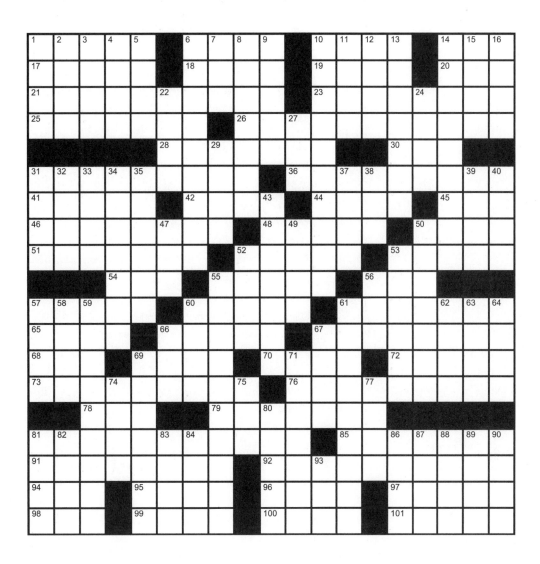

82. Smell terrible

83. Banff landmark: _____ and Basin National Historic Site

84. See 48-A

86. South African antelope

87. 1982 A Flock of Seagulls single

88. Thermal Infrared Scanner (abbr.)

89. Backyard entry point

90. Forget to mention

93. Setting for *Good Will Hunting* (abbr.)

69 Has a Nice Ring to It

Appealing place names

ACROSS

1. Ski resort tow
5. Whisperer's summoning sound
9. Currency in 31-D
13. Canadian Pointers and Newfoundlands
17. Trucker's truck
18. Horse's colouring
19. Long-time cosmetics company
20. Land mass
21. Opposin'
22. Like a teetotaller
24. Exchange (var.)
25. Ladder step
26. Permissive response
27. Sign of September
28. Calgarian Bret of wrestling fame
29. More white, in winter
31. Primer for a canvas
32. Metamorphic rock layers
33. Surge
35. **Town on Lake Simcoe's Kempenfelt Bay**
37. Allen who quarterbacked for five CFL teams
40. CNE locale: Exhibition _____
42. Canadian _____ Workers
43. Eludes
45. Habituate to (var.)
47. Canadian media entrepreneurs Turner and Drabinsky
51. Former Romanian politician Iliescu
52. Practice for the Calgary Philharmonic
55. Short-horned Asian antelope
56. War wound relic
58. Sylvester, to Tweety
59. Peter MacKay, vis-à-vis Elmer
61. Like severe straits
62. Principle
64. Scotiabank user, say
69. Actress Ortiz

70. It precedes cling or electricity
72. "The Divine Comedy" poet
73. Thingamajig
75. Spirited horse
77. Some body parts
79. Religious reverence
80. **Northern New Brunswick village**
84. Reach a personal goal
86. Skirt around
87. Partitioned, like urban areas
89. Fischer's finale?
93. Canadian poetess Robertson
94. Old-style word for nitrogen
95. A sib
96. Swollen spot
97. Temper tantrum
98. Surgical tool
100. Dry
101. Proactiv treats it
102. Larch or loblolly
103. Con
104. End of the _____
105. Data storage capacity, in brief
106. Casino computations
107. On the South China, say
108. Wolfish glance

DOWN

1. Old Russian monarchs
2. Started
3. _____ acid
4. **Ontario town north of Markham**
5. Orison
6. Come clean?
7. Cheek
8. Blasting crew's explosive
9. Flour storage spots
10. "Be it _____ humble, there's no place like home"
11. **Northern neighbour of Kawartha Lakes**

12. Passionate about
13. Shamed one's family, say (var.)
14. JFK's killer
15. Stuart who starred in *Titanic*
16. Like some nasal deviations
23. Acclaimed Canadian film: _____ *Heard the Mermaids Singing*
30. Victoria waterfront area: _____ Harbour
31. African nation
32. Greek cheeses
34. Neither rained nor snowed
36. Schlep
37. Religious rationalists
38. Bird with long legs
39. Tomorrow, in Toledo
41. Mangy dog
44. Band's playlist
46. Most facile
48. EMS prioritizing system
49. Royal Canadian Air Force fighter plane name
50. Dripping with perspiration
53. Possessed
54. Nephew of Abraham
57. Exacts revenge
60. Holiday beverage, for short
63. All tuckered out
65. Certified inventors, say
66. Yoko who married John
67. Shortened name for a famed violin
68. Fleet of foot
71. Human heel?
74. **Cape Breton coastal community**
76. **Small Saskatchewan place**
78. Say again
80. Fir found in Canada
81. Display emotion
82. Not in the lead
83. Made a hangman's rope

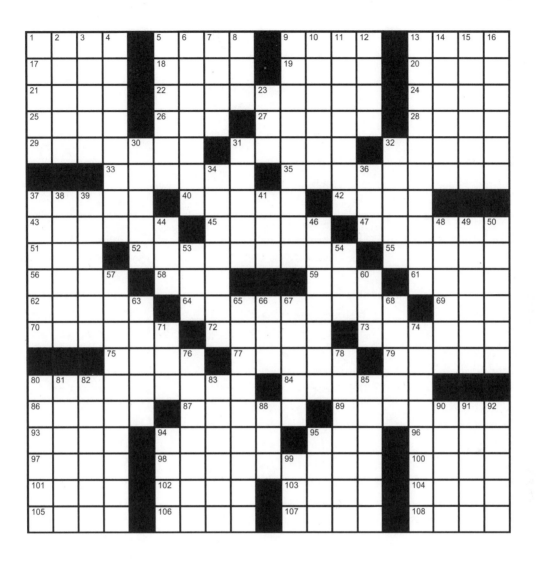

85. Symptom of amnesia
88. Energy Efficiency Ratio (abbr.)
90. Roost for an eagle

91. Québec neighbour
92. First Nations VIP
94. She sings in a lower clef

95. Canadians Heppner and Mulroney
99. Lamb's bleat

ACROSS

1. Orderly grouping
6. Tied down a sail
12. Winnipeg's Doug Henning excelled at this
17. Junky car
19. Petroleum hydrocarbon
20. Ontario gorge near Guelph
21. Margaret Atwood novel: *The _____ Woman*
22. Gap in a parapet
23. Nostrils
24. He trumped Hillary
25. Girls' school principal
27. Textile worker, sometimes
28. Monotonous, colloquially
29. Canadian singer Cochrane
30. A princess slept on one
32. Father figure?
34. High school equivalency completion certificate (abbr.)
35. Pedants
39. Phoned
41. BC-born NHL defenceman Shea
43. Viscid substance
44. Canadian actress Mitchell nominated for a 2016 People's Choice Award
45. Arise
47. Reince Priebus' White House role (abbr.)
48. Earl Grey's trees?
50. Southern Ontario polytechnic
52. Not enlightened?
53. Moist
54. Canada is a member of this organization
57. Bit of grain
60. 2006 Brian De Palma film: *The Black _____*
61. Naturally, from birth
65. British novelist J.B.
67. _____ in "vacation"
68. Peoples Jewellers parent company
69. Cash register drawer
70. Malarkey
71. Arachnid's poison
73. Donated
74. You might do this on a Saturday morning
76. Clef notation
77. Heart of a matter
79. Title for him
80. Shoot the breeze
81. Song from *Oklahoma!*: "_____ New Day"
83. Beau's daring deed?
85. Razing
89. Old dances in France
92. Slight abrasion
93. Half a deer's rack
94. Nail varnish
95. Compare
96. Ancient cemetery markers
97. You can spend this in Spain
98. Expel phlegm
99. Zimbabwe city
100. Bird with long longs

DOWN

1. Not yet stirring
2. Change the decor
3. 1971 Guess Who hit
4. Cornered, in a Canadian store?
5. Shouted
6. Ness and Lomond
7. Farmlands
8. *Titanic*, for example
9. Passed on: _____ down
10. Adversary
11. Kosher market
12. Coach
13. False fire info?
14. Impale, at the bullfight
15. Information and Real Estate Services (abbr.)
16. Mama _____ Elliot
18. Change map boundaries, say
26. Caviar source
30. Canucks and Jets, say
31. Apiece
33. Canada's Warner won Rio Olympic bronze in this
35. English physician who shares his name with a disease
36. Long-time CBC offering: *The Wayne and Shuster _____*
37. Home of the UK's art collection
38. Process (abbr.)
40. Philosophy maven
42. Ossicle or anvil
43. Occurring every 48 hours
46. Orange peels
48. Meadow bleat
49. Ball's TV and real-life husband
51. Rant
52. It's used for paternity tests
55. Bryan Baeumler hosted this show: *Disaster _____*
56. Guys only party
57. Picks
58. Liar anagram
59. Scrabble piece
62. Neoprene, for one
63. Blue jeans pioneer Strauss
64. French Flanders river
66. Composes a mournful poem
67. Extremely close
71. Neapolitan ice cream component
72. Robbed a coffee drinker?
75. Black _____ leather
76. Blue Jay who's up next?
78. 1990s collectible: _____ Baby
81. Underseas ray
82. Come to terms
84. Street talk

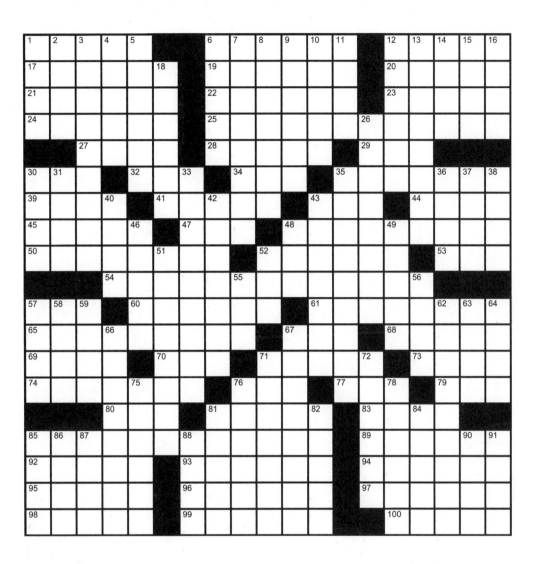

85. Take a good long look
86. Cell on a ship

87. Great Slave _____
88. Poison ivy effect

90. Family man, in Montréal
91. Opening for a token

Forecast: Fun!

Weather you like it or not

ACROSS

1. Pinnacles
6. Strew
13. Red tape, et al.
20. Metallic noise
21. Sicilian seaport
22. Driveway covering
23. **Light for the eye of the storm?**
25. Japanese massage
26. "Abominable" humanoid?
27. Alternative to Windows
28. Hillary Clinton, _____ Rodham
29. April Wine hit: "Just _____ You and Me"
30. Valley on Everest
32. Shakespeare work: "Why _____ thou promise such a beauteous day"
34. Perfect gymnastics score, previously
35. The Ducks play here
39. Ontario-born NHLer Gagner
40. Menswear item
41. Musical repeat sign
46. How you conduct yourself (var.)
48. **Fisherman's protection?**
51. "Stop!" at sea
52. Granola bar flake
54. Old Chinese currency
55. Linda Ronstadt hit: "You're _____"
56. Cat or dog
57. Answered evasively
60. Vacillate
62. Purpose
63. Flashes of time
65. Words to live by?
67. Threatening
69. Site for West Coast aquatic tourists
71. _____ ligation

73. Math abbr.
74. Intact provides it
78. Gets up
80. Casual wear
84. 2011 Bruce Cockburn song: "Each _____ Lost"
85. Tarzan, for example
87. Kenya's largest ethnic group
89. Neighbour of Swe.
90. Ranter's rant
92. Give up the goods?
94. Canadian's federal government ID no.
95. Minnie or Mickey
97. **Dangerous locale for bowlers?**
100. Ants, old style
102. Lend _____
103. Be overly inquisitive
104. Coastal European fish
106. Like sandals
107. North Sea bird
108. Vicious Dickens character
110. _____ *Doubtfire*
111. Botch, at the bingo hall?
116. Gemini-winning news anchor Hanomansing
117. Svelte
119. Shania Twain bio: *From _____ Moment On*
123. Blow up a photo, say
124. **Pleasant BC locale?**
127. British Columbian's northern neighbour
128. You might break up a block with this
129. It can be acute or obtuse
130. Prepare a press job, old style
131. Shawls for Mexican men
132. Buttes

DOWN

1. "_____ Breaky Heart"
2. Mrs. White board game

3. Western Canada pharmacy chain: Value Drug _____
4. Improves one's financial situation?
5. Half a pair for the slopes
6. Bridge over untroubled waters?
7. Dog or wolf, for example
8. Joan Collins' *Dynasty* character
9. _____ Aviv
10. Send
11. *Slap Shot* star, M. _____ Walsh
12. Lasso
13. One whose popularity has perished
14. Like a chimney sweep's face?
15. Barbecue tool
16. Canadian telecommunications firm
17. Not on schedule
18. "If all _____ fails . . ."
19. Leave dumbfounded
24. Cousin of parsley
31. **Corporal O'Reilly's forecasting tool?**
33. Spotted canine, for short
34. Names
35. Accommodate alterations
36. At no time
37. Pricey violin
38. Atmosphere
40. "We stand on guard for _____"
41. **Spurge that's an oxymoron?**
42. Easter hunt find
43. Tile installer's mortar
44. Hangman's lethal loop
45. More uneven?
47. Ravi Shankar musical selection
49. WWI protective gear
50. Just plain silliness
53. Message, electronically
58. Broke out of the joint
59. Active when it's light out
61. Family sib

64. Canadian Golf Hall of Fame inductee: Dawn _____-Jones
66. Sash for a *Star Wars* stalwart?
68. "Zip it!"
70. Era or epoch
72. Lanai garlands
74. Panna _____
75. Fried ring filling
76. Glass, in Gatineau
77. Get on board
79. Bypass curling practice?
81. Get accustomed to
82. Valentine's Day gift
83. Rapunzel's pride

86. Close confederate
88. Building block?
91. American Nurses Association (abbr.)
93. Tyro
96. Blade sharpening device
98. Ritzy
99. Tibetan beast
101. Significant WWI battle for Canada
105. Send again
107. Pond surface build-up
108. Sundae topping

109. Canadian specialty TV channel
111. Carnivore's staple
112. Towards the centre, old style
113. _____ on the wrist
114. Lawyer's assignment
115. Big biblical boats
116. Sister of Osiris
118. Signs a deal, say
120. Beldams
121. La Palma, for example
122. Holy French females (abbr.)
125. Place to get 25-A
126. Rotating shaft component

ACROSS

1. Cook in broth
5. Whine
9. Fragrance first produced in 1932
13. Hit hard
17. Opulent
18. Opportune for the picking?
19. Is under the weather
20. _____-and-seek
21. Appetizer, in Ancona
23. Devoted
24. 1975 ELO hit: "_____ Woman"
25. Some Canadian Armed Forces personnel
28. European Nuclear Society (abbr.)
29. Actor's audience comment
30. Acrophobia and arachnophobia
31. Flippant
33. It airs *The Voice*
35. On one's own
37. _____ test
38. Light switch switch
40. Little bit of Greek?
42. Pesky insects
44. More conclusively, to Octavius
46. 2017 federal Conservative leadership hopeful Michael
48. Impervious to sensation
50. Plaything
51. Cut down to size
52. Goofs
54. No longer living
56. Alphabet letter, in Arkansas
58. River in the Netherlands
59. CANDU reactors produce this
63. Tax pro, for short
66. Male bud
67. Activity on *Property Brothers*
68. _____ Leone
72. 55-D, for example
74. Type of tide
76. *Carpe* _____
78. Ice rain
79. Pine extract, for one
82. Glitch
84. Struggle to catch one's breath
85. This acting Al joined Canada's Walk of Fame in 2016
86. Old union: Communications, Energy and Paperworkers of Canada (abbr.).
88. Dreary
90. James _____
91. Massages
92. Cell disintegration processes
94. Tumbler
96. Grad student's goal (abbr.)
97. Highly charged weather event?
102. They wriggle under the sea
104. Ivy League university
105. Temporary cessations
106. Fundraising event
107. Done with, colloquially
108. 1994 Alice Munro collection: _____ *Secrets*
109. Sashes for geishas
110. Organic chemical radical
111. "Untouchable" Eliot
112. After deductions, in Derby
113. Whispered letters?

DOWN

1. Entree side salad
2. Albacore or ahi
3. Exhaust fan, for example
4. Stream dams
5. Manitoba city
6. Eavesdrop
7. _____ no good
8. Depart
9. Regina-born Maslany who won a best actress drama Emmy in 2016
10. WestJet has a fleet of these
11. Colourful music genre?
12. Rehab attendee
13. 1962 hit: "_____ Cried"
14. California city
15. Temporarily, to Tiberius
16. Brooks and Blanc
22. Bucket
26. Government employee, for short
27. _____ and polish
32. Radiate
33. Pleasant French place?
34. Physicist Niels
36. Musical composition
38. Some Kenmore appliances
39. Edges
41. In a little while, old style
43. Defame, say
45. Seep
47. Wormlike larva
49. Showed all?
53. Canadian _____ Awards
55. Canadian talk show stalwart Marilyn
57. Cuirass part (var.)
60. Tennis techniques
61. With _____ in sight
62. Pound sound
63. Dinner for a Chinese dog?
64. Toonie mammal
65. How some plants reproduce
69. Soaks up for a second time
70. American actress Sofer
71. ABA member
73. Resting place?
75. Travels via two wheels
77. Manitoban Laurence who penned *The Diviners*
80. Level, in Lancashire
81. They might feel empty?
83. New Brunswick's 33rd premier Brian
87. Apiece

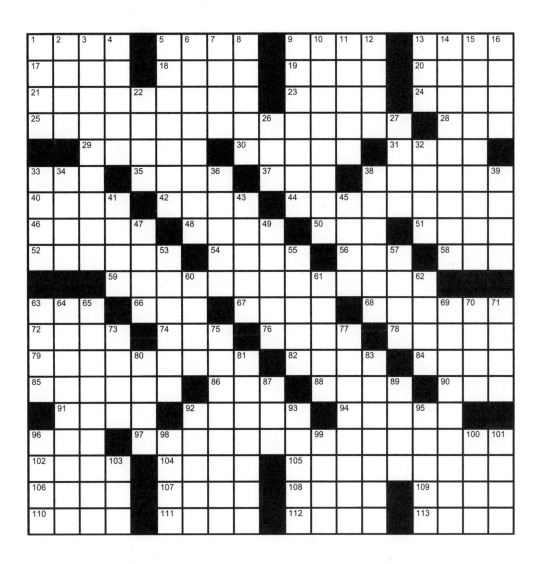

89. Strong fibre
92. See 8-D
93. BC academic institution: _____ Fraser

95. Posture problem
96. Huge, in slang
98. Former prime minister: William _____ Mackenzie King

99. Get along okay
100. Former NDP MP Nelson
101. Crow's nest locale
103. Mineo of *Exodus*

73 Mmm Mmm Good!

A taste of Canada

ACROSS

1. Boast like a bird?
5. Dining room furniture piece
10. Québec-born pianist _____-André Hamelin
14. Surveyors' documents
19. Traditional Maori war dance
20. Offers employment at the root beer plant?
21. Viva voce
22. Sketchily obtained profits, say
23. Join together
25. Etna output, in 2015
26. Wheat used for feed
27. Eccentric behaviour, say
28. **Wild Rose province meat**
30. They're optimistic
31. H1N1, et al.
32. Peace and quiet
33. *Tiger Beat* readership
35. Touches up an essay
37. Least refined
41. Mythological war god
42. Horse's tress
45. Second Cup staffer
46. Greek letters
47. They come first?
48. No score, on the soccer pitch
50. Register for a draw
51. Reykjavik citizen
53. Show one's emotions
56. Clarified butter for Asian cuisine
57. _____ nouveau
58. Desert shrubs (var.)
60. Golfer Ernie who's won four majors
61. **East Coast seafood**
66. Be in debt
68. Competitor
69. Cap for a lass
70. Vets do this to stallions
72. Alabama city

73. No ifs, ands or buts statements
79. Surgeon's tool
81. Cosmetics queen: Mary _____
82. Québec locale: Pointe-_____
83. Bustle or fuss
84. Call forth, old style
86. Covers a road with tar
89. Skiers' tow
90. Indicate
91. Vancouver Island bus service: West _____ Trail Express
92. Type of park
93. Royal Canadian _____
95. Lake bottom sediment
96. He or she stocks stockings
99. **Popular provincial spuds**
103. Plants popular in Tokyo?
106. Town in Ontario
107. Harness component
108. You might stay here if all else fails?
109. Paul Simon hit: "Still Crazy After All _____ Years"
110. Locker room powder
111. Red sign outside a studio
112. The Bee Gees, for one
113. Emulated a carrier pigeon
114. Old World language
115. Canadian sprinter Williams who won double gold at the 1928 Olympics
116. Lose one's temper

DOWN

1. Plug of tobacco
2. Chippewa First Nation in Ontario
3. **Québec dairy product**
4. Bit parts
5. Macbeth, for example
6. To adore, in Abitibi
7. Petite restaurant
8. Gives permission to rent?

9. Abbotsford, directionally from Vancouver (abbr.)
10. Slug or snail
11. Bedouins
12. Great party?
13. Western Ireland county
14. Business before _____
15. Like an ungraceful logger?
16. Opposite of nadir
17. Kids' playhouse locale
18. Middle Ages worker
24. Rips off (var.)
28. Palo _____
29. Snack in Seville
31. Son of Sept-Îles?
33. Joni sang about a big yellow one
34. Ex-Dodgers pitcher Gagné from Québec
36. Precious ruminants?
38. 1940s movie star Williams
39. Nickname for Hamilton and Sydney: _____ City
40. Shipping weights
42. Apparition, old style
43. Roulette table bet
44. Use a prie-dieu
45. Dust jacket copy
47. Egg–pupa connector
49. _____-Chinese
52. Indochinese language
53. Give your two cents' worth
54. "Excellent," in street-speak
55. Church service leaders
58. Literary citation abbr.
59. Time-worn
61. British Columbia city
62. Uttered
63. Canadian Intercollegiate Baseball Association (abbr.)
64. Some Hindus
65. It never gets off the ground?
66. Looked at amorously
67. Use a loom

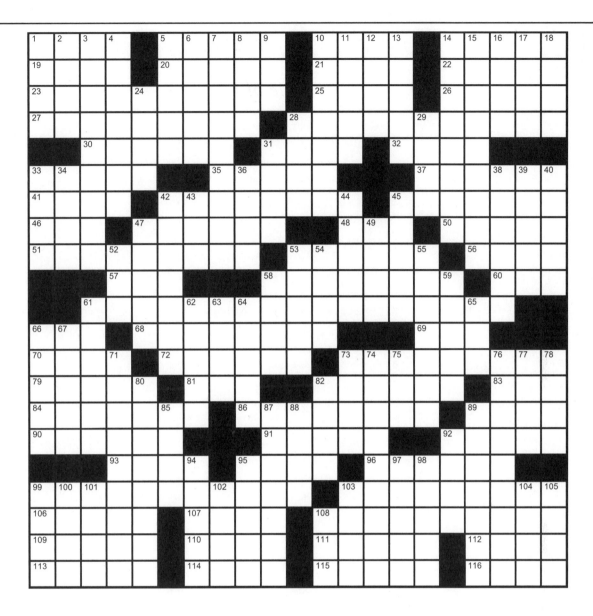

71. Rot

73. It precedes ". . . poor Yorick!"

74. He was a wise guy?

75. Pose for an artist

76. Sweet summer treat from Alberta

77. Dutch dairy export

78. Like lousy losers

80. Restricted the use of resources

82. Internet conversation, say

85. Shelter for campers

87. Toronto attraction: Ontario _____ Centre

88. Tories and Libs

89. Believers

92. Trident end

94. French pastry: _____ Tatin

95. Gets dirty

97. Vision-related nerve

98. Apologetic

99. Bicyclist's trail

100. Sound that lingers

101. Collector's thing?

102. Shred into strips

103. Canadian author Urquhart

104. Opera performance highlight

105. Cease moving

108. Cut

ACROSS

1. Funny pages strip
6. Use a letter opener
10. Starch for chefs
14. Short order order?
17. *La Bohème*, for example
18. Top-rated number?
19. Happily _____ after
20. Type of loaf
21. Ontario county popular with tourists
23. Not so warm
24. Coffee dispensing appliance
25. Car industry magnate Ransom
26. Salé and Pelletier, et al.
27. Without enough sleep
29. Assignment in the Old Testament?
30. Like a gold-digging girlfriend?
32. Fissure
33. 65, perhaps?
38. Sketch out details
43. One kind of influenza
44. Chutzpah
46. Back off, tactfully
47. Like some artists' models
49. Fey
51. It precedes jacket or storm
52. Early rounds, for Eugenie Bouchard
53. Solo songs
54. _____ story goes
55. Slangy "sure"
56. Big hit from 94-A: "_____ Days"
57. TD foyer machine (abbr.)
58. Bends out of shape
61. Fifth Dionne quintuplet
62. Bug an electrician?
66. Absent from roll call
67. Sprite's sister?
68. Quebecer Louis Quilico, for example
69. Adulterates
71. Long-time US film critic Judith
73. Plume
74. Exactly the same
76. Comes into view again
78. Work unit
79. Michael Morpurgo children's book: *This Morning I _____ Whale*
81. Stop sign colour
82. Way to go?
86. Sign on a lavatory door
88. Evidence for Miss Marple
92. Insect type
93. Cooper/Kelly western: *High _____*
94. Popular 1970s Canadian band
96. Odd sight in the sky
97. Encircle
98. American self-improvement guru Carnegie
99. _____ sprawl
100. River that runs through Calgary
101. Birds you might see at the beach (var.)
102. Phillips University Oklahoma city
103. Beast's short friend?

DOWN

1. You might catch this in BC
2. Alberta town or Ontario lake
3. Play a canasta
4. Tennessee state flower
5. Discovery channel show: *Cash _____*
6. Old court dances
7. He wrote *Madame Chrysanthème*
8. Good to go, say
9. On edge, emotionally
10. Safe
11. US romance novel publisher
12. Large Ontario bay
13. Ottawa suburb
14. Brand of men's toiletry products
15. Ancient Greek harp
16. Care for a flock, say
22. Fairy tale preposition
28. Dashboard display instrument
29. Female donkeys
31. Barbershop quartet song: "Sweet _____"
33. Sound from a surprised person
34. _____ and done with
35. Bright green shade
36. Canadian Discovery channel show since 1995
37. "Fancy that!"
39. Necklaces for Oahu visitors
40. Summer month, in Montréal
41. Bum
42. Small suffix?
45. Scale on a scale
48. Baseball game arbiter
50. Canadian-born 1933 *King Kong* star Wray
53. Heart part
54. Like zebras
56. Kenny G instrument
57. Balloon filler
58. Dry African riverbed
59. Amazed
60. Supreme Court of Canada justice's attire
61. Assorted category (abbr.)
62. Drainage basin
63. Host of 36-D Ziya
64. _____ *of Green Gables*
65. Crop grown in Canada
67. Sexy ladieswear
68. Cattle disease first seen in 1986 (abbr.)
70. Not normal
72. Tehran resident
75. Makes it right?

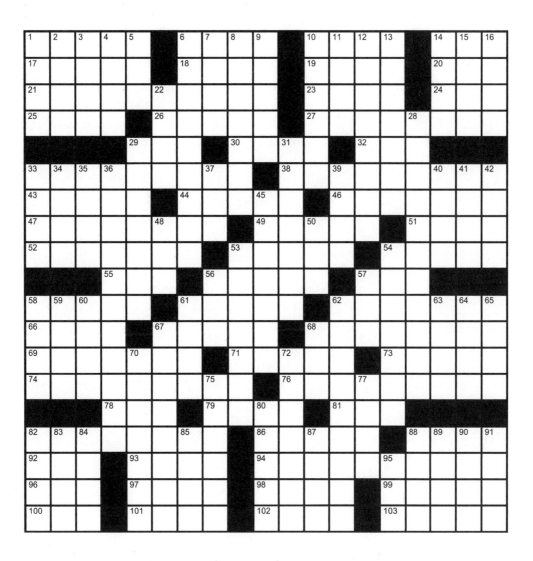

77. Judy Garland musical: _____
Me in St. Louis

80. Diacritical language symbol

82. Fingerpaint

83. Facts

84. Stash

85. See 65-D

87. It's not a pretty fruit?

88. Middle of a Mac

89. She won three female vocalist
Junos in the '80s

90. Genesis sibling

91. Left a location

95. Centre

Geisel's Gaggle

Dr. Seuss characters

ACROSS

1. Helmet part
6. Puts up a painting
11. Non-flying bird
14. Stumble
18. Rodeo animal pen exit
19. Old Greek gathering place
20. Henry VIII's circumference (var.)
22. Activity for Canada's Holmes and McGillivray
23. Suit for a Knight of Columbus?
24. City famed for its shroud
25. Nursemaid in Tianjin
26. _____-roll bar
27. Barmy bird?
28. Starting a par 5, say
29. Petty whose talk show aired from 1989–99 in Canada
30. Long-time Boston Red Sox star Yastrzemski
31. Historic Québec place: Plains of _____
33. Tiller's plot
35. **A little Who who was no more than two**
37. **Eponymous environmentalist**
39. Moncton optical illusion spot: Magnetic _____
41. Alcohol and Gaming Authority (abbr.)
42. _____ centre
45. Where Germany surrendered on May 7, 1945
47. Greetings of Gaius
49. Lethargic
54. Positive public reception
56. Plaster backing
58. Books printed before 1501
60. *Basic Instinct* star Stone
62. Northern art piece medium
64. Goddess seen in hieroglyphs
65. Best bun?

67. Genetic substance (abbr.)
68. US investor's option (abbr.)
69. Labour Day falls this mo.
70. 1955 Guinness/Sellers comedy: *The* _____
74. 11-year Maple Leafs captain Sundin
78. Bro alternative
79. French pronoun
80. Kind of civic race
86. "Immediately!" abbr.
87. Orion's celestial neighbour
90. Oscar-winning actor Robert
91. Mutually beneficial, say
93. Professional club payment
95. *Global National* weekend anchorperson Gill
96. Bite from a Russian Blue?
97. Significant historical periods
99. Small, in Sorel-Tracy
101. Reverse of NNW
102. 1971 Olivia Newton-John cover: "If _____ for You"
104. Goes dark
106. **Her brother narrates** *The Cat in the Hat*
108. *The Cat in the Hat* **tandem member**
113. What you might call a lady?
115. Shone
119. Took transit
120. Michelin product
122. Wallops, old style
124. Wintry window coating
125. Declare with conviction
126. Arthurian legends lady
127. Animal skins
128. Synthetic material
129. Stephen King thriller: *The* _____ *Zone*
130. Oboe mouthpiece component
131. Bird of prey
132. Royal Italian title

133. Additions to buildings
134. Ball game: _____-pitch
135. Used one's olfactory sense
136. Geek

DOWN

1. Rossini opera: *La* _____ *di seta*
2. Pulsate
3. TMZ tidbit (var.)
4. Hard on the ears
5. Individually
6. Nasty correspondence
7. Old-style illness
8. Irrigation apparatus
9. **His heart was two sizes too small**
10. Sweetened red wine
11. "Yikes!" old style
12. Imitator
13. One of the Greek Muses
14. Canadian ex-race car driver Paul
15. Kidney related
16. Short musical opener?
17. WWI French infantryman
21. **See 108-A**
28. Container weight, in shipping
32. **The Wickersham Brothers tormented him**
34. 1990s Canadian skating star Stojko
36. Raw information
38. Dec. 25th
40. Progresso product
42. "No _____ for the wicked"
43. 2014 film: _____ *Park*
44. Thunderous sound?
46. Film director's road map
48. Get a goal
50. Wetlands bird
51. Sixth-longest river in the UK
52. Freud's fall?
53. Compass point
55. _____ of the Covenant

57. Baseball great Aaron
59. Render weaponless
61. Net Operating Loss (abbr.)
63. Thomas who wrote *Common Sense*
66. Unacceptable in society
71. Cap type for a numbskull
72. George Harrison classic: "My Sweet _____"
73. Blue
74. Astronaut-turned-MP Garneau
75. Adrift, on the Adriatic?
76. Mediator's forte
77. Wheels do this
81. Turtle who winds up as King of the Mud

82. Yoko's sad interjection?
83. Swiss Chalet serving
84. Magnate Onassis, et al.
85. Solo
87. I-dotter/T-crosser in *Did I Ever Tell You How Lucky You Are?*
88. Allegation about Intact?
89. Catches sight of
92. Engine knock sound
94. Broadway props
98. Big hits?
100. Colds and coughs
103. Packing ropes
105. *Green Eggs and Ham* advocate

107. Perennial herb
108. Part of NAFTA
109. Shanty
110. It's perfect?
111. Eggheads
112. Architectural window projection
114. Cousin of a skeeter
116. Tigger's creator
117. Overdramatize, at the theatre
118. Bright Cygnus star
121. Tuber type
123. Alice Munro collection: *Something I've Been Meaning to _____ You*
128. Hoarder's disorder, for short

ACROSS

1. Tabbouleh ingredient
7. Dull impacts sounds
12. Board game with a 16 x 16 grid pattern
17. Some person
18. Benzene-based radical
19. Eye part-related
20. Rock piles
21. Saudi _____
22. Early homeopathic medicine term
23. Raspy voiced
24. Some financial institutions
26. Arranging groups of students?
28. Teacher's favourite
29. US magnate Forbes
33. "_____ sell his own mother!"
34. Bean, in Beauceville
38. Botanical angle
39. Engages in espionage
41. Shorten trousers
42. Unrestrained revelry
43. Former Canadian senator Dallaire
45. Finale
46. Scoundrel's mutt?
47. Lewis Carroll character
48. Canadian who flies south
50. Provoke public opinion
52. Students' spelling contest
53. Jane Austen's emotions?
56. Nickname for *Playboy* founder Hugh
59. Canadians Virtue or Moir
60. Insurer from 1887–2013: _____ of Canada
64. Narrow mountain ridge
66. Character actor Glass
67. Scotiabank Saddledome game official, for short
68. Rocket fuel ingredient, for short
69. He tells little white ones
70. Bra size for 71-A gal
71. Zaftig
73. CNE or PNE
74. Soft-bodied sea creature
76. Beverage type, in Baie-Comeau
77. Tear away
79. You might be a stick in this
80. Lacking saline
82. Tim Hortons order
86. He's on board?
91. Toronto CFLers
92. Small stream
93. Mississippi city
94. Québec-born ex-NHLer Simon
95. Fall flowers
96. They cause puffiness
97. Some plums
98. Tops
99. Sponge or teabag description (var.)

DOWN

1. Hearty party
2. Odd, in Scotland
3. Constellation name
4. Busy bee
5. This org. nominates World Heritage Sites
6. Puts on the market again
7. Trounced, in competition
8. Large thugs?
9. Set free
10. To one's _____ day
11. Insult, in Ipswich
12. Toronto college or river
13. Air Canada industry
14. Not fatty
15. Movie starring Canada's Jim Carrey: *The* _____
16. Donations, in Dickens-speak
18. Backstage _____
25. Canned meat brand name
27. Some punctuation marks
29. Red planet
30. Neurotransmission site
31. Chauffeur's wheels
32. Balls of yarn, old style
34. Until now
35. Kvetching crustacean?
36. Fiend, in fairy tales
37. Little kid
40. Put into words
41. Meteorologists use this Canadian invention
44. Overweight
46. Op-ed piece
47. You might raise one at Oktoberfest
49. 74-A produces this
50. One of BC's tallest trees: Douglas _____
51. Matchsticks game
54. Twin or king
55. Smell
56. Circle above a saint
57. *Corner Gas* actor Peterson
58. Daring accomplishment
61. _____-TASS
62. Spanish fishing town
63. 1970s Maple Leaf Ullman
65. Canadian Brass instrument
67. Cattle thieves
70. Guy, colloquially
71. Little plant part?
72. Blunder
75. Throbs
76. Pleasure trips
78. Not genuine
80. Tippler
81. Permits
82. Hammarskjöld, et al.
83. Toothbrush brand: _____-B

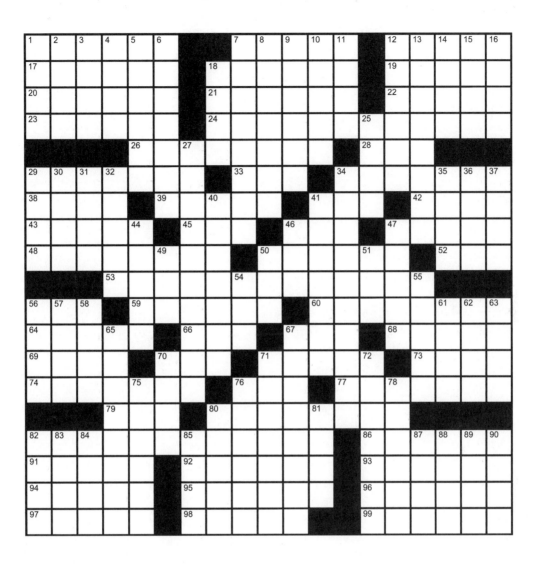

84. Not at all pretty, in Internet slang

85. Unexciting

87. Impersonator, say

88. Exec's msg.

89. "With regret" expression

90. Prominent facial feature

Rocking in Rio

Sports for our 2016 Olympics stars

ACROSS

1. Canadians' winter wear (var.)
7. Settled a debt
11. Toddler's early word
15. Fungus, in Fresno
19. Genetic combination
20. Back blemishes
21. Model host of *Project Runway Canada*
22. Small case, in Calais
23. **Our women won bronze in this debut event**
25. **Andre De Grasse shone in this sport**
27. Grp. for US lawyers
28. Ersatz copies
29. Marshy tract
31. Provides relief
32. Track meet official
33. Like a verdant landscape
34. Unagi
35. "My kingdom for _____"
38. *Doctor Zhivago* star Omar
40. Golden ager
44. Utah indigenous people (var.)
46. **Penny Oleksiak swam to silver in this event**
48. WestJet traveller's info
49. Latch (onto)
50. _____-European
52. *Star Trek* genre
53. Become obscured
54. Lingerie garment
55. Moved menacingly toward the weaver?
58. Chef's spoonful (abbr.)
59. _____-de-camp
60. Brouhahas
62. These share turf with Canada lynx
64. **Canada won bronze again on this pitch**

66. American singers Rawls and Reed
68. "Say what?"
69. Eat like a bird
70. **Meaghan Benfeito won bronze from the platform in this**
73. The only way you should be driving
76. Org.
80. Golf club
81. Computer hackers' application (abbr.)
84. Desert-set Bogart film
86. Currency spent in Apia
87. 1960s crooner Jerry
88. Ancient Peruvians
90. RBC Canadian _____
91. She might have regrets
92. Sens' city
93. **Damian Warner scored a bronze in this**
96. Russian tea urn
98. Flower for an Assam aficionado?
100. Praised precipitation?
102. Compares
103. Overwrought (with "up")
104. Drink or eat excessively
105. Answer for one's sins
107. Gutters
110. Tithing denomination
111. Bland colour
112. Walter Cronkite's network
115. **Erica Wiebe won gold on the mat in this**
117. **Canadians won bronze at the velodrome in this**
120. See 111-A
121. Sheath for a seed
122. Loosen shoelaces
123. In a wicked way
124. Niagara Falls MP Nicholson, et al.
125. Disavow

126. Hammer component
127. Dakota subgroup

DOWN

1. Juno winners: Tegan and _____
2. Sierra _____ Canada Foundation
3. Pond organism
4. Civil War "Gray"
5. Lure the trout
6. Asian cuisine flavour enhancer
7. Patio stones
8. Top pilots, colloquially
9. B&B's brethren
10. Nanaimo bars, say
11. Arouses enmity
12. With plenty to spare
13. Challenge
14. *Wheel of Fortune* vowel purchase
15. Zinc and nickel
16. Blues musician Rush
17. Moon, to Michel
18. Archaeological sites
24. _____ out a living
26. Destitute
30. Bides one's time
32. **Rosie MacLennan won her second gold on this**
33. Canadian poet Evelyn
34. Orbital path
35. Anxiety
36. Gelsenkirchen greeting
37. Shaped like a football
39. Bikini Atoll blast weapon
40. Murders, à la the Mob
41. Having an end goal
42. Practice piece for a pianist
43. More difficult to find
45. Elitists
47. Tease Adam?
51. Bombardier product: Ski-_____
53. **Masse and Caldwell swam to bronze in this**
56. Audible reverb

57. Applies plaster, say
61. Brett, to Bobby Hull
63. Former CTV *etalk* host Andrews
65. Ontario Chiropractic Association (abbr.)
67. Least pretty
69. Combustible heaps
70. Fairway chunk
71. Boiling mad
72. Ghana river
73. In an unsparing manner
74. French wine region
75. Where some small dogs sit?
77. 1980s Governor General Jeanne
78. New York state city

79. Canadians Emily and Shirley
82. Back then
83. Institute of Chartered Accountants (abbr.)
85. Watches with dials
89. Kipling line: "Can't! Don't! _____! Won't!"
93. Old-style verb contraction
94. Debby Boone classic: "You _____ My Life"
95. Cheer for Atlético Madrid?
97. Roman goddess of wisdom
99. Monkey used in medical research
101. Evil being (var.)
104. Neighbour of Nigeria

106. Gratuity
107. Jug
108. With the bow, in the strings section
109. Action word
110. Canadian _____ money
111. Commanded, old style
112. Group for zealots
113. Liver secretion
114. Eyelid infection
116. Pre-teen boy
118. Moose Jaw-to-Regina direction (abbr.)
119. Sloth or gluttony

ACROSS

1. Lying in, say
5. Smashing show?
8. Muskoka ON town
12. Davis of *Highway Thru Hell*
17. Arnaz, Sr. or Jr.
18. Orangey drink suffix
19. Allen who writes for *Maclean's*
20. In the midst of
21. Tolkien tale soldiers
22. Pays attention?
24. Approximately, in appraisals of antiques
25. Most nattily dressed
27. Royal Automobile Association (abbr.)
28. Prep pizza dough
29. Forte, on a musical score
30. Tip-off
32. Requiem Mass hymn: "Dies _____"
34. Kid's modelling substance
37. Medical diagnostic test
38. Title for a spouse
41. Ore source
42. Resort town in England's Kent county
44. Long-time Vancouver Canuck Sedin
46. Bizet work
48. Masons who smoke marijuana?
50. Kim Mitchell classic: "_____ Lanterns"
51. Ouija board response
52. Connect the _____
54. Vandalism
56. Big sport in Japan?
57. Bump on the body
58. It holds roses
59. Retail robber
63. Barn roof topper
64. Austin Powers or James Bond
67. French painter Claude
68. Computer programming language
70. Old photo finish
72. Child-friendly international org.
74. In Judaism, where the wicked go
76. Cadet or captain
77. Acquire
78. *As For Me and My House* scribe from Saskatchewan
80. Canada's Marion Orr, et al. (var.)
82. Message via iPhone
83. You're solving one
84. Fashionable fury?
85. Former Governor General Léger
88. Not at the peak of health
90. Exercise machine, for example
94. Odds' opposites
95. Paper type
97. Tear, violently
98. Landlord/tenant agreement
99. Bettor's bereavement?
100. "Revolting!"
101. Black cat, to some
102. Puts cargo on board
103. Got by on very little
104. Earnings
105. Archie Goodwin worked for this Wolfe

DOWN

1. Brouhahas
2. 2016 presidential primaries slogan: "Feel the _____"
3. Cadillac SUVs
4. Garbageman, say
5. Mystical Jewish sect members
6. _____ *fixe*
7. Clothing items that often have logos (var.)
8. At the plate implement
9. Cancel a rocket launch
10. She had a romance with Han
11. Asian language family
12. Nicholson's nincompoops?
13. Nitrogen compound
14. Oliver's seconds
15. Anagram for Cain
16. Old-style oath
23. Potent ale, to a Brit
26. Well-_____
31. Early humanoid
33. Circle meas.
34. Gambit
35. Run slowly
36. Fisherman's hand-me-down?
37. Olden days slave
38. Minute insect
39. It might prevent horsing around?
40. Opening
43. Adolescent
45. It's always a proper noun
47. They cuckold
49. Subtropical region grassland
53. Old Japanese title
55. _____Con
56. Hamiltonian's newspaper, for short
57. "As you _____"
59. Complacent
60. Sharpen
61. Reacting immediately
62. Duds
63. Canadian interuniversity football trophy
64. Four-dimensional continuum description
65. Type of tree
66. Talks about Tibetan bovines?
69. Variety shows
71. Fleabane
73. AB-born *Family Ties* star Michael J.

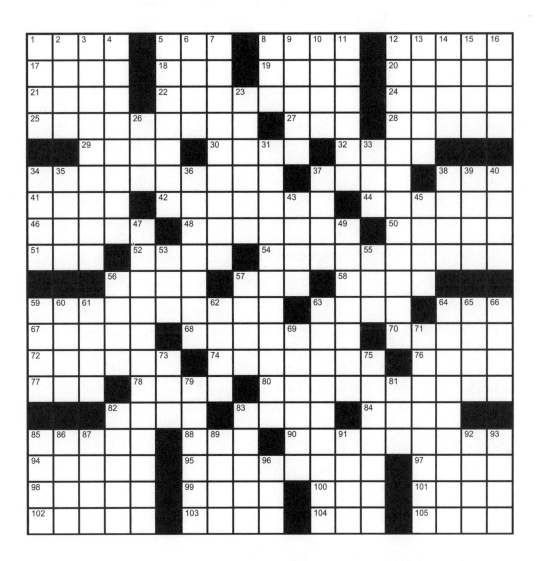

75. Weaken through degeneration
79. Smother
81. Animal world male
82. Uptight about verb conjugation?
83. Near and dear, say

85. Set
86. Eye part
87. Guide the way
89. Take a gander
91. "Bad Romance" singer: Lady _____

92. 2009 single from Toronto's Drake: "Best I _____ Had"
93. Canada's Walk of Fame inductee Ginette
96. Drug to take on a trip?

Footy Fun

English soccer team nicknames

ACROSS

1. Misleading dancer?
6. Thoroughfares (abbr.)
10. Tex-Mex menu item
14. Instinct
18. Food poisoning source
19. Fence crossing device
20. Soul singer Redding
21. Lacking value
22. Canadian telecommunications company
23. CBC Radio Happy Gang player Eddie
24. Bada Bing! on *The Sopranos*
26. Stir-fry
27. Powders
28. Blasphemous behaviour
29. Rodent remover
32. "Crazy" singer Patsy
33. Golfer's gadget
34. Not for
35. They might follow rags?
37. Lingerie garment
40. Segment of a circle
42. *SCTV* brothers: Bob _____ Doug McKenzie
44. Sandpaper texture
45. **Chelsea**
47. **Arsenal**
51. _____ Lanka
53. Like oil in water
55. Like some managers' policies
57. Cake covering
59. Japanese city
60. Stand in good _____
61. Idling, at the bakery?
63. Bird that transported Sinbad
64. Canadian-bred Northern Dancer
65. HVAC outlet
66. American vocalist Suzanne
68. Limestone landscape formation
73. Contest
75. Las Vegas resident
77. Outback holler
78. Like volunteer labour
82. Show a designer's dresses, say
83. Sweet vegetable?
85. Hamlet speech, for example
87. _____-tac-toe
89. **Stoke City**
90. **Tottenham**
91. Facebook reader, say
93. Justin, to Hadrien, Xavier and Ella-Grace
95. Trade partner of Canada (abbr.)
96. QC-born former NHLer Fleming
97. African antelope
99. Approximately
101. Type of flour
104. Fire emergency warning
106. Sorry state, say
110. Romped with a bird?
114. Blood component
115. Yell
116. Without good fortune, at the casino?
117. Whack, old style
118. Hindustani stringed instrument
119. Indian tree
120. Ablan who founded a major Canadian retailer
121. Dubai dignitary (var.)
122. Anoint, old style
123. Precious jewels
124. Marine eagle
125. Guff
126. Actress Oberon

DOWN

1. Elite Air Canada passengers?
2. Mountain climber's tool
3. Gastropod's spiral shell
4. Remove with a solvent
5. Stage set component
6. Calgary Flames former US city
7. **Aston Villa**
8. Choose to cast a vote?
9. Security system part
10. Fling a horseshoe
11. Affixing to
12. Jewelled headbands
13. Egyptian god of the underworld
14. The man was from here on '60s TV
15. Precept to be obeyed
16. Guzzler's noise
17. European river
19. Fabric for a shimmering gown
25. TD ATM no.
30. Computing shortcut
31. Leduc #1, in Alberta
36. Winced
37. Tuberculosis swelling
38. Count (on)
39. Out on the ocean
40. Actresses Faris and Paquin
41. **Manchester United**
43. Wandered aimlessly
45. **Sunderland**
46. Haul
47. Surprised expression: "Oh my _____!"
48. Engaged in no good?
49. _____-do-well
50. Finish this puzzle, say
52. Here, in Hochelaga
54. Lennon's second bride
56. Caviar source
58. See 21-A
62. Pestered
63. "The mouse _____ the clock"
67. Product at some Canadian Tire outlets
69. Major artery
70. Climber's twine
71. Nostradamus, for example

72. Irish and English Breakfast
74. Bride or groom's declaration
76. Doc for a Doberman
78. Brezhnev's nation (abbr.)
79. Slangy turndown
80. Drain blocker
81. _____ Transat
82. Cantaloupe, for one
84. Fruit that can double as an instrument
86. More eccentric

88. **Norwich**
92. Purged (of)
94. Transfers authority to an underling
97. Become cloudy, archaically
98. Hershey's love bites?
100. To like, in Laval
101. Rabble-rouser
102. 1978 Exile song: "Kiss _____ Over"
103. Swiss Chalet serving

104. Dalhousie grads, for short
105. _____ La Biche AB
107. Logical proposition
108. NE India state
109. "To _____ own self be true"
110. Performed a cappella
111. Leg part
112. Big Bang theory matter
113. Physics unit

ACROSS

1. Pub libations
5. League for Roughriders and Redblacks (abbr.)
8. Sonny's '60s missus
12. Drug pusher
17. Icy covering
18. *Richard* or *Rocky* follower
19. River in England
20. Troy tale (with "*The*")
21. Eye drop
22. Former Calgary-based energy company
24. Unaccompanied
25. Sol's rays?
27. Fruit stone
28. World's richest man, as of 2016
29. Garnish for a meat dish
30. Some rifles, for short
32. Verve
34. National tax (abbr.)
36. It follows Nova in Canada
38. The Government of Canada apologized to this Maher
39. Way back when
42. Hawaiian garlands
44. Like chow chows
46. Group of Seven member A.J.
48. Part of AECL
50. Prickly plant
52. Former Irish Rover Millar
53. Regal house adjective
55. Leprechauns' land
56. Chewy candy
57. Anagram for diddle
59. Forward mail, say
61. Blockheaded gardeners?
64. Jungle dwellers
66. Most strict
70. If you're this you need 15-D
71. Grandfathers' favourite whale?
73. Butterfly's markings
74. Very much, to Dorothy Gale
76. Partially bearded
78. Céline or Stéphane
79. Edmonton Oilers season ticket holder, say
80. Massive
82. Sagan PBS show
84. Final letter in Florida
85. Military cap with a visor
86. Zip
87. Hindu teachings principle
89. Former Ontario premier Miller
92. Legislative Assembly of Ontario (abbr.)
94. Pakistan capital
98. She might dress in a saree
99. Eponymous botany classification system
101. Sandwich board info
102. Island type
103. Curlers' conclusions?
104. Explosive AC/DC hit?
105. It released 62-D in 1669
106. Big tops
107. Iron oxide
108. Boars and rams
109. It's made with lentils (var.)

DOWN

1. University course genre
2. Stead
3. Apparition
4. Some Europeans
5. It's found in some fruits
6. Total failures
7. Bounce in the air?
8. Math ratio
9. Camels' features
10. *NYPD Blue* actor Morales
11. Tenant
12. It's -on-the-Lake?
13. Former *Maclean's* columnist Fotheringham
14. Public fracas
15. Mobility aid
16. Dose anagram
23. 2016 NBA all-star Thomas
26. DHL competitor
31. Couric or Holmes
33. String shoestrings
34. 1970s rockers' style
35. Bristle
37. Book's beginning
38. Canada's Ellen Page and Rachel McAdams
39. "Dream on!"
40. Sport for Canada's Brooke Henderson
41. The "O" in SRO
43. Burn without a flame (var.)
45. Militant Middle Eastern group
47. Moved aimlessly
49. Camera part
51. Pre-Easter period
54. Sixth Jewish month
56. Celtic jewellery piece
58. Short presentation?
60. These offset the smell of sweat
61. Treble or bass follower
62. See 105-A
63. Prophetic sign, to some
65. The final frontier
67. Canadian-born cosmetics queen Arden
68. Gin flavouring
69. Pointy fork part
71. Ascend
72. Ideal place to live?
75. Kibbutz coinage
77. Board a 747
81. Canadian literary prize
83. Juno-winning vocalist Roberts
85. Prepared to propose
86. Ducks' milieux
88. Christened
89. Campus hangout for him
90. Assess

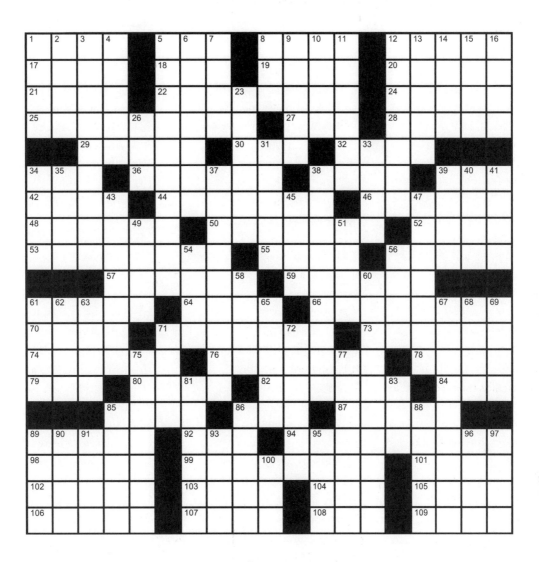

91. Name of an unknown author?

93. Ethnicity of some Japanese

95. BC-born *Knocked Up* actor Rogen

96. *Pitch Perfect* star Kendrick

97. Twofold

100. Nonstress test (abbr.)

81 And the Province Is . . .

Québec

ACROSS

1. Dance that leaves you hanging?
6. Tobacco plug
10. 1990s Philippines president Fidel
15. *Teen Mom* reality star Bookout
19. Passion, in Papineau
20. All the vogue, perhaps
21. Not with the crowd
22. Four Seasons song: "Walk Like _____"
23. **Sweet export**
25. Using one's wiles, say
27. _____ nitrate
28. Distressed
29. **McGill University city**
30. Peak near Jasper: Mount _____ Cavell
32. Benefit to Daniel?
34. Finely woven hosiery fabric
35. Hurries
38. Some scouts hunt for this
41. Young male
42. On stage
43. Certain courses cleanse it
44. They follows las
45. It comes after Christmas?
48. Glossy
49. _____ *delicti*
50. Holiday in Vietnam
51. Supplicate
52. Pierre Trudeau-era deputy prime minister Gray
53. Salad for an emperor?
54. Jail, informally
56. Honours bestowed by Queen Elizabeth (abbr.)
58. Show that's featured drivers in NT and MB: _____ *Road Truckers*
59. Stock transaction option
60. **He's feted every June 24th**
63. Tyrannical ruler
65. Most famous Egyptian king
66. High or low shoe part
67. They're required for fashion models
68. Forewords, for short
70. Support for the poor, old style
74. Tennis court calls
75. Street in 29-A: _____ Sainte-Catherine
76. Diacritical mark over a vowel
77. Nosy Parker
78. Emergency services vehicle acronym
79. Pets' medic
80. Paddled like a voyageur
81. Spacecraft component
82. Disencumber of
83. Pudding-like dessert
84. WestJet employees, in flight
85. Ohio city
88. Peddle goods
89. Online cash-back offer
90. **Official provincial bird**
92. Miniature, in miniature
94. Stag's scent
98. Formal processions
101. **Major waterway**
103. Cake baking appliance
104. Attentive
105. "Gosh!" old style
106. Invest with powers
107. Media mogul Turner, et al.
108. You might put this to the metal
109. Capacious carryall
110. Put your foot down?

DOWN

1. Dalai _____
2. Head of a mosque
3. Down (var.)
4. Notice-posting places
5. Miners lode up on this?
6. Underground chambers
7. Like draconian laws
8. Malarial illness
9. Shed tears
10. Knock aggressively
11. Roddy McDowell played one in several movies
12. Alberta ski resort: _____ Basin
13. *Citizen Kane* star Welles
14. Bowl over
15. City in the centre of Spain
16. Gatineau girlfriends
17. Rideau or Welland follower
18. Fireplace, in Folkestone
24. Taking to court for damages
26. He bore the sky on his shoulders
31. Turn down a request
32. Gamblers' stakes
33. *A Chorus Line* number?
35. Illicit drug, for short
36. Stomach woe
37. Get up, say
38. Indonesian primates
39. Andes animal
40. **One of the oldest mountain ranges in the world**
41. Long lists of complaints?
43. Edgar Allan _____
44. Annual Easter Seals fundraiser
45. Weaken a berm
46. Place to put a bouquet
47. Observer, in olden days
49. Excommunicates
50. Gordie who hosted CBC's *Country Hoedown*
51. Building material from Oregon?
53. Bleeped a bad word
54. Vestibule stand
55. Audio equipment brand
57. *Total Recall* actress Jessica
60. Espies a Dalmatian?
61. Josh

62. Some scams
63. Look at lustfully
64. Al Purdy's "The Country North of Belleville"
69. Canadian TV sports announcer Black
71. Sullen expression (var.)
72. Spicy Mexican sauce
73. Egest
76. Handle too roughly
77. Classify
79. 45s were made of this

80. Military rank (abbr.)
81. Sound from a Siamese (var.)
82. Shrubs for actor Atkinson?
83. Went down, in canasta
84. Scour away
85. Type of tie
86. Poker table scoundrel?
87. Wandered aimlessly
88. Low-lying wetland
89. Positive reviews, say
91. Ontario Coalition of Aboriginal People (abbr.)

92. Security providers on 101-A: Marine Security Enforcement Team (abbr.)
93. *Frozen* song: "Let _____"
95. Word processing menu command
96. Gunk of the earth?
97. Retain
99. MLB game stat
100. City of the Cardinals and the Blues, for short
102. They precede mis

ACROSS

1. *Intelligence for Your Life* radio host John
5. TELUS competitor
9. Treads the boards on Broadway
13. Walter who wrote *A Night to Remember*
17. Water colour?
18. Shoshonean language
19. Created animated characters, say
21. Sound of a contented cat
22. Pumps up the volume?
23. Sincerely
24. Brit Morgan who had a show on CNN
26. Ubiquitous palindrome you've seen before in crosswords?
27. Created mood lighting?
28. Canadian Cancer Society fundraising month
29. She receives May flowers
30. Jacket fastener
31. Type of mitt
35. Muscovite's metal urn
38. *From Here to _____*
40. Golden Canadian Olympian Montgomery
43. Compositions for old court dances
45. Poetic offering
46. *A Series of Unfortunate Events* character Arthur
47. Pose anagram
49. Radio Interface Layer (abbr.)
50. Grasp
52. Tony-winning Canadian actor Carver
54. This lights up your life?
56. Stop
57. Juno winners: _____ Lady Peace
58. Sandbars

59. "_____, Rattle and Roll"
60. Examining in detail (with "over")
63. Tease
64. Busy bees
65. Early Halifax stronghold
66. One half of a 45
68. Hawk's hatchling
69. Mouth, colloquially
70. Wedding dress trim
71. 17th Greek letter
72. It produces *Where Canadian Rockies* guides: _____ Publications
74. Sleepwear (var.)
77. Encrypted Key Exchange (abbr.)
78. It sold for $11.2 million in 2016: _____ *Forms*
81. Monroe's *Gentlemen Prefer Blondes* character
83. Kind of blah
84. Bread to dip in dal
86. "Let me ponder that . . ."
87. Construction site sight
91. There's one of Queen Elizabeth on Parliament Hill
93. Kernel
94. 1935 Civil War-era picture: _____ *the Rose*
95. Steve Jobs first marketed this in 1984
98. Large number
100. Serbian city: _____ Sad
101. He cheats on her
102. It's also known as ladies' fingers
103. Long-running TV comedy: *How _____ Your Mother*
104. Ellen DeGeneres voices this animated fish
105. He bartered his birthright in the Bible

106. Fishing boat gear
107. Hondas and Hyundais

DOWN

1. Paper-like cloth
2. Outfit with gear
3. More certain
4. Group of Seven artist who painted 78-A
5. Singing group: _____ Na Na
6. Family viewing?
7. Seal of _____
8. Melchior, for one
9. Caustic liquids
10. Elkhound's eye tooth?
11. Mollusc parasite
12. Affixed a seal
13. Western University city
14. Queen classic: "Another _____ Bites the Dust"
15. Abode (abbr.)
16. Banned pesticide
20. Bonanza find
25. _____-happy
32. Venomous snakes family
33. Prince William attended this school
34. Security Council veto from Russia
36. Actress Helgenberger, et al.
37. Cast's run-through
39. Shut down and start again, in computerspeak
40. Some wear 69-D
41. Moonfish
42. Infamous Bergman/Grant movie?
44. Drenches
48. Sober
51. World's third-largest stock exchange (abbr.)
53. Not urban

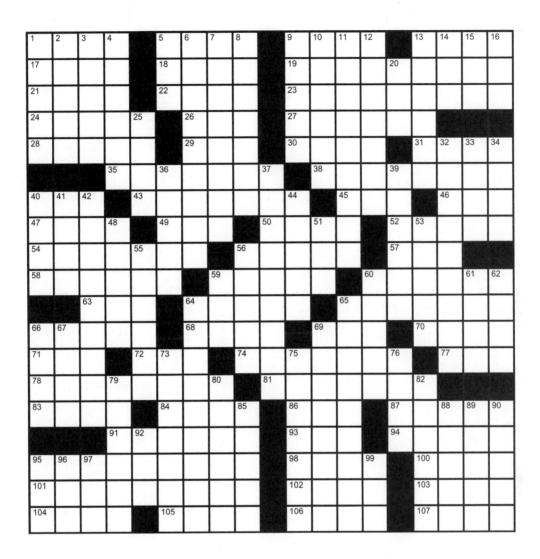

55. Saskatchewan city: Prince _____

56. Like shoddy goods

59. Savoury cooking sauce

60. Indian fig tree (var.)

61. Make out in the back seat?

62. Joy

64. They go off the beaten track

65. Cheese type

66. Former House of Commons role for Kevin Vickers: Sergeant-at-_____

67. "Scram!"

69. Skullcap

73. Underseas mammal

75. Kennedy's successor

76. Bits of time, for short

79. In a meddlesome manner

80. Bad tummy symptom

82. Sarcastic

85. India's first prime minister

88. Bouquet

89. 1985 Corey Hart Juno-winning single: "_____ Surrender"

90. Rewrites to amend

92. Toluene compound, for short

95. Word repeated in a 1991 Tom Cochrane song title

96. Flap

97. Junkyard dog, perhaps?

99. "I _____ robbed!"

Legislative Levity

Poking fun at politics

ACROSS

1. CTV daytime program: *The Marilyn Denis* _____
5. Brief presentations?
10. Downtown Hamilton landmark: _____ Park
14. Gardener's aid: Miracle-_____
17. Lab worker, for short
18. Not suitable
19. Workplace for non-union employees
21. Dead set against
22. Lobbies made of glass (var.)
23. Most irritable about an exam?
24. Bit of a hitch?
25. Neighbourhood pub goers?
27. Midway workers (var.)
28. "O that thou _____ hearkened to my commandments!"
30. Outer space streak of light
32. Table part
33. Daily word game in many Canadian newspapers
35. Country bumpkin
37. Beck who brought hydro to Ontario
41. Oxidized coatings
44. Kosher shopper's shop
45. Joe Clark government cabinet minister MacDonald
46. Recording device
47. Potato bud
49. Output from an ovary
51. Albanian spending money
52. Kids' science fair display
55. Flip-flop
56. Donald and Marla; Donald and Ivana
58. **Conservative's vessel?**
60. Circular ocean current
63. Itinerant Saharan
65. Eternal
67. Call from a cote
68. Small warships fleet
71. It might be bitter?
72. University of Alberta online education option: _____ Portal
74. Former Ontario TV network: _____ Broadcast System
75. Doctor's diagnostic process
77. Just fine
78. Day to remember, for Caesar
79. "Hardly!"
80. Great gabfest?
82. Average, on the golf course
84. Canadian-born Pittsburgh Penguin Kris
86. Irish playwright's contemptuous expression?
90. It makes the heart grow fonder
94. Ascended the stairs
96. Sonata's last section
97. Décolletage displays this
99. Like confused seniors
100. European freshwater fish: Common _____
101. Scars and spots
102. *Chinatown* director Polanski
103. Archipelago part
104. Summer, to a Montrealer
105. Pierre Berton classic: *The _____ Spike*
106. Severe, aboard ship?
107. Kokanee makes it

DOWN

1. Secret supply
2. Body art dye
3. Group of eight
4. **Politician's happy dance?**
5. Having two purposes
6. Buries
7. 1992 Hockey Hall of Fame inductee Dionne
8. Painkilling medication
9. Like day-old bread
10. Inherited
11. Angola and Algeria are members of this (abbr.)
12. Used car purchase, for example
13. Between, in Bécancour
14. South Asian cuisine ingredient
15. Like red cheeks
16. Makes a choice
20. 1960s CBC show: _____ *Jubilee*
26. Cold _____
29. Synchronized the strings, say
31. Golden precept?
34. Of matrimony
36. Brownish-yellow pigment
38. Pet lover's leftovers?
39. Frequently used verb
40. 1988 Leonard Cohen record: "I'm Your _____"
41. Heap of dirty laundry
42. MasterCard rival, for short
43. Pay close attention
44. **US senator's stone?**
45. Not to
47. "To _____ is human"
48. 2002 movie: *Divine Secrets of the _____ Sisterhood*
50. "Physician, heal _____"
53. Lots
54. Port on the Red Sea
57. "As it were," said the orator?
59. Government program: _____ Age Security
61. Too quick to scratch?
62. Nunavut, directionally from the Northwest Territories
64. Sino-Tibetan language category
66. Discard a small piece of paper?
68. Its motto is "Fidelity, Bravery, Integrity"
69. Boy
70. Branch angle
73. **Left-winger's hangout?**

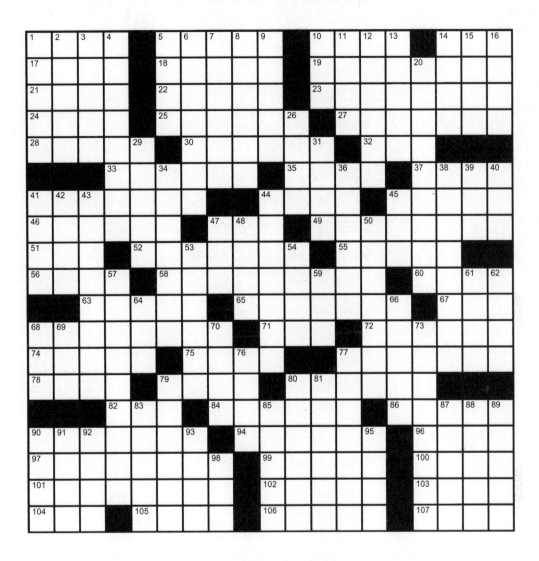

76. Some
77. Like a gaunt geometrician?
79. Sect's secrets
80. Is incapable of
81. Prompt
83. Ear bone

85. 1985 Canadian fundraising song: "_____ Are Not Enough"
87. Margaret Laurence CanCon classic: *A Bird in the* _____
88. Cause confusion
89. One of a fisherman's pair
90. Peak point?

91. Honk of a horn
92. All dried out
93. Coop crop
95. Magical entertainers: _____ & Teller
98. Ontario clock setting (abbr.)

ACROSS

1. She loved Narcissus
5. Cause injury to
9. Ooh and _____
12. You might ride this in Montréal
17. Wander aimlessly
18. "That's fine"
19. Drooled like a dog
21. Highest level
22. Early Canadian railway pioneer Donald
23. Sophisticated lady, perhaps
24. Polished, in appearance
26. Singalong activity
28. Does some landscaping
29. Scottish landowner
31. Cattle farm young'uns
33. Preschooler
35. Hamlet
37. Confederate of Calista Flockhart?
38. Golden Horde member (var.)
43. Asian buffalo
45. When the sun is at its highest
47. Buckingham _____
48. Mexican music superstar Rivera
50. Dress with elaborate care
51. Renters
52. Doctor of Nursing Practice (abbr.)
54. City in Germany
56. "I've _____ a Crush on You"
57. Repeated musical motif
61. Some teeth
63. Arapaho enemy
64. Ready to do battle?
68. Heading at sea (abbr.)
69. "Easy peasy!"
71. Defensive trenches
73. Put in stitches?
77. Some punctuation marks
78. Old-style layout technique
80. Prima donna
81. You might spot one on a safari
82. Database command
83. Count on for support
85. Age when you enter your second decade
86. Microscope eyepieces
89. Instruct in a classroom
91. Canadian financier Jackman, et al.
95. Type of summertime market
97. Surrounded by
100. Sometime reason for visiting Vegas
102. Surveys
104. *Star Trek: The Next Generation* counsellor Deanna
105. "I Just Want to Celebrate" band
106. Weather _____
107. Make money
108. Canadian furniture retailer: The _____
109. Some UBC degs.
110. 1980 "The Dukes of Hazzard" spinoff
111. Elite police team (abbr.)

DOWN

1. Rase anagram
2. Canadian model Rocha
3. U.S. Steel Canada headquarters city
4. Greek letter
5. Cause for cheering at Rogers Centre
6. Rap sheet abbr.
7. _____ and file
8. Asian starling (var.)
9. Attacker
10. In a remote manner
11. Toronto attraction: _____ Hall of Fame
12. Wharton graduate's achievement (abbr.)
13. Underwater wrigglers
14. Huey, Dewey and Louie, say
15. No longer part of the workforce (abbr.)
16. Lofty works
20. Catafalque
25. Tip of a pen
27. Book lover
30. "Good to the last _____"
32. Subs
33. _____ Mahal
34. _____ *Flew Over the Cuckoo's Nest*
36. "Sundown" singer Lightfoot
39. Steamed: _____ *vapeur*
40. Former Air Canada subsidiary
41. Occupation of 96-D
42. Takes it easy
44. *The King* _____
46. Prefix for Georgian or Gothic
47. US VP Mike
49. Nasty jibe
51. Cask
53. Nova Scotia's Denny Doherty was one of these
55. 1960s sitcom: _____ *Ed*
57. Whisky measurement
58. Ottoman
59. Electromagnetism unit
60. _____-for-tat
62. Origin of a flower
65. Pigweeds, by another name
66. Speakers' platforms
67. This welcomes you home?
70. Finished first
72. Bird feeder filler
74. Secede
75. Bette Davis movie: *All About _____*
76. Ontario-born NHLer Boyle who's played on four teams

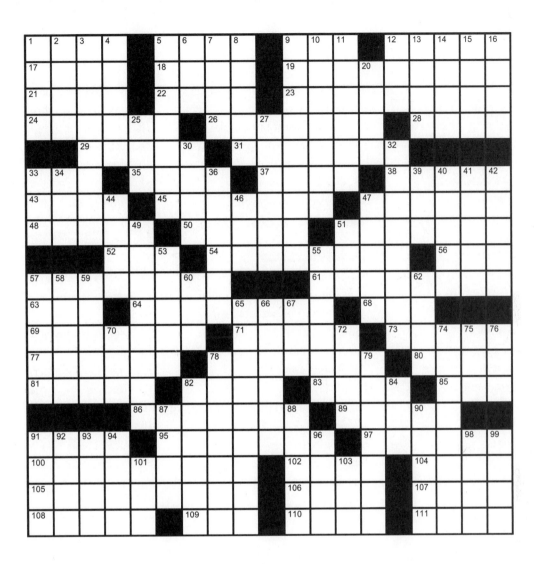

78. Grits, Italian style
79. Makes happy
82. Fantastic
84. Sweet potato
87. Induced state of sleep
88. Colander
90. Lists one's resources

91. Thyme, for example
92. Banned apple orchard spray
93. *Footloose* actress Singer
94. Build as per particular requirements
96. Canadian-born 2017 Golden Globe winner Gosling

98. Eastern North American bird
99. Bit of colour
101. Mouse-sighter's cry
103. British musician/composer Brian

85 Digging Deep . . .

For top Canadian exports

ACROSS

1. 1996 game: Trivial Pursuit _____ IV
6. Actor Robert's pile?
11. They always agree?
17. **Canada is the #1 world exporter of this**
18. Car cleaning products brand: _____ All
19. Night sky "eagle"
20. Drool
21. "Great" Muppet
22. Neutron star
23. Without purpose
24. Like a good dog
27. In an appropriate manner
28. Feel regret
29. Finished
31. Frank Sinatra film: *The Manchurian _____*
36. Coal, in Canada
40. Old-style spreads for breads
41. Wash away soap
44. WWII attack type
45. **Gemstones mined in the North**
47. Commits a cyber crime
49. Pixar films FX
50. Large, low cloud
51. They live in Novi Sad
52. Usurp control from
54. 2013 Michael Bublé single: "_____ a Beautiful Day"
55. Canadians go to these at least once every four years
56. Exercise regime: _____ Bo
57. There's a lot of this in bat caves
60. She might wear these in the family?
61. Cartilage discs
65. Runway tower work grp.
66. _____ Hawkins dance
67. **Light bulb filament metal**

68. Instructional books
71. _____ of the crop
73. Absorb information
74. Amontillado and manzanilla
76. Goes under, like a U-boat
78. Dictatorial leader
81. Managed the troops
82. ". . . _____ came a spider"
85. Untanned leather
87. Speech problem
91. Singer Rucker of Hootie & the Blowfish fame
93. Sots who prefer Chablis?
94. Early Greeks gathered here (var.)
96. Sponge apertures
97. Devoured
98. **Alloy production ingredient**
99. Aquatic "carpet"?
100. Flippant
101. Concert at Calgary's Saddledome, say

DOWN

1. **Export that shines**
2. Bibliography abbr.
3. Blue for an able seaman?
4. Put to good _____
5. Cover up?
6. Philosophy mentor
7. Like grapes in vats
8. Pregnancy procedure, for short
9. Deceive
10. Scandinavian currency
11. Bark like a Bichon
12. Canada lies far north of this "line"
13. **Fertilizer ingredient**
14. Fog
15. Israeli airline
16. None, at Loch Lochy
17. Second-to-last Greek letter

25. NHLers grow these during the playoffs
26. Makes minor adjustments
28. Arborio rice dish
30. Horus' mother
31. Some delivery types (abbr.)
32. Hopped off a horse, say
33. In the vicinity
34. Eminent environment?
35. Xmas song contraction
37. TV reality show: *The Amazing _____ Canada*
38. Fags
39. Word processing menu option
42. Safe haven
43. Canadian restaurant chain since 1982
46. They come before xis, in Greek
48. *Hawaii Five-0* network
51. Part of SST
52. Achieved through trickery
53. *Mad About You* actor Paul
55. Hippies' home
56. Former Leafs Apps and Armstrong wore this number
57. Groups of whales
58. Speed skater Marc Gagnon won Olympic gold twice in this state
59. Cane anagram
60. Some old Toyotas
61. Speak indistinctly
62. Tundra animal
63. Prepare for burial, archaically
64. Quaint places to stay
66. Sexy skirt opening
67. It comes after sigma
69. **Nuclear reactor fuel source**
70. Bitter salad leaves
72. Description of Fifi's cycle
75. Unstressed middle vowels
77. Dennis is this, in the comics
79. Indian yogurt-based dish

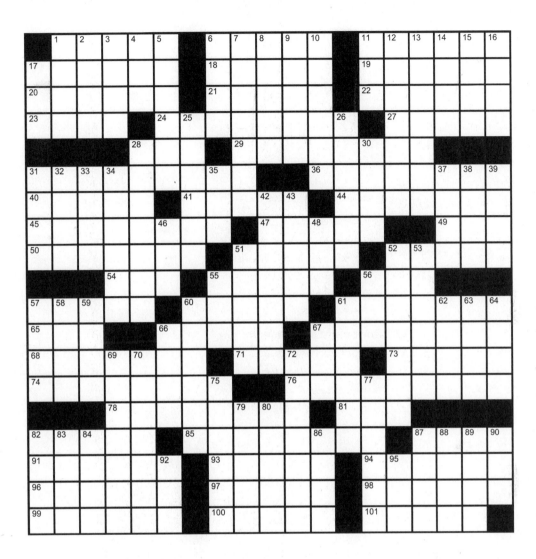

80. Canadian political trailblazer MacPhail
82. Hubbubs
83. Repair a detached retina
84. West Coast sea mammal

86. Spot, old style
87. Brain component
88. Canada's Ken Taylor was ambassador here
89. It's mined across Canada

90. Initials of a former 24 Sussex Drive resident
92. Convened
95. Jeb Bush's FL job

ACROSS

1. Château Frontenac, for example
6. Arched blade tool
10. Fast food joint: _____ Bell
14. Mates' meeting place
17. Lickety-split, say
18. Tilt to one side
19. Check the sleeping kids: Look _____
20. "N," in Spanish
21. Canadians Donald or Kiefer
23. Occasional Sicilian spewer
24. Eighteen-wheeler
25. Telephone operator's accessory, for short
26. Creepy
27. Takes away from
29. BC destination: Pacific _____ National Park Reserve
30. MacDonald co-star, in '30s movies
32. Lecher or libertine
33. Classifieds for some lovelorn folks
38. Gross
42. Honshu port city
43. Fertilizer component
45. Early Guess Who hit: "Shakin' _____"
46. Olympus cupbearer
48. Some criminal trials
50. Apportion resources (with "out")
51. Broad scope of a plan
52. Canadian singer Sainte-Marie
53. Merry-go-round animal, to a toddler (var.)
54. Toronto's prov.
55. Tim Hortons treat
56. Cotillion VIP
57. Imitating
60. Joins metals
61. Large-billed seabird
65. Bit of fluff
66. Brusque
67. Montréal landmark: Notre-Dame _____
68. Canadians give thanks in this month
70. Groups of three
72. Long-time CBC Radio personality Gzowski
73. Like an Asian island native
75. Toss off the boat?
77. YMCA word
78. Impulse
80. Place for two peas?
81. They're squirrelly?
84. Take advice, say
86. _____-in
90. Leftover bit
91. Hullabaloos
92. Name of two places in Nova Scotia
94. Genealogy word
95. Subject of some paintings
96. Ink _____ test
97. Canvas holder
98. "_____ Save the Queen"
99. Top spot, say
100. Puts into the pot
101. Dilettantish

DOWN

1. Leftovers dish
2. Creator's masterful output
3. *Argo* actor Donovan
4. Genuine, in Germany
5. Poe poem: "Annabel _____"
6. Suite movement
7. Column since 1956: _____ *Abby*
8. Most goofy
9. Completed
10. Cloth colouring technique
11. The "A" in AM
12. Handles the remote?
13. Hot, at the craps table?
14. Psychic, perhaps?
15. Complex place to live?
16. Pleads
22. Equestrian's restraint
28. Members of the Cars drive these?
29. Travelocity mascot: _____ Gnome
31. Emmy-winning actress: Julia Louis-_____
33. Canadian corn dog brand
34. Biblical twins: Jacob and _____
35. Verbal bluster
36. Niagara Falls landmark
37. Fairway ball position
39. Diversify
40. Earns
41. Annual Canadian event: _____ Cup
44. Like chubbier cheeks
47. Sinus doc
49. Little amphibian
52. Support with a pillow?
53. Rooftop landing spot
55. Crosby moniker: _____ Bingle
56. From, in France
57. Immensely
58. Linear printing unit
59. Hinted
60. Beyoncé hit: "If I _____ a Boy"
61. Canadians need these to travel abroad
62. New York Mets ballpark: _____ Field
63. Executed a perfect serve
64. Nostril, old style
66. Got edgy about verb conjugation?
67. Feathery neckwear
69. Cowboy's attire item
71. Freezing
74. Rideau Hall is on this Drive

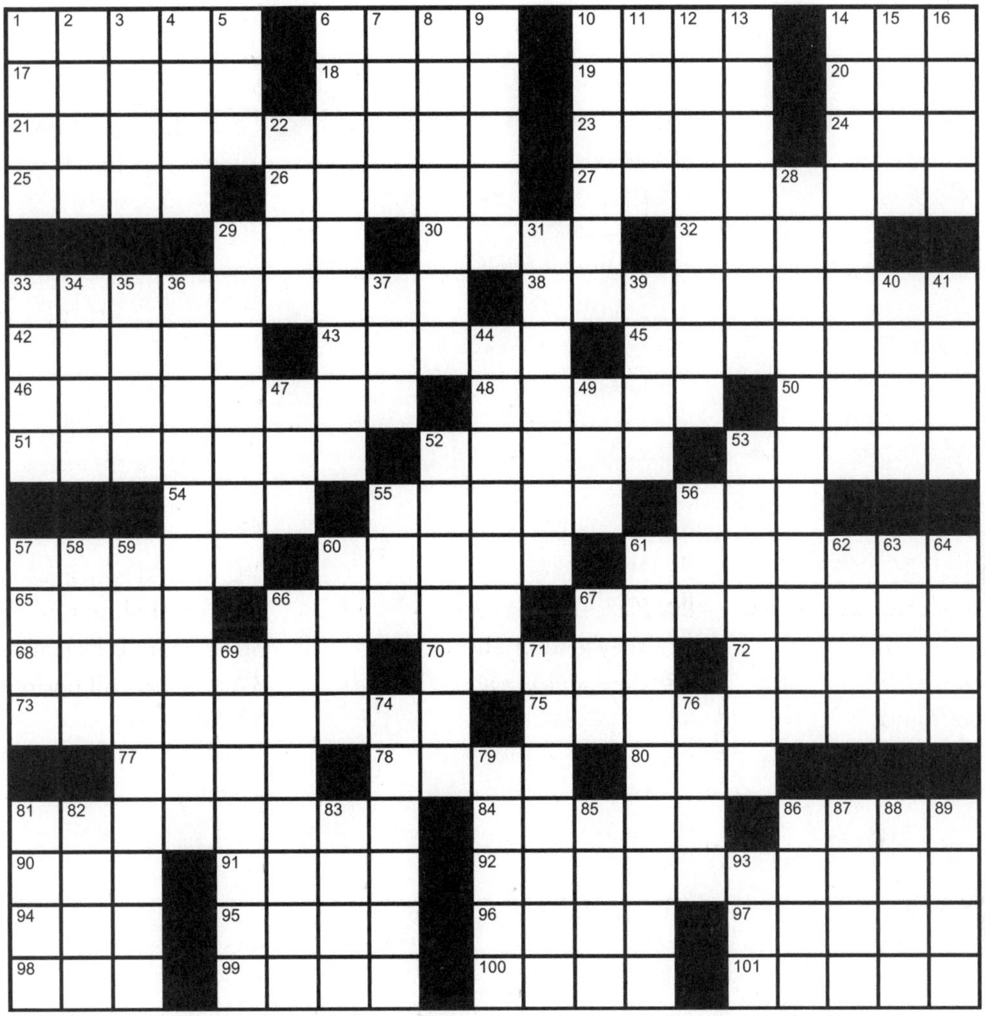

76. Singers Tennille or Braxton
79. Viola da _____
81. _____ Kong
82. Store-bought cookie type
83. Went by bike
85. Walked
86. Polaris or Sirius
87. 72-A, for example
88. Needs to pay up
89. Justin Bieber song: "_____ Thing I Ever Get For Christmas"
93. Black or Yellow

Solution on page 229

Where You Live?

A little home-based humour

ACROSS

1. Holy war
6. Adjust an instrument?
12. Alaska Dispatch News (abbr.)
15. 15-year comic strip: *The _____ Side*
18. The nose knows these
20. Less fatty
21. Celeb's bestseller, often
22. Signature song from Vancouver's 54-40: "_____ Day in Your Life"
23. 1994 Rush single: "_____ Agent"
24. One way to ship stuff
26. Ribonucleic Acid (abbr.)
27. Stored fodder
29. Daring
30. Confessed
32. Dry up
34. Twinkles
35. French religious figures
37. Cleaners' cloths
38. Maritime fog: _____-souper
39. At hand
43. Mercury barometer pressure unit
44. Smarts
45. Pleasing to the ear
47. Hardly cooked
48. Decorators' timepieces?
50. Bonanza at The Brick?
51. Unwelcome electronic messages
52. Bard's sunset contraction
53. Sue Grafton book: _____ *for Deadbeat*
54. Pine for a little lady?
55. Private yacht's staff
57. "_____ had it!"
58. Passions, in Pennsylvania
60. Pasture baby
61. Charged particle
62. Enlarge one's domicile

64. **Domestic work for the self-employed?**
68. Indian area known for its tea
71. Sash for a kimono
72. Swallow a big 7-Eleven drink?
73. Constructs a structure
77. Like veggie tray veggies
78. H.H. Munro pseudonym
80. Elizabethan era instrument
81. US inventor's monogram
82. Curve
83. Bikini tops
85. Student leaders?
87. Workout rooms, in olden days
89. Grimm giant
90. Canadian poetry anthology: _____ *Form*
91. Pouches for yolks
92. Impale
93. 11-year Ottawa Senator Wade
95. Compass point
96. Asian cuisine thickener
97. Some pickles
98. Rut on a record
100. Rock that falls from space
102. Opposite of first class on old steamers
105. Lisbon lady
106. Inuit legend whale
109. Bricklayer's box
110. Embittering
113. Former Liberal MP Copps
114. One of a common dozen
115. Never, in Nuremberg
116. 1751 Henry Fielding novel
117. Sitting room, in Scottsdale
118. July holiday: Canada _____
119. CFL game scores
120. Search for clues?
121. Hot sandwiches

DOWN

1. Semi-precious green gem
2. _____ Ore Company of Canada
3. **Grocery savings option for a rancher?**
4. He fluctuates between exhibitionism and reticence
5. Texas city
6. Piz Bernina, for one
7. Tetley squares
8. Fortune teller's cards
9. _____ *Tom's Cabin*
10. "All You _____ Is Love"
11. Express Rail Link (abbr.)
12. "Humble" lodgings?
13. Take apart the fireplace?
14. Guess Who hit
15. Nova Scotia National Historic Site: _____ Edward
16. Grammy and Juno winner Murray
17. Crazy Canuck Ken
19. Leak out
25. **Trouble for the Queen?**
28. Rowing boats
31. They ruled in Russia
33. "Darn!" to the exterminator
34. Neuter, at the stable
35. On the Caspian, say
36. 1960s Maple Leafs goalie great Johnny
38. Small dogs
40. At a speedy pace
41. Canadian specialty cable channel
42. Oman neighbour
44. Trick-taking card game
45. Mar
46. Deserves a raise, say
49. Data discs
50. Liver secretion
54. Wise biblical guys

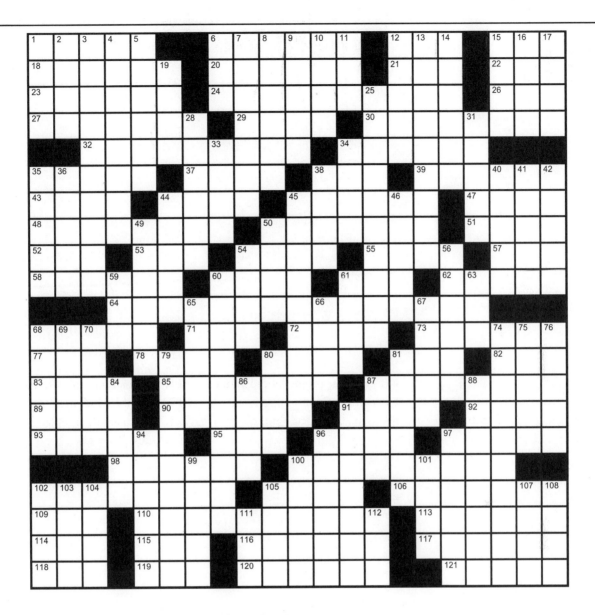

56. QB Moon who won five Grey Cups with the Eskimos
59. Goose, in Granada
60. Malady for backwoods dwellers?
61. With nothing to do
63. Clairol hair product
65. Insignificant coin?
66. Superfans who love filberts?
67. Redblacks and Senators
68. Shady garden spot (var.)
69. Boot camp boss, for short
70. Ground cover

74. Scenic spot for Newfoundlanders?
75. Accused's courtroom proceeding
76. Union foes' wound reminders?
79. Tryptophan, for example
80. It precedes ranger or wolf
81. Business bigwig
84. Grasslike plant
86. Sticking point?
87. Guarantee, old style
88. So to speak, in the past?
91. Rushdie novel: *The* _____ *Verses*
94. Not on the mark
96. Mentally weak, in old age

97. United Arab Emirates currency
99. Gothic mouldings
100. Choral composition
101. Hoarse voice sound
102. Small storage building
103. Roman Forum attire
104. Avant-garde, in fashion
105. *South Pacific* song: "There Is Nothing Like a _____"
107. Several used cars?
108. Metallica drummer Ulrich
111. Naughty
112. Gangster's gun

ACROSS

1. _____ Québécois
5. Berry used in smoothies
9. Box for theatre patrons
13. 1975 Bachman-Turner Overdrive song: "Take It Like _____"
17. Bulgarian money
18. Hopeless, in bygone days
19. Copied 86-A?
20. Window part
21. Above
22. Saliva
23. Choppers end their flights here
25. River that passes by Cairo
26. 1960s abstractionism
28. Event impetus
29. It opens the door
30. Fortune and fame
32. Long-time Yugoslavian leader
33. Loud crowd's sound
35. Church cleric
37. Disparities
41. Stitched again
44. 1911 Nobel Prize winner in chemistry Marie
45. Radiator covering
47. Humpty Dumpty shaped
48. Illuminated from behind
50. Samuel Woodworth poem: "The Old _____ Bucket"
51. Venus de _____
52. Roadside pylons
53. Scientists' milieux
55. Little isle in a lake
56. Camera apparatus
58. Alberta-born author W.P.
60. Some magazine pages
61. "_____ on Down the Road"
62. Papyrus plant family
63. Opera first produced in 1871
65. Glove box or trunk (abbr.)
67. Eaton of Canadian retail renown
69. Physics units
70. Fireplace
72. Splinter groups
73. Most hurtful?
74. It might soar by the shore
75. Require
77. Movie theatre, in Trois-Rivières
78. Automatic Display Call Indicator (abbr.)
80. 42-D, perhaps (var.)
82. African chieftain
86. Monkeys and gorillas
90. Parkinson's treatment
91. Actors Carvey or Delany
92. 2016 Grey Cup champs
94. Brownish-red colour
95. "-zoic" periods
96. Chemical compound
97. Unpleasant odour
98. Exploitative person
99. Tee off
100. Cold North or South place
101. See George Smiley?
102. Colorado locale: _____ Verde National Park
103. Auctioneer's final word

DOWN

1. Like a clean slate
2. Allow entry
3. Moulding style
4. The Canso Causeway connects this to the mainland
5. Foot race loser?
6. Canadian export
7. Suffix with sect or Unit
8. Announced something new
9. "Well, _____-di-dah!"
10. Intl. oil grp.
11. Italian sorbet
12. Textual tinkering
13. Written defence of one's beliefs
14. Actress Pickford who was born in Toronto
15. Termites' kin?
16. Cozy home, colloquially
24. Former Canadian NHLer Verbeek
27. Moves like Miley?
31. Metal tack
34. Be indebted to
36. Gaelic gatherings
38. With a high pH
39. Taurus constellation
40. Mailed
41. TO attraction that opened in 1914
42. Villain
43. Product pitcher
44. Canada's Mark de Jonge, for example
46. Kennedy family matriarch
48. Jump-start
49. Tart to the tongue
52. When doubled, a Latin dance
54. Mad cow disease acronym
57. Badgers' home
58. Timpani instrument
59. Some church speakers
60. American College of Healthcare Executives (abbr.)
62. Twitter or Tumblr: _____ media
64. Clock setting in 4-D (abbr.)
66. First words?
68. *Beowulf* beverage
69. Harron who created Charlie Farquharson
71. Acre, metric style
73. Crooner Frank
76. Female family members
77. Thickets
79. Vancouver's "King of Swing" Richards

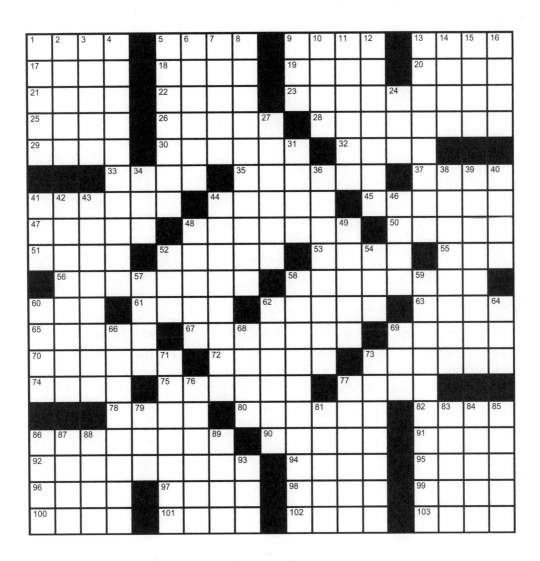

81. Rodent
83. Hockey great Lemieux
84. Totally
85. Destroyed, in Derby

86. _____ school
87. Nevada city
88. "White Wedding" rocker Billy
89. Beehive made of straw

93. BC route: Sea-to-_____ Highway

89 Special Deliveries

Here's the birthplace; name the prime minister

ACROSS

1. Animals' "hands"
5. Actress Blanchett, star of *The Aviator*
9. Takes a little off
14. Prodded
19. Pasty-faced
20. Former LA Laker Lamar
21. "Diamond Mine" group: Blue _____
22. Sycophant
23. Notable New Mexico town
24. _____ of the above
25. Flip over
26. Ammonia compound
27. Like a perfect Dalmatian?
29. **Montréal, Québec**
31. Venezuelan plains
32. Oomph
33. Without any mirth
34. Analgesics relieve this
35. Illusory hope
38. Fruity cocktail: Mai _____
39. Panelled altarpieces
43. You do this at The Keg
44. Printer brand name
47. Sad
49. It comes after "soh"
50. Shoppers _____ Mart
52. Amarone and Asti
54. Lambs' mamas
55. Tender and loving concern?
56. Absolutely necessary
58. Staffs the guys' locker room?
59. Jeweller's magnifying glass
60. Mediators
62. **Grand-Pré, Nova Scotia**
63. More conventional, in attitude
66. **High River, Alberta**
67. National Ballet of Canada dancers, sometimes
68. **Amherst, Nova Scotia**
69. Canadian Armed Forces ranks
71. Opera highlights
72. Spur on
73. Dental procedure numbing agent (var.)
77. Shatter with a hammer
78. Floozie's pastry?
79. You might keep your dog on this
80. Oaf (var.)
81. Escape, Evacuation and Rescue (abbr.)
82. Business person's injustice?
85. C-3PO, for one
87. Appeared in print, say
88. Shipbuilding sites
90. Cheerleaders' shout
92. Frequent federal election issue
94. Manipulates
95. Leaves a black-and-blue mark
98. Many millennia
99. iPad, for example
102. **Newtonbrook, Ontario**
103. Like a punch-drunk pirate?
106. Use TNT
107. Old Finnish currency
108. Harry Belafonte signature song
110. Install ceramic flooring
111. End of a shoelace
112. Privet
113. Maple genus
114. Was aware of
115. Pink hit: "_____ Your Glass"
116. Laundry or hair appliance
117. Order to an Otterhound
118. "I haven't seen you for _____!"

DOWN

1. Canadian light infantry unit, briefly: Princess _____
2. Lickety-split, for short
3. Party hearty
4. Organized method
5. Gretzky won this twice: _____ Smythe Trophy
6. Benedick and Beatrice's brouhaha?
7. Lone Ranger's companion
8. Board for a manicurist
9. **Ottawa, Ontario**
10. Entices, at the Calgary Stampede?
11. "Don't get any funny _____!"
12. List of diners' choices
13. Add grass
14. ENMAX or ATCO
15. Gypsies' tongue
16. Add flab
17. Type of Caribbean taro
18. Goes platinum blonde, say
28. Org. that impacts Canada's oil price
30. Of last month (abbr.)
31. Some Scandinavians
33. Building maintenance employee
34. Church organ adjuncts
35. Cash to spend in Accra
36. Injure
37. Despoiler
39. Morning breaks?
40. Former Québec Liberal leader Ryan
41. **Toronto, Ontario**
42. Glossy finishes
45. "You can bank _____"
46. Religious order newbie (var.)
48. Listened
51. South American fruit tree
53. Closed an envelope
55. 2017 poetry collection from Canada's Crosbie: _____ *of the Future*
57. Counsels, in olden days
58. Mere human being?
59. Unwilling to
61. Greek letter

62. Of the sea bottom
63. Made one's claim
64. **Richmond, England**
65. Beehives' building
67. See 10-D
69. Stanley and Grey
70. _____-death experience
72. Stares at rudely
74. Like a tightly packed crowd
75. Middle Eastern religious officiant

76. Rabbit
78. Musical direction to not play
82. Horse show ribbon
83. Take care of the catering, say
84. **Saint-Lin, Canada East**
86. 10-year Manitoba premier Gary
89. Edible seaweeds
91. Belonging to that chap
93. Sound or island, in BC
95. Like sippy cup straws
96. Fizzy drinks

97. Portray
99. One way up, at Whistler
100. Pond plant
101. Indonesian vacationers' island
102. House of Lords member
103. Like slasher movies
104. Jolly TV show until 2015?
105. Evergreen shrubs
107. Carleton prof's deg.
109. Assenter's vote

ACROSS

1. Streisand's stinging remark?
5. Senegal neighbour
9. Reynolds of *Deliverance*
13. Egyptian deity
17. Sounds like 2-D?
18. Saudi Arabia neighbour
19. On the ocean
20. _____ *kleine Nachtmusik*
21. It's not so much
22. Quaker _____
23. Town north of Toronto
25. William Lyon _____ King
27. Most maudlin on a rainy day?
28. Gists
30. Girl Guide knot type
31. Spoiled one's copybook?
34. Freshly bottled, like wine
36. "_____ it seems"
40. Groucho hosted this: _____ *Your Life*
41. Donnybrook
42. Sometime British Open venue: Royal _____
43. *Entourage* actress Debi
44. Judicial order
45. _____ of First Nations
48. Organic compound
49. Fireplace piece
50. Farley Mowat book: *People of the _____*
51. _____ appeal
52. Mercifulness
54. Language family that includes Finnish
56. Long-time Canadian equestrian Millar
59. Gigantic
60. Traffic tie-up
61. Falling out between friends, say
65. Italian macaroons
67. Butts
68. Bread or gravy (var.)
69. Penny-pincher
70. Eastern Europeans
72. Scenic points of view?
73. Hillside in Scotland
74. Take a drag
76. Leave in the lurch, say
77. Craps cubes
79. Nova Scotia town
81. Confederate
85. Extra payment on a payment
89. Wealthy ruler
90. 2.54 centimetres, in Chicago
91. Bridge crossing fee
92. Identical
93. Spring religious observance
94. You might buy one at Christmas
95. "Rise Up" Canadian band: Parachute _____
96. Studied, say
97. Old Ireland language
98. Some Hebrew letters
99. Blood compound containing iron

DOWN

1. Soothing substance
2. Space
3. Reduced Instruction Set Computer (abbr.)
4. Sport invented by Canadian James Naismith
5. Evening horizon happening
6. In awe
7. *A mari usque ad mare*, for example
8. Lack of confidence
9. Musicians' tool?
10. Cannabis aficionado
11. Fix the electrical
12. Pressed down
13. Gaseous
14. *Holmes on Homes* star
15. Loonies, say
16. Bottom line, in Bath
24. Jungle animal
26. Fruity-smelling chemical compound
29. Related on one's mother's side
31. 1986 movie: *Stand _____*
32. You might get one from Scotiabank
33. Clear liqueur
35. Happy dresser's duds?
37. Former mayor Ford, et al.
38. Bottom of the foot
39. Cameo stone
41. Not well-behaved
42. *Tootsie* actress Garr
44. You might get a slap on this
46. US retailer in Canada
47. What 46-D does
49. Minuscule insect
53. Endless amount of time
54. Waterloo or Western
55. Mark with parallel intersecting lines
56. Poetic foot
57. Important person, in the Arabic world
58. US org. that hires Canadian astronauts
60. Famed Milan building: La _____
62. Letter before kappa
63. Type of jacket
64. Stun with a gun?
66. Fine-tuned text for a second time
68. Merriment
71. Newborn's accoutrements
72. Gives a guarantee
74. Eavestrough adjunct in winter
75. Not as far away
76. Coerced
78. Labour concerns arm of the UN

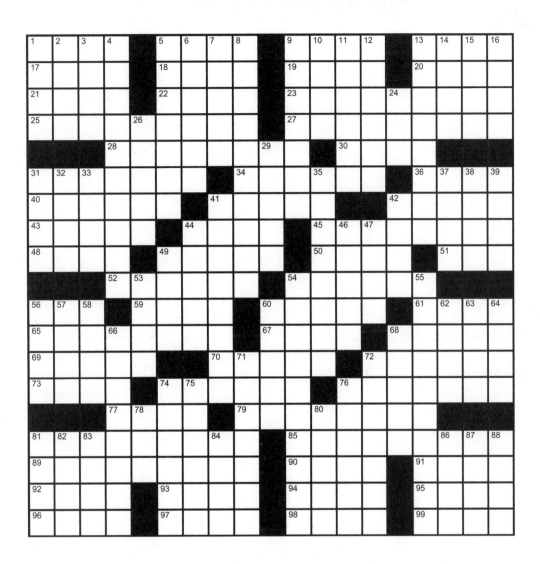

80. Atwood literary contemporary

81. Abbey area

82. Scold celebrity chef Bobby?

83. Get smoking mad?

84. Enjoys a sun bath

86. Jack Bauer, for Canada's Kiefer Sutherland

87. Down in the dumps

88. Major European river

91 Eponymous Adjectives

Match the word with its namesake

ACROSS

1. Brief bit of news?
5. Pat down, at the police station
10. Canadian singers Connors and Cochrane
14. Actress Kelly who became a princess
19. Russian legislative assembly
20. Assisted: _____ hand
21. Not so much?
22. Short scouting mission?
23. One who pronounces properly
25. Soft, wet soil
26. Beethoven composition: "Für _____"
27. Creamy Italian cheese
28. Besides
29. Armour plates, of old (var.)
30. Sheds
31. European Economic Community (abbr.)
33. **Like Don's deeds?**
35. Capsules, in Colorado
38. Veneer on fancy furniture
40. Minister's msg.
41. Darlings
42. Some McGill degs.
43. "No" vote
44. _____ of the Lost Ark
49. Small French case
50. Centre of a plum
51. It's at the end of a cigar
52. Tabbies' trees?
53. Like puffins and petrels
55. Pronoun for a female
56. Teensy, in Troon
57. Actress Bridget Fonda, to Jane
58. Made up of three
59. How long johns keep you warm
62. Gestures made by Churchill
63. **Like cut-throat politics?**
66. Arizona flatland
70. Precedes, in time

71. Roman "Ars Poetica" poet
76. Pleasant smell
78. Acclaimed 1982 Canadian film: _____ Plouffe
79. U of C teaching aides
80. Prague currency units
81. Dangerous current
83. Google rival
84. *Just Watch Me*, for example
85. Storage totes
86. See 30-A
87. Greek letter
88. Victoria tourist attraction: Fan _____ Alley
89. Sparkly stone
90. Possesses
91. Summer cooler, for short
93. Knight's flag
94. **Like some slips?**
98. Before, old style
99. Poetic phrase?
100. Like an exhausted person's eyes
101. Canadian actor Ted, to actress Megan
103. Like silver that's not sterling?
108. Brightly coloured loincloth
109. Toronto Blue Jay Bautista beginning in 2008
110. Molson XXX, for example
111. *The Jungle Book* wolf
112. Ottawa landmark: National _____ Centre
113. Regional flora and fauna
114. It's adjacent to the humerus
115. Legendary Swedish forest creature
116. Lacking vigour
117. More cunning
118. "_____ does it"

DOWN

1. The same (Lat.)
2. Fish food?
3. Big Aussie birds
4. **Like some candidates?**
5. Coquettes
6. Harvests
7. Jump _____
8. Druggies
9. Former LA Laker Abdul-Jabbar
10. Diplomacy
11. Public state of disgrace
12. Cat's cry (var.)
13. Dump of a dwelling, say
14. **Like some chants?**
15. Got a fire going again
16. Advisory Committee on International Students and Immigration (abbr.)
17. Term used in trig
18. Some compass points (abbr.)
24. Embryonic membranes
29. Leave for a cleric
32. European arts school
34. Tel Aviv citizen
35. Masterful
36. Taxi time tracker
37. He succeeded Catherine the Great
38. Grain morsel
39. _____-di-dah
42. Pen brand name
45. 554, to Caesar
46. Sword for a sport
47. Sprinters' competition
48. See 18-D
50. Rice dish
51. Race leader's status
52. Prisoners' phones?
54. Leg
55. Backs away from
56. Charles became prince of this in 1969

59. Tossed
60. Genre of Canadian bands Helix or Anvil
61. See 83-A
64. Larger-than-life statues, say
65. It's adjacent to Swe.
66. Ravage
67. Northwest Ireland river
68. Pepsi or Coke
69. Congregation's common word
72. Like Peter Paul's models?
73. Electrolysis particle
74. Positive attitude at Bruce Nuclear Generating Station?

75. North Rhine-Westphalia city
77. Like some legends?
80. Your family members
82. Herpetologist's sycophant?
83. See 2-D
84. Prevent from participating
87. Group of seven in an eponymous card game
88. In might be ingrown
89. Gordon Pinsent won several of these?
92. Orts
93. Architectural column
94. Coincidental

95. Quebecers Lévesque and Simard
96. Bald bird
97. Love
99. 1962 Academy Award nominee Lenya
100. Spill a secret
102. Office workstation
104. Clever tactic
105. Hip-swaying dance
106. Geological ages
107. Cart without sides
109. Moose _____ SK

ACROSS

1. Turns around?
7. Vinegary
13. Rigid
18. Canadian coin
19. Hoity-toity
20. Ethical no-no
21. Vodka cocktail
22. Sci-fi trailblazer Isaac
23. Getting the last drop, say
24. 1971 Canadian hit: "_____ Flasher"
25. Little lump
26. Takes time off
27. Brew camomile
29. Guinness, et al.
30. Lah preceder, in a scale
31. "Pipe down!"
33. More wry
35. Controversial discussion
39. Troubles and traumas
41. Parts of blinds
42. Library and Archives Canada (abbr.)
43. Glorified gofer
44. Deck on a ship
46. "The Holly and the _____"
47. Stabbed with a slender blade
49. Olden days bolt thrower
51. Family meal moment
52. It's between Fogo and Morton's Harbour in "I'se The B'y"
54. Canada Day celebrations, say
58. Hacking grass
63. Surpassed a sergeant?
64. Band that performed 24-A: The Guess _____
65. Host of a roast
66. With the bow, to a violinist
67. Lake Muskoka musical venue: The _____ to Bala
68. Hindu men's loincloth
70. Make kittenish noises
71. Put back on the payroll
73. Crunchy confection: Peanut _____
75. Non-profit BC legal services grp.
76. Currency code for the Saudi riyal
77. Eliminates a debt
78. Top male?
80. Hold tightly to
83. They might be dressy or casual
85. Ogres
88. Hawaiian patio
89. Lapis _____
90. Francophone regions of the Maritimes
91. Make improvements
92. Online group
93. Super skilled people (var.)
94. Some amphibians
95. Short fellows?
96. Votes for an MP

DOWN

1. Daughter of Nicholas II
2. Churn
3. Blonde who explodes onto the scene?
4. BC Coast locale: Sechelt _____
5. Wedding cake description
6. Some Irish dogs
7. Shepard who went into space
8. Injured person
9. Vittles
10. Canadian export
11. They're worshipped by fans
12. Castleguard is Canada's longest this
13. Insoluble molecule
14. Buck up
15. Bird with a down-curved bill
16. Calibri or Cambria
17. Mists
28. Hit the hustings
30. Canadian Cancer _____
31. Mop the deck (var.)
32. Jewish wedding dance
34. Calixa who composed "O Canada"
35. Moulded Italian dessert
36. Noon, in Nice
37. Anagram for dime
38. Give in
40. Roman deity
42. Risky venture for Canada's Graham DeLaet?
45. Brightly coloured Asian bird
47. BMO foyer machine no.
48. Where glacial valleys meet
50. More chi-chi
51. Roman underworld god: _____ Pater
53. Light Emitting Diode (abbr.)
54. Fly aloft
55. Unrefined
56. Make an art piece
57. Rich roll
59. Hesitant person's interjection
60. Like Reykjavik residents
61. Nightly CBC offering
62. Coloured sheets for spotlights
64. BC ski resort
68. Practice sessions
69. Unhealthy reputation?
72. St. Lawrence landmark: Lachine _____
73. Gaming tables fabrics
74. Like some sagas?
77. Stage
79. Heft

80. Group related by blood
81. Unconvincing, colloquially
82. Turn over _____ leaf

83. You might find tenements here
84. Meets, like a committee
86. Blow, old style

87. Saucy response

They Came to Play

Swedish stars of Canadian teams

ACROSS

1. Killed, old style
5. Pass a bill in the House of Commons
10. Peanuts or popcorn
15. Dofasco dross
19. Joni Mitchell hit: "Big Yellow _____"
20. Pizza order size
21. Shrub for a fairy's garden?
22. Irving Berlin composition: "_____ Be Surprised"
23. Shipboard affirmatives
24. Like a chef on the move?
25. Old CBC show: *Man _____*
26. Former Italian currency
27. Without ostentation
29. Salad dressing served on a California island?
32. Weight for some freight
33. Adjacent area
34. **Henrik or Daniel of the Canucks**
35. Accountants' books
37. Remains behind
38. Laureen Harper, _____ Teskey
40. Grammy winner Erykah
42. "Slavonic Dances" composer
43. Laid lawn
46. 1996 Bryan Adams hit: "_____ Make It a Night to Remember"
48. To be, to Octavius
49. 15th-C. French satirical play
52. Your brainstorm
54. Film critic, say
56. David who played Poirot on TV
57. Frighten
59. **1970s Winnipeg Jets forward Anders**
63. Ann-Marie MacDonald Giller nominee: *Fall on Your _____*
64. Swing musician Benny
66. Colony insect

68. In a lazy way
69. Actor Carvey, et al.
70. "That is _____ happening!"
72. Phoenician fertility god
73. British Pre-Raphaelite painter John Everett
75. Iranian city (var.)
77. They might give you the chills?
78. **Kent who was a Calgary Flame in the '80s**
80. US president William, et al.
81. Tuxedo wearer's neckwear
82. Robber
84. Quizzical grunts
85. Firebug's felony
86. Canada's third-largest lake: Great _____
89. Ponce de _____
91. Minimums
93. The Queen's preferred pooches
95. Fall, like prices
97. Street, in Lisbon
98. Chinese au pairs
103. Gets a sense of direction in Asia?
105. **The Jets retired this Thomas's number in 1995**
107. Bequest recipient
109. Barfly, perhaps
110. Pliers and tongs
112. Holey Swiss cheese
113. Gloom
115. Eyed
116. Long, loose shirt
118. Prepare loins?
119. Curved moulding, in architecture
120. Oyster's jewel
121. Web reading
122. About
123. 1970s hairdo
124. Theatrical?

125. Famed Canadian battle site: Vimy _____
126. Come across as

DOWN

1. Calgary CFLers, for short
2. Magazine art director's forte
3. Semicircular room in old Rome
4. With much sagacity
5. Put on a happy face?
6. **Seven-year Vancouver Canucks captain Markus**
7. Chi-chi
8. It generates special FX
9. Canonical hour
10. Involving area?
11. **1990s Calgary Flames centre Michael**
12. Angle, in botany
13. Parliament passed this in 2005: _____ Marriage Act
14. Lamented loudly
15. Maple Leaf Apps who became an MPP
16. Hangs around
17. Night lights in the North
18. City where Solidarity was born
28. They might be scared of their siblings?
30. Advanced Digital Broadcast (abbr.)
31. Parts of speech
34. Cover for a kernel
36. Green lights, say
39. He held 1,093 patents
41. Nevada neighbour
44. Office of Engineering and Technology (abbr.)
45. Absolutely against, say
47. Push a pedal
49. **Mats who spent 13 seasons as a Maple Leaf**
50. Markings on butterfly wings

51. Comic strip from 1929–2008: _____ *Do It Every Time*

53. Provide with a pistol

55. Remove film footage

56. Milk type

58. Relaxing

60. Forms into an arch, old style

61. Venice commercial area

62. **Thomas who's #6 on Vancouver's top scorers list**

64. Fuel that's heavier than kerosene

65. Band from Saskatoon: The _____ Pikes

67. "What _____ can I get you?"

69. Deep _____ pizza

71. Caribbean capital city

74. Sinatra song: "I've Got the World on _____"

76. Triumphant cry

77. Prom night pinning

79. 1977 Leo Sayer smash: "When I _____ You"

81. Club for a cricket competitor

83. **Peter who started his career with the Québec Nordiques**

86. East York prior to 1998 in Toronto

87. Asmara nation

88. Mature, like wine

90. Duke Vincentio response to Lucio: "Most _____, sir"

92. **16-year Leafs defenceman Börje**

93. Sunflower family flower

94. Sharpens shaving equipment

96. Part of rpm

99. Some tropical fruits (var.)

100. Duds

101. Funeral vehicle

102. Not very often

104. *Full House* actor Bob

106. Perfume compound

108. Host

111. Irish breakfast bun

112. Writer Bagnold

114. Big barrel for beer

117. Israeli made submachine gun

Solution on page 231

ACROSS

1. Glower
6. Wacky
10. Door handle
14. Flock female
17. Big tippler (var.)
18. _____ the roost
19. Genial
20. Manitoba-born Gabrielle who wrote *The Tin Flute*
21. Harasser
23. Early Peruvian tribe
24. "_____ You Lonesome Tonight?"
25. Tit for tat deal?
26. Love for a Quebecer?
27. Matisse, among others
29. Run along smoothly
30. Sort
32. Cygnet's mother
33. Assume a claim is true
38. Edible vegetable spears
43. Abdominal pain cause
44. Guilt or innocence determiner
46. Performing live
47. Former Governor General Adrienne
49. Sirloin tip or cross rib
51. Alternative to hardwood
52. More ragged
53. Canadian jazz singer Cole
54. Become inured
55. *Superman* character Luthor
56. Traveller's stopover
57. See 56-A
58. Calf's milk source
61. Fake
62. James Cameron's manifestations?
66. Natterjack
67. Some of 62-D prosecute for this
68. Not the norm
69. Neurological condition
71. Skilled
73. WWI fighter in France
74. It's not light?
76. Livestock chow
78. Stretch resources
79. Spicy food type
81. Colour on our flag
82. Warp, say
86. Tea tray item at the Empress
88. First name of Canada's first prime minister
92. Intense anger
93. Vacation destination
94. Exploding stars
96. 20th Bond film: _____ *Another Day*
97. Fellow's formalwear accessory
98. Pretentious
99. Like some gases
100. Doctrine suffix
101. Actresses Tilly and Ryan
102. Disorderly conduct?
103. Popular video game: Angry _____

DOWN

1. Exhausts of energy
2. Evidence for Sherlock Holmes
3. Southern US cooking pod
4. Will-o'-the-_____
5. *To Kill a Mockingbird* author
6. Marching band leader
7. Vehicle
8. Show-off
9. Legendary Canadian goalie Sawchuk
10. Stabs
11. 1492 ship
12. Recipient of junk mail
13. They're on our nickels
14. Chapters in history
15. St. John's _____
16. 2013 Michael Bublé single: "Close Your _____"
22. Amniotic sac
28. Lack of focus
29. More muscular
31. Releases from Springhill Institution
33. Ancient Briton
34. Earthenware pot
35. 1D or 24C, on an Air Canada flight
36. Two Christmas birds
37. Barrel
39. Ring-around-the-rosy flower
40. Pace
41. Jamaican fruit
42. 2008 Bryan Adams song: "I Thought I'd _____ Everything"
45. Bombastic
48. Fair _____
50. Old W Network show: *Candice Tells* _____
53. Baloney, in the pigsty?
54. Lost control of oneself
56. Cattle call?
57. Climbing vine
58. Osmond family home state
59. Venetian judge
60. *China Beach* actress Delany
61. Bluff in the Highlands
62. Members of the CBA
63. Battery _____
64. Unhealthy inhalation
65. Speak disparagingly
67. Film fan or filmmaker
68. Fourth month (abbr.)
70. Punjab religion founded in the 16th century
72. Foodie
75. War horses
77. Careen
80. Indian tea-producing region
82. Lunchtime, in Longueuil

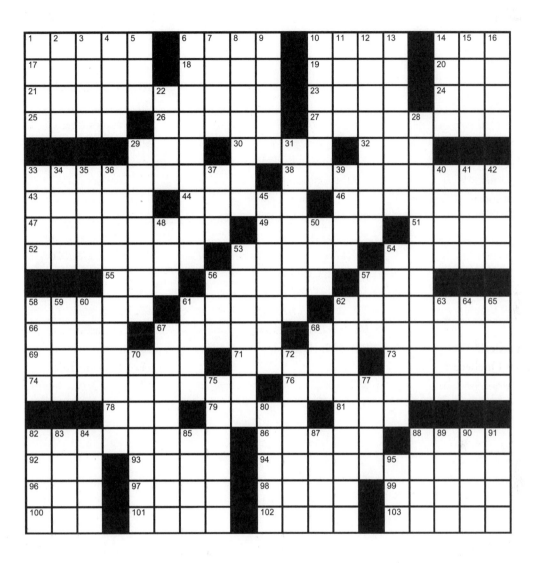

83. Greek goddess
84. Look as if
85. Actor's pitch, say
87. Makes a decision

88. Canadian Mitchell who sang "Help Me"
89. _____ and out
90. Difficult

91. NBA team: Brooklyn _____
95. Pen point

Music to Your Ears?

Tuneful twists of phrase

ACROSS

1. Canadian Tire money, e.g.
6. Credit card giant
10. Seats a jury in Seattle
18. Neither Liberal nor Tory?
20. _____ Intensive Care Unit
21. **Chair for a Goth musician?**
22. Group of emissaries
23. Courtroom combatant (abbr.)
24. Footnote note
26. Joke writer
30. Fairy tale people eater
31. Plays together?
36. Mug on stage
37. Nebraska city
39. Bats' cave, say?
40. Unexciting
41. Strong gust of air
42. Musical instruction to slow down
43. Person making a plea
45. Skin bumps
46. _____-lock brakes
47. Ocean Research and Education (abbr.)
48. Roughly
49. Golden Jamaican sprinter Usain
50. It's under the rooftop
51. Pastry fat
53. Region's animal life
55. Swami or sibyl
56. Tense, like a termite?
58. Twisted
59. Jackson 5 sibling
61. Slangy affirmative
64. Afrikaans village
65. Maroon 5 front man Levine
66. Component of some VIA trains
68. French king's coin, circa 1640
70. Underwater explorer
71. *Born Free* lioness
72. Contest ballots
73. Little ones
74. It holds oil or vinegar
75. Fix shoes
76. Ontario's Niagara Region produces this
77. Move awkwardly
79. Spicy turnover
81. _____ *ex machina*
82. More substantial, like a meal
86. **Benny Goodman set?**
92. Esso product description
93. Some floor lamps
94. Pilots' communications devices
95. Bucket-carrying frame
96. Southern Ontario county or town

DOWN

1. Easy mark
2. Central Processing Unit (abbr.)
3. MacLean who rejoined *Hockey Night in Canada* in 2016
4. Sort
5. Blackbeard or Black Bart
6. Phonographs
7. Gross
8. Freelancer writer's submission encl.
9. Stevie Wonder single: "Uptight (Everything's _____)"
10. Musical genre of Canada's Arcade Fire
11. Old-style reward
12. Smelly mammals
13. Buttercup-like bloomer
14. Fault-finder
15. Greek letter
16. _____ La Hache park in BC
17. Cunning
19. Storage bin
25. Lingerie item
26. Painter's plaster
27. Love, in Longueuil
28. **Church choir's beliefs?**
29. Quit
30. Kiln for brewers
32. Paternal relative
33. **C&W fans' group?**
34. Little Richard classic: "_____ Frutti"
35. Disengaged, emotionally
38. Floating terror, in the sea
39. Clue
41. Heron or hawk
42. Niece or nephew
44. Colourful Australasian bird
45. Finished in first place
49. Purchase
50. Eternity (var.)
52. Set a goal
54. Limb
55. Whip up
56. Canadian media man Charles
57. Herman's Hermits vocalist Peter
58. Disturbances
60. Basically, to a perfume producer?
62. Jan Steen's stand
63. Jabber
65. Toronto street named for William IV's wife
66. Levee's cousin
67. Disease causer
69. Tijuana snoozes
70. Pierre and Justin, perhaps
73. "_____ the season to be jolly"
74. Two-time Olympic women's hockey gold winner Campbell
76. Crossword books have a lot of these
78. Canadian *Barometer Rising* author MacLennan
80. Bump into at the track competition?
81. Scot's blade
82. "Say again?"

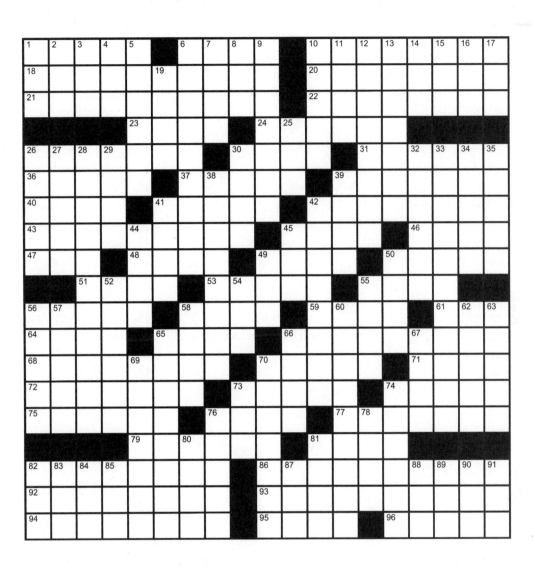

83. The wind might blow this direction (abbr.)

84. Pie _____ mode

85. Manitoba river

87. Make amorous advances

88. "For _____ a jolly good fellow"

89. US taxman

90. Banking charge

91. Toronto trading floor (abbr.)

Solution on page 231

ACROSS

1. Hit from Canada's Colin James: "Back in My _____ Again"
5. Kind of tissue
9. Preowned
13. Top of the top
17. Half of a faun
18. Rabbit's relation
19. "_____ But the Lonely Heart"
20. You might have one in your throat?
21. Music style for a sitar player
22. "Nessun Dorma," e.g.
23. U of T residence
25. Early cinematic offering
28. Head topper
29. Barbecue accessories
30. BC smelter town
31. Silvery salmon
33. Clock standard (abbr.)
35. It can be more?
37. Lady of the lea
38. She published *Coming of Age in Samoa* in 1928
39. Blades for boaters
41. Sending again
46. Speak from a soapbox
48. Beaufort, for one
49. Amy who wrote *The Joy Luck Club*
50. *Inter* _____
51. Eye membrane
53. Pronto, in the ER
56. Furrow
58. Decline in intensity
59. Like those of Arabic origin
63. Canadian sports award: _____ Marsh Trophy
66. Nigerian people
67. Clan in ancient Ireland
68. Workboot component
72. Shania Twain song: "I _____ No Quitter"
74. Colorado Native
76. Large parrot
78. Vascular skin layer
79. Some Lindt bars
84. Othello, for one
85. Bear anagram
86. Journal for a captain
87. Animal skin
89. Saskatoon-to-Regina direction (abbr.)
90. Bleated
92. Ex-premiers Vander Zalm and Davis
94. Onions' kin
96. 1999 Barenaked Ladies single: "_____ All Been Done"
97. Lack of focus
102. Hindu mysticism teacher
104. Out on the water
105. Colonial India household helper
106. Drained a radiator
107. Kardashian clan matriarch Jenner
108. Go-_____ (var.)
109. Lyra's brightest star
110. Auto industry pioneer
111. Novel from Canada's Hugh MacLennan: _____ *Man's Son*
112. Old World language
113. Netherlands dairy export

DOWN

1. Taj Mahal site
2. Shade in a stable
3. Authoritative
4. Canada Post purchase
5. Smash into pieces
6. Strokes
7. Dry like a desert
8. Flinch, perhaps
9. Like a holstered weapon
10. Most blackened, like a chimney
11. Sign up at Dalhousie
12. New software showing, for short
13. At the back, on ship
14. _____ tears
15. Ethical
16. Suez Canal country
24. Atlas feature
26. Have a bug
27. Neck of the woods, say
32. Hari of espionage notoriety
33. Sticky substances
34. Juno-winning singer Jordan
36. Bargain for a Blue Jay?
38. Musical suite component
40. Flower stalk
42. Bulldozes, in Brighton
43. Western Canada retail chain: Peavey _____
44. Bit of licorice
45. Prattle
47. Great Lake
52. Offer up evidence
54. Association of Energy Engineers (abbr.)
55. Like Francis' decrees
57. Put a foot down?
60. "The lady _____ protest too much"
61. It attaches to a guitar
62. Tree in India
63. Pool loop
64. Edmonton _____ Kings
65. Not at all embarrassed
69. Bleary from puzzle solving?
70. Bible book
71. Canadian Jean of *Company's Coming* cookbooks fame
73. Canadian retailer: Kal _____
75. Of the Stone Age
77. Artists' studios
80. Point of greatest despair
81. Like a frolicking foal?

82. Loge anagram
83. Raise to great heights?
88. Shirt type
90. Dumb blonde
91. "That's _____ order"
92. Iraqi city

93. River name in Yukon and Ontario
95. Jack
98. Serena Williams promotes this brand
99. Peter I or Nicholas II

100. Multigenerational epic
101. Fakery
103. Marketing pitches

97 | Short and Sweet . . . Provincially

Abbreviations x2

ACROSS

1. Capable
6. Blue Jays squad headgear
10. Underworld river
14. Believer's suffix
17. Vancouver's *Sun* or *Province*
18. Lie next to
19. Saws
20. Parliament Hill vote option
21. Fold of skin
22. Canadian Conservative, say
23. Chemical radical
24. Tub type
25. Time away from work
27. **Yellowknife church bible?**
28. Calendar abbr.
29. Be of one mind
30. Had supper
31. California place: Santa _____
32. **Trillium province communications system?**
36. Eye, to a bard
37. Maintains
39. **Halifax port visitor?**
41. Kittens' cries
43. Canada Savings Bond owner, for example
45. Assail
47. Calgary's Saddledome
48. "Gotcha!"
49. Hits the spot
51. Informal writing style
55. Workstation shared by several staff
56. Ladies' partners
57. 1970s tennis star Chris
59. Interrupting (with "in on")
63. Absorbed by the Borg
69. CUPE principles?
71. Marshalled the parade
72. Radiate
73. Barbaric
74. Took advantage of privileges, say
77. Indented
78. "Don't change," in proofreading-speak
79. Pre-raid action, for short
81. Where surgeons work (abbr.)
83. Obligation
84. Miners dig it?
85. Catch a crook
86. Quartz kin
88. Hamburg waterway
89. ***La belle province* British barrister?**
90. Most graceful, old style
95. The _____ is cast
96. Maui gathering
97. Rhett didn't give one
98. Bronfman family philanthropist
99. Gallivant around
100. Herb for stuffing
101. Manitoba indigenous group
102. Olympian Hughes who cycled and skated for Canada
103. Mom's malady when the kids have left home (abbr.)
104. Colours one's hair
105. Summit Series rival of CDA
106. Pres. Roosevelt

DOWN

1. You might download these to your iPhone
2. Surrealist artist Salvador
3. Huge, colloquially
4. Oscar-winning actor Gregory
5. Part of a musical refrain
6. Nasal membrane inflammation
7. Honest, on ship?
8. Blender setting
9. Piglet's place
10. Strews
11. Canada's prime minister in 1984
12. **Whitehorse dog breed?**
13. Xtreme Soccer League (abbr.)
14. Devoid of feeling
15. Some Fred Astaire performances
16. Fledgling aerie denizen
26. _____-ideal
27. Main part of a church
28. Classified section notice
32. It's next to Yemen
33. Fictional detective Wolfe
34. Ontario city: _____ Sound
35. **The Rock night sky phenom?**
37. Month that precedes Nisan
38. Stage of enlightenment for a Zen Buddhist
40. **Prairie province service for the homeless?**
42. Travelling on the sea
44. Tibetan dog breed: _____ Apso
46. Minute amounts
50. Interruption sound
52. More chic
53. Joule components
54. Permissive responses
58. Pac-Man and Minecraft
59. Smooch
60. Eastern Turkey native
61. They're usually silty
62. Small beard
64. Swerve (var.)
65. Fired a forester?
66. Nobel Peace Prize winner Desmond
67. Rephrase phrases?
68. Refuse a plea
70. Rock of Gibraltar monkeys
75. **Lotusland citizen's ID?**
76. Colander or sieve
80. Lock up
82. Depot (abbr.)
86. Cuisine gelatins

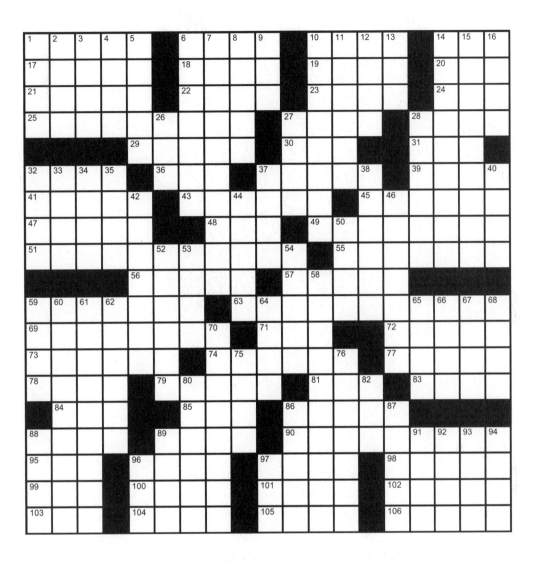

87. Vote in an MPP
88. Leading boundary?
89. Underground Toronto streetcar station: Queens _____

91. Without busy hands, say
92. "My goodness!" old style
93. See 86-A
94. Server's salver

96. Hit for a hippie, for short
97. Democratic Canadian Union (abbr.)

ACROSS

1. Fairy godmother's gift
5. Lightfoot classic: "The _____ of the Edmund Fitzgerald"
10. Remove, surgically
18. Her magazine in Montréal?
19. Munich greeting
20. Canada's 150th falls in 2017
21. *Dreamgirls* star Sharon
22. Venomous snake
23. Organism that doesn't need oxygen
24. Painter Leonardo
26. ON-born Morgan who starred in *Really Me*
28. Beatles hit: "Back in the _____"
29. Caulking substance for wooden ships
31. "I need to see a man about _____"
33. A dog does this with its tail
36. Flat-topped land features
38. Rank for a sailor (abbr.)
39. "Oops," I said
44. Grad who attends a reunion
46. NHL on-ice official
48. Brave, like Beyoncé?
49. Backyard bloomer
51. Alarming femme fatale?
52. Rainwater storage tank
53. Long, loose dress (var.)
55. No longer in vogue
56. Large coffee pots
57. Like a rainy day, say
58. Pipeline in the news in 2016
62. Dan Rather anchored for this network
65. Sewing case
66. NAFTA partner
67. Like a soused sharpshooter?
71. Flaps
73. Skin flake
75. Micronesian land mass
76. Jerusalem country
77. Caribbean commonwealth
79. Xmas drinks
80. Your monies owing
81. Malaysian Armed Forces (abbr.)
82. Hades river
84. Lush
85. Performers' platforms
88. Francis who wrote *Fighting for Canada*
90. Cheats out of
94. Landing site for Noah
96. 1970s AMC auto
100. Gunwale adjuncts
102. Clean a spill
104. Adriatic wind
105. Does damage to a nose
106. Projecting window
107. Ramis played this Spengler in *Ghostbusters*
108. May West's final film
109. Like 24-A?
110. Madrid madam

DOWN

1. Actress Tuesday
2. International Law Enforcement Agency (abbr.)
3. Eastern Europe resident
4. 2007 *Dancing with the Stars* champ Castroneves
5. Weed _____
6. Lines, in math (var.)
7. Antiquity, once
8. Ball of yarn for Miss Marple?
9. Canadian troops served here in the 1950s
10. Gastropod with a pearly interior
11. Men of the Deeps choir members
12. Says grace
13. Union of Taxation Employees (abbr.)
14. Discovery TV show: *Highway _____ Hell*
15. See 71-A
16. You might run these in bars
17. Ogler, old style
25. Where US vets fought in the '60s
27. Lustrous finish
30. Sicilian crime cartel members
32. Environmentalist's release?
33. Canada's _____ of Fame
34. Canadian womenswear retailer: _____ N Tan Jay
35. The St. Lawrence is one
37. Blood fluid
40. To this point
41. Strange quaff for the McKenzie brothers?
42. Green plot?
43. Fender-bender result
45. Canadian-born Christian singer Maher
47. Fix photos, say
48. Last match of a tournament
50. Without a concern in the world?
52. Old PC component
54. South African area
56. Without any weapons
59. Some Greek letters
60. Commonplace
61. Indian bakery product
62. Scolded (var.)
63. Audio products retailer in Canada
64. Old World fruit tree
68. Pairs
69. Thus
70. _____ bunny
72. 1980s Mulroney cabinet minister Carney
73. Toronto-born *60 Minutes* stalwart Morley

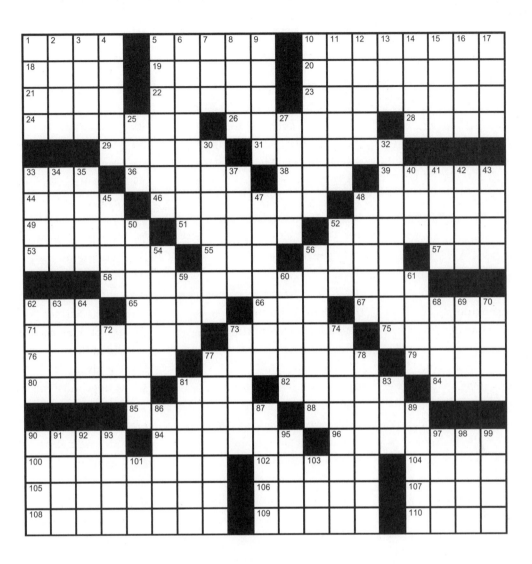

74. Tired old clothes?

77. Sugar cane pulp

78. How a scolder speaks

81. Canadian retailer rebranded in 2016: M&M Food _____

83. London-to-Kitchener dir.

86. Understood, non-verbally

87. Place in Polynesia

89. Put securely in place

90. Lots of saliva?

91. Connecticut university

92. Next month, for short, to Caesar

93. Assign into a schedule

95. Unit of vacuum pressure

97. Corporate letterhead graphic

98. Club for a golfer

99. The Darlings' governess

101. Form of some poems

103. Hole in the ground

Solution on page 232

99 Creature Comforts

They're not immaterial materials . . .

ACROSS

1. Carpentry files
6. Yucca
11. US broadcasting watchdog
14. Cashed out?
19. Fibre _____ cable
20. Kathmandu country
21. Segment of Santa's postal code
22. Aspirant
23. *The Beachcombers* star Gerussi
24. Ball-shaped cheese
25. Some scale notes
26. Nobel Prize-winning Canadian writer Munro
27. **For a duck hunter?**
29. You'll find yaks here
31. Like mountains in BC?
32. Guileful
33. Eur. kingdom
34. Canada's Wonderland, for one
37. Sovereign's ceremonial gear
39. Solo dance: _____ seul
40. Break out of the joint
45. Cape Verde money
48. It precedes Sunday or egg
50. Like some putts
51. Herring
52. "_____ to Billie Joe"
54. Big load
55. Relating to two algebraic variables
56. Bullfighters
59. Ancient theatre
61. Canada's 1995 female figure skating champ Kim
62. Son of Clytemnestra and Agamemnon
63. Spruce up
66. Harass
67. **For an angler?**
68. Some consonants, for example
74. Aquarius or Aries
76. Southeastern Europe country

77. Sandbar
82. Come to pass as a result of
83. Most severe, at school?
85. Military exercises
87. Louisville Slugger wood
89. Stars' public appearances: Photo _____
90. Mere
91. Accepts at face value
92. Bury in a crypt
94. More rigid
96. "Poetry Man" songstress Snow
97. Erie, to a Quebecer
98. Bill remittance
100. Like canny plans
103. Poetic "night"
104. Belgium city's airport code
107. Metal fastener
111. Pennsylvania folk
112. **For an equestrian?**
115. Poetry Muse
116. Abode for a bear
117. 1985 film starring ON-born Kate Nelligan
119. Tripoli country
120. Chocolate source
121. RBC rate
122. Part of NIMBY
123. Perfect
124. Odour
125. O.J. trial judge
126. Make a link?
127. Farmers' computers?

DOWN

1. Judges' housecoats?
2. Long-time Canadian band: _____ Wine
3. Prepare for a final
4. Cabinetry wood
5. Treated contemptuously
6. **For a rabbit owner?**
7. Siamese's sound

8. Cactus type
9. Young fellow
10. Bring a smile to someone's face
11. Abstain from, old style
12. Nest noises
13. _____ Rica
14. **For a diver?**
15. Horseback sport
16. Like some proportions?
17. Adam's apple spot
18. *South Park* co-creator Parker
28. Social reformers, say
30. About to occur
35. "_____ thou slain the Jabberwock?"
36. Not fake
37. Most socially offensive
38. Wanton glance
41. Bamboo stem
42. Aid
43. Survey map
44. Strange (var.)
45. Prevent, in court
46. Vancouver enclave: North _____
47. Shows concern
49. Like the most dazzling smile?
50. Sussex Drive building: Royal Canadian _____
53. John _____ Passos
55. Yacht or yawl
57. Had a bite
58. To-dos
60. Balances things out
64. Outputs
65. Army newbies
67. Beliebers, for example
69. Agatha Christie mystery: *The _____ Murders*
70. Didn't play
71. With regard to, in olden days
72. Hosiery material

73. Narnia's Mr. Tumnus, for example
75. Golfers' gadgets
76. Dadaism doyen Jean
77. Trade
78. Corned beef dish
79. Around about
80. Influenza, old style
81. **For the shepherd?**
84. Ontario MPP Barrett first elected in '95

86. 1962 CBC show: *Making Ends* _____
88. US indigenous people
92. Corrode
93. Vegetation cutting knife
95. Earthworm, for example
97. Grieve
99. **See 81-D**
101. Spokes in a wheel
102. City in Belgium
104. Biblical tower

105. Qatari currency
106. Russian range
107. Tiny bits of time
108. Stuff stuff
109. Yukon River Trail Marathon, for one
110. Common Latin abbr.
113. "Step _____!"
114. Stay out of sight
118. Law, in Lachine

ACROSS

1. *Maclean's*, for short
4. Pick
7. Farm Credit Canada (abbr.)
10. Quit what you're doing
14. Climb to new heights?
16. He preceded Hua
17. Way out of a room
19. Don Moen was this when he set the record for most CFL games played
20. Erne or tern
22. Ottoman Empire title (var.)
23. Long-time role for Canada's William Shatner
24. Fan
26. Skimpy garment for ladies
28. Canadian singer Heppner, et al.
29. Box for bricks
30. Lacking refinement
32. Lewdness
34. Be crazy for
39. Accustom to (var.)
43. Part of a pedestal
44. Pardoned, old style
46. Canadian government group
48. Top of Canada description
50. There's nine in this kind of group
51. 1850s Can-Am author Eliza
53. Half of Gretzky's long-time number
55. Guesstimating phrase
56. Grabbed some grub
57. Sexy ballroom dance
59. Rust, for example
61. Provide with clothes
62. Ogle, like a Shakespearean king?
64. Middle Eastern capital
66. Goat-like
68. Baltimore bird?
70. Hello, in Hilo
72. British monarchy bodyguards
73. They exchange letters
75. Air Canada Centre, in Toronto
77. Nail filing board
78. Rims
79. Some smoked meats
82. Powerful Greek city state in olden days
84. Vietnamese new year
85. It precedes "nationale" in Québec
89. US state or river
93. Something to look at in 75-A
96. Only daughter of Elizabeth
97. Disorderly situation
99. Provided nourishment
100. Mix
101. Anne Murray's voice
102. No. for a good or bad Canadian
103. Enlighten
104. BC place
105. Second person pronoun
106. Took for a ride?
107. Amusement

DOWN

1. Montréal morning
2. Actor Baldwin, et al.
3. Spice Girl Halliwell
4. Like forbidding forebodings
5. Delivery that falls from the sky
6. Winnipeg-born ex-NHLer Kevin
7. US drugs gov. overseer
8. French brandy
9. Sticks to it?
10. South American monkey
11. Subj. for math students
12. Manlike monster
13. Jab
14. Cotton-tipped stick
15. Small restaurant
18. Scott Joplin compositions
21. Nobel-winning physicist Niels
25. Spots on butterfly wings
27. Take in info
31. Reciprocal pronoun
32. Tiny, in Trois-Rivières
33. Dissident
35. Fred and Wilma's pet
36. NHL "extra"
37. Long-time *60 Minutes* journalist Harry
38. Growth from within, biologically
39. Meat slice
40. Fixed Fifi
41. Blind
42. Cheer syllable
45. Farmer's prosperous time?
47. It covers a crown?
49. *National Post* columnist Murphy
52. Serengeti animal
54. Twitch
58. US girls' grp.
60. Fencers' blades
63. You might find soap on this
65. Major arteries
67. Royal Ontario Museum (abbr.)
69. Cowboy's circle
71. Peninsula that forms part of Turkey
74. Done without ornamentation
76. Pertaining to US Natives
80. Upper-cruster, for short
81. Thing
83. Cougar's cousin
85. It's served in a shared pot
86. Kitchen style
87. Not kosher (var.)
88. Nelson or Duane
89. Sitcom set in Korea
90. Common preposition
91. Cut short?
92. Dry

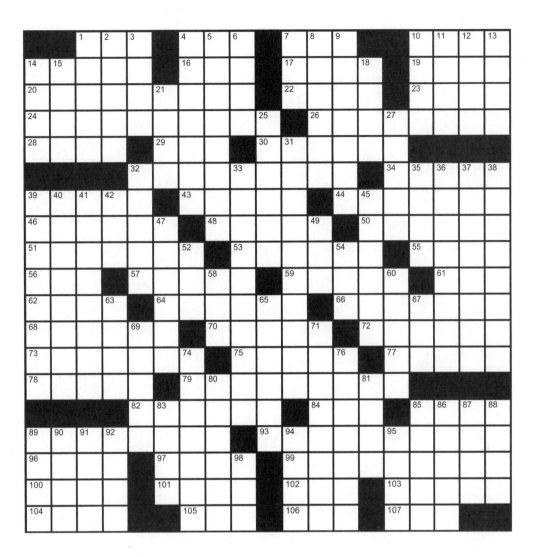

94. Loonies or toonies

95. Alberta export

98. Parisian pittance?

Bonus question: One horizontal line of answers contains a hidden message. Can you find it?

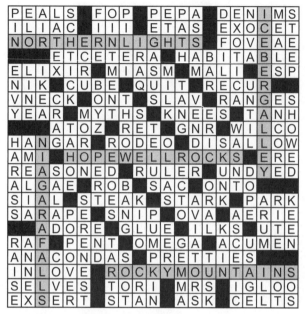

1 ■ *Au Naturel*

2 ■ *Canada Cornucopia 1*

3 ■ *For the Man of the Family*

4 ■ *Canada Cornucopia 2*

5 ■ *Quotable Notables*

6 ■ *Canada Cornucopia 3*

7 ■ *Dancing with the Wordplay*

8 ■ *Canada Cornucopia 4*

9 ■ *Making It Right*

10 ■ *Canada Cornucopia 5*

11 ■ *Old Occupations*

12 ■ *Canada Cornucopia 6*

13 ■ *Destination: Hamilton*

14 ■ *Canada Cornucopia 7*

15 ■ *How Swede It Is*

16 ■ *Four-Square 1*

17 ▪ *Yes, Sirs!*

18 ▪ *Canada Cornucopia 8*

19 ▪ *Repetitious*

20 ▪ *Canada Cornucopia 9*

21 ▪ *Either/Or*

22 ▪ *Canada Cornucopia 10*

23 ▪ *Once Upon a Time . . .*

24 ▪ *Canada Cornucopia 11*

25 ▪ *Who Am I? 1*
Unscramble: COLVILLE

26 ▪ *Canada Cornucopia 12*

27 ▪ *Double Ws*

28 ▪ *Canada Cornucopia 13*

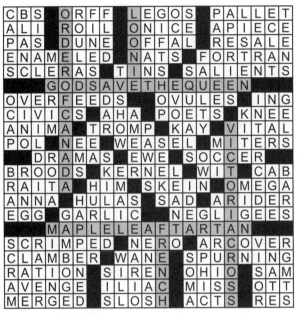

29 ■ *Half and Half*

30 ■ *Canada Cornucopia 14*

31 ■ *Just For the Pun of It*

32 ■ *Four-Square 2*

33 ▪ *Witty Women*

34 ▪ *Canada Cornucopia 15*

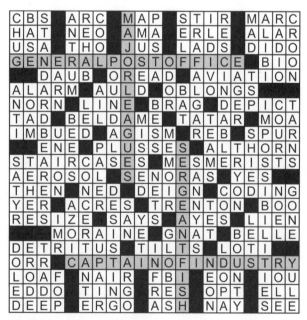

35 ▪ *Rank and Guile*

36 ▪ *Canada Cornucopia 16*

37 ▪ *Happy Birthday to Us!*

38 ▪ *Canada Cornucopia 17*

39 ▪ *Yes You Can...*

40 ▪ *Canada Cornucopia 18*

41 ■ *Who Are We?*
Unscramble: FAMOUS FIVE

42 ■ *Canada Cornucopia 19*

43 ■ *Sounds Fishy to Me* ⋯

44 ■ *Canada Cornucopia 20*

45 ■ *They Hail from Vancouver*

46 ■ *Canada Cornucopia 21*

47 ■ *On the Diagonal*

48 ■ *Four-Square 3*

49 ■ *Great Scotts!*

50 ■ *Canada Cornucopia 22*

51 ■ *Loud Enough For Ya?*

52 ■ *Canada Cornucopia 23*

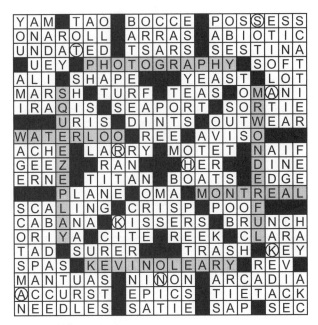

53 ▪ *Who Am I? 2*
Unscramble: SHARK TANK

54 ▪ *Canada Cornucopia 24*

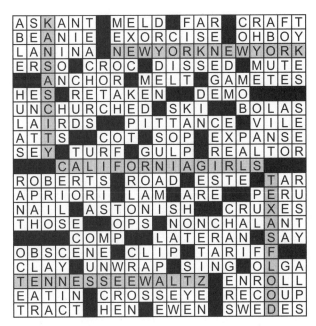

55 ▪ *Stately Songs*

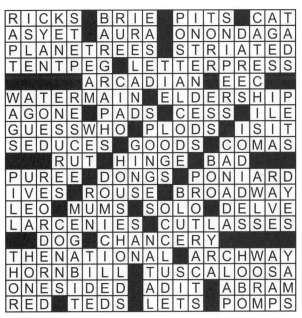

56 ▪ *Canada Cornucopia 25*

57 ■ *Spice Up Your Life . . .*

58 ■ *Canada Cornucopia 26*

59 ■ *Called It Macaroni . . .*

60 ■ *Canada Cornucopia 27*

61 ■ *Canadian Capes*

62 ■ *Canada Cornucopia 28*

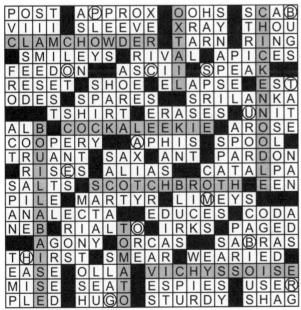

63 ■ *Soup's On*
**Unscramble: BORSCHT, GUMBO,
PEA**

64 ■ *Canada Cornucopia 29*

65 ■ *In*undated

66 ■ *Canada Cornucopia 30*

67 ■ *Suit Yourself*

68 ■ *Canada Cornucopia 31*

69 ■ *Has a Nice Ring to It*

70 ■ *Canada Cornucopia 32*

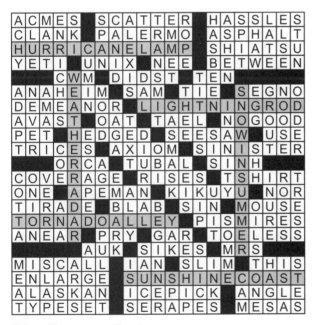

71 ■ *Forecast: Fun!*

72 ■ *Canada Cornucopia 33*

73 ▪ *Mmm Mmm Good!*

74 ▪ *Canada Cornucopia 34*

75 ▪ *Geisel's Gaggle*

76 ▪ *Canada Cornucopia 35*

77 ▪ *Rocking in Rio*

78 ▪ *Canada Cornucopia 36*

79 ▪ *Footy Fun*

80 ▪ *Canada Cornucopia 37*

81 ■ *And the Province Is . . .*

82 ■ *Canada Cornucopia 38*

83 ■ *Legislative Levity*

84 ■ *Canada Cornucopia 39*

85 ■ *Digging Deep . . .*

86 ■ *Canada Cornucopia 40*

87 ■ *Where You Live?*

88 ■ *Canada Cornucopia 41*

89 ■ *Special Deliveries*

90 ■ *Canada Cornucopia 42*

91 ■ *Eponymous Adjectives*

92 ■ *Canada Cornucopia 43*

93 ■ *They Came to Play*

94 ■ *Canada Cornucopia 44*

95 ■ *Music to Your Ears?*

96 ■ *Canada Cornucopia 45*

97 ■ *Short and Sweet . . . Provincially*
Abbreviations:
NTNT – Northwest Territories New
Testament
ONON – Ontario Optical Network
NSNS – Nova Scotia Nuclear Ship
QCQC – Quebec Queen's Counsel
YTYT – Yukon Territory Yorkshire Terrier
NLNL – Newfoundland Northern Lights
SKSK – Saskatchewan Soup Kitchen
BCBC – British Columbia Birth
Certificate

98 ■ *Canada Cornucopia 46*

99 ■ *Creature Comforts*

100 ■ *Canada Cornucopia 47*